The Search for Miss Deal and The Early Raiders

To John & Nancy

Front cover painting by A.A. Jansen
The last minutes of Miss Deal
The B-17F 42-30049 from the 384th Bomb Group, 544th Bomb Squadron
Lost to fighters and flak after a gallant fight to the end by her gunners on 25 June 1943

25 June 1943 MIA

The Search for Miss Deal and The Early Raiders on The Reich

This book is dedicated to the men of the 379th, the 384th and other bomb Groups who fought and lost in their effort to deliver their bombs to their assigned targets and bring their flying Fortresses back home. Most of all to the relatives of the fallen flyers that are lying in some foreign land and recorded by The American Graves Registry Service as Missing in Action.

Of course to Betsy and Erin. To Erin, who set an example of motivation and hard work in the initial search to wrapping up the editing. To Betsy who supported twelve years of searching and going down so many disappointing trails. Standing with me at Bomb Group reunions and travels to all the POW/MIA family updates plus the visits to meet the relatives of Charlie's Air Corp friends and crewmates. The trips to Europe to assist in searching for any clues that might lead to a bit more information and to another trail.

Also, a special thanks to my big brother Joe and his wife Carolyn for their encouragement, proof reading, and editing, when they had their own issues to deal with. To Shirley Bevers, the retired teacher who can't give up on teaching, for her editing, and her notes on grammar rules and spelling.

A special hats off to the historians who have passed on, for sharing and directing our searches. These include Lenny Schrik, Sicco de Vries and John Hey.

To the Dutch writer and artist Ab Jansen, my mentor whose letters were always fascinating and a rewarding experience. A professor of history and composition he should be.

To the German air war historian, Olaf Timmermann, who shared so much of his research along with numerous original images. He went out of his way to search church records and interview old Germans on the east side of the Dollart.

Finally, a thank you to Harm and Andrea Pastoor for continuing the search on the east side of the Dollart, the area of Germany where Harm and his wife may find the clue that will locate Miss Deal and her two missing crewmembers, John Way and Charles Crawford.

Preface

It was a nice day at Kimbolton as the 379th Fortresses began their take offs. The gunners in the back of 42-3148 gathered around the open waist ports during taxi. Following Group procedure the boys in the cockpit timed the previous Fortresses' thirty-second takeoff run. The pilot likely turned toward Cochran, his copilot, who would have nodded that all engines and their instruments were a go. Releasing the brakes while all four engines were at full power, the heavily loaded B-17 slowly began her run. The roar from the four big Wright Cyclone engines made the most experienced flyer pause and gaze toward the big Boeing. While standing by the waist gun stations, the four gunners waved at the men watching the Forts take to the air. The flyers felt their pride grow as the ground crews and even the executive officers up on the control tower waved back.

Watkins, the engineer in the top turret standing behind the pilots, calls out the airspeed as Brinkman's B-17 accelerates. With his Fortress racing down the runway, Brinkman hears the number one hundred and he eases back on the wheel. At one hundred and ten miles per hour, the ship is airborne and accelerating rapidly toward her climb out speed. Reaching one hundred and twenty her gear is up and locked.

At one hundred and forty miles per hour, the pilots start their first 90-degree turn as they work their B-17 to assembly altitude. With their route in hand, the navigator keeps the pilots abreast of their waypoints and on course.

Prior to reaching twelve thousand feet, Andrews was directed to arm the bombs. Once in the bomb bay, the bombardier removed the pins from the arming vanes mounted on the nose of each bomb. Returning to his station, he secured the pins as evidence that their bombs were armed. By now all the gunners have donned their masks and connected to their oxygen outlet. With fifty percent cloud cover the gunners get an occasional good view of the North Sea and the distant coast of Holland on their right.

The journey toward Bremen is a comfortable ride for all the young flyers on their way toward their target. With the 379th forming up behind their Group leader, the crews catch glimpses of other Groups of B-17s forming up into a growing Wing. Most of the rookie crews probably have a nice confident feeling knowing they are traveling with over two hundred and fifty B-17's to Northwest Germany.

With towering cumulus clouds, the Brinkman's tail gunner is probably reminded of funerals back in Alabama. The preacher would occasionally quote the 23rd Psalm: "Yea though, I walk through the valley of the shadow of death, I will fear no evil." Frank Murphy Jr. has never had a problem with controlling his fear per his old buddy Chester Graham from Benevola. "Frank was always quick to defend himself no matter how big the other boy was". Chester continued, "Frank carried his lunch to school in a syrup can and bent up a good number of buckets hitting the bullies upside the head".

Meanwhile the 379th Group leader directs his four commanders to bring their squadrons of B-17s into a tight formation. On this mission the 379th has launched thirty-one Fortresses within the Wing of two hundred and fifty-two ships. The "Brinkman" crew can see the other B-17s as the Groups merge. The tail-gunner, Frank Murphy Jr. has an excellent view of the "box formations" following his ship.

The formations begin heading northeast toward the North Sea as all groups join-up with the mission leader from the 303rd Bomb Group. Slowly the B-17s gained their required altitude and the various groups and squadrons form their defensive box formations.

Approaching the Island of Heligoland, Brinkman had to throttle back his Fortress as other lead ships were slowing down. Fortunately, he heard his Group leader's warnings that the Wing was slowing and turning to the secondary target, Wilhelmshaven.

With the German barrier islands in sight, the Brinkman crew witnessed black puffs of smoke indicating that the flak stations on the Frisian Islands were attempting to engage the Wing. As the formations turns toward the IP or the inital point of the bomb run, the fighters came into view. The top turret gunner, Watkins warned his gunners that fighters were on their right and racing past their Squadron.

The strength of the enemy fighter opposition was formidable. It was estimated that approximately two hundred enemy fighters took part in the action including Fw 190s, Bf 109s and Ju 88s. Even the German night fighters, the Bf 110's, were reported at debriefing as attacking the Fortresses.

Within the next few minutes, the fighters could be seen banking into the front of the formations. Quickly the fighters began their head-on attacks in an attempt to break up and scatter the tight formations. The attackers were Focke Wulf Fw 190s and Messerschmitt Bf 109s. The Brinkman crew, while watching their sister ships under attack may have felt Lady Luck was with them.

The officers and the turret gunners of the crews under attack were probably terrified by the fighters blitzing head-on. These men observed the bright orange flashes from the 20 mm cannons of each fighter that came charging in toward the formation's leading Fortresses.

In the meantime a Staffel of Focke Wulfs from Hosum, Germany have been ordered to intercept the American bombers that are retreating from Wilhelmshaven. The Focke Wulfs are racing south across the North Sea. With Hosum northwest of Kiel, it is apparent that these fighters were not released by the German controllers until it was certain that Kiel was not the target.

Departing Leeuwarden airfield a Schwarm of Messerschmitt Bf 110 night fighters from NJG 1 have also been ordered to intercept the departing Fortresses. These twin-engine, twin tailed fighters are climbing to the B-17s altitude. Streaking to the northeast their interception point is near the Ostefriesland Islands.

Cochran has been flying now for over six stressful hours and is watching for fighters. He notices a number of Focke Wulfs has started a frontal attack directly on their ship.

This was the Brinkman crews' second raid against the heavy concrete structures of Germany's submarine pens. In retrospect air war historians considered attacking these enormous naval bunkers a waste of machines and men.

The men that made up the crews were skilled and courageous warriors. Most flyers in 1943 dreaded the missions. They knew that it was just a matter of time before death and destruction from the flak and the German fighters visited their B-17. The lucky ones that survived a few missions had witnessed the morgue details pack up the kits of the missing upon their return to base. The empty bunks of their friends were soon claimed by replacement flyers with unfamiliar faces.

Of all the old B-17 crewmen that I interviewed, not a single one described combat as enjoyable. Rather, they realized it was a necessary job to rid the world of an evil leader. Most of the survivors expressed their grief to me for the loss of their friends. They all considered that the real heroes were the boys that never came home.

Those that survived the required twenty-five missions in 1943 were not only rare but extremely lucky. The fortunate escaped the flak fields both going to and away from the target. In addition to this, they were shot at by a 350-mile-per-hour fighter hell bent on destroying any bomber in German airspace, and still somehow managed to make it back. Indeed many of them seemed to return to base on nothing but the proverbial "wing and a prayer".

On the 23rd of September, the 384th attacked the submarine repair ship in the Nantes port. This was the Groups 25th mission while losing the Fortress *Jolly Roger* 42-3459. This ship represented the loss of the Groups 43rd B-17. Since their arrival with thirty-six new bombers the odds of surviving twenty-five raids was dismal.

The Estes crew was the first of the 384th to survive twenty-five missions and receive their free ticket home and out of the Air Corp. They lost one Fortress in the North Sea and on their final raid, their radio operator fell out of the bomb bay. This was on 4 February 1943, during a raid on Frankfurt. After fifty-eight raids, the 384th Bomb Group had lost seventy-three Fortresses.

This book includes stories gathered throughout my search for my uncle Charlie and his pilot beginning in 1999. In 2006, after thousands of phone calls and letters to air war researchers, meetings with acquaintances and families of the flyers, the assembling of the work began. The searching and the writing has never stopped.

Thanks to Bomb Group reunions, help from DPMO (Defense POW/Missing Personnel Office), JPAC (Joint Prisoner of War, Missing in Action Accounting Command) and AHRC-PER (U.S. Army Human Resources Command) in searching and sharing Department of Defense records, parts and pieces of the puzzle began coming together. Included in the sharing of copies of documents was National Archives. This agency's personnel assisted in advising possible search areas for documents in other countries.

The Netherlands Air War Study Group members shared a number of stories, pictures, paintings and documents concerning the raids studied. Additionally German researchers shared invaluable information, documents, and photographs that helped bring these historical air battles to life.

TABLE OF CONTENTS

Appendices Contents

25 June 1943 MIA
The Search for Miss Deal and The Early Raiders on The Reich

Chapter 1

Her Final Raid

Eight Boeing B-17s are approaching the German island of Heligoland. At twenty-five thousand feet, with a strong tailwind, they are furiously racing at a ground speed of over two hundere and fifty miles per hour. The Group leader is intent on striking the industrial city of Hamburg. He recalls his Commander lecturing the Squadron leaders that their Group must complete more missions.

Pilots from his Group have been struggling to stay within sight of each other; now the sweeping turn to the southeast allows them to temporarily gain on their leader. Climbing to twenty seven thousand feet has helped the navigators to find their waypoints and the bomber pilots to locate their comrades as the cloud cover again approaches 100 percent.

Fighters from the tiny island of Heligoland are airborne and being directed toward this small Group of Fortresses. German ground controllers are now convinced the target is Hamburg rather than Kiel.

The eight B-17s are all that make up the contingent now racing toward the Elbe estuary, the IP (initial point of the bomb run) and at last, on to the target.

Suddenly, a large concentration of 8th Air Corp B-17s appear on German radar, turning toward Bremen. The surprised ground controllers must redirect their fighter Gruppes toward this rapidly approaching storm of bombers.

Meanwhile, a *Staffel* or Squadron of German fighters has caught up with the small band of raiders climbing above and ahead of the high flying Fortresses. The Group leader's plane is instantly met by attacking enemy fighters. One by one the fighters strafe the Fortress head-on and she is riddled by 20 mm cannon fire. The officers in the lead B-17 are overcome with helpless fear as they witness bright orange flashes emanating from the cannons of each fighter.

The Commander in the lead B-17 pushes his throttles to war power, giving the Fortress another fifty miles per hour. He is intent on getting his bombs on the target. While the enemy fighters continue to take their turns strafing the lead bomber, the gunners in the back of the Fortress can only get off a few return volleys to the Germans. The small, wicked fighters bearing down from 12 o'clock high suddenly roll upside down, streaking underneath the big Boeing, diving down and away from the gunners. The toll on the lead plane is high. The fighters knock out two of her engines from their attacks, and one of the exploding 20mm shells catches the top turret gunner in the face killing him instantly.

The fighters move away from their target as the raiders approach the flak fields surrounding Hamburg. As the leader drops his bombs, he turns west with his struggling B-17 notifying the other Forts they are on their own. Some of the other bombers have dropped their bomb loads while two of the Fortresses fail to find the target.

Leaving the Hamburg area, one Fortress is struck by flak smashing the ball turret and setting the number four engine on fire. Falling back, she continues her trek west with a guesstimate of a heading toward Emden as her secondary target. Somewhere along her route to Emden, she is met head-on by a Focke Wulf 190. The attacker rakes the nose and left side of the B-17. A well-placed 20 mm shell strikes the number 2 engine and a fire ensues.

Diving into the nearest cloud cover, the B-17 is now tracking a bit more to the south of her secondary target, Emden.

South and east of Leer, Germany, fly four of the Boeing B-17F bombers that had attacked Hamburg, and they are now heading west toward Holland.

A number of the town's residents watch in awe as four of the big Fortresses are flying close together while the fifth plane was lagging behind. The people of Leer are entranced. While observing this event they can see that two of their fighters are in pursuit of the crippled plane. Two engines are apparently afire as they stream trails of black smoke.

The pilot puts his heavy Fortress through various turns and gyrations in his attempt to shake the attackers. The two fighters, which had swept in from the north, begin their attack at three o'clock high. They are immediately engaged by the right waist gunner and the engineer in the top turret.

As the two intimidating fighters flash over the Fortress the left waist gunner picks up the leading Messerschmitt for a couple of seconds.

The engineer spins his turret a full 180 degrees, getting off a few shots as the two Messerschmitts streak out of range. In the distance, he keeps his eyes on the two fighters as they bank into a long sweeping turn back to the east. Relaying their movement over the intercom as the distant enemy aircraft continuing their turn, he quickly alerts the tail gunner that the fighters are coming his way at 6 o'clock low.

Outbound from the wounded B-17, the two fighter pilots decide to change their tactics by attacking her instead from the rear or the six o'clock low position. They had noticed the ball turret's guns were pointing straight down indicating it was inoperable. So, with those other two B-17 gunners firing their fifty calibers like madmen, the change of attack certainly seemed prudent. Hopefully, a quick victory would follow
.

The German flight leader directs the nervous rookie, piloting the Messerschmitt Bf 109 G-6, to lead the attack. The Leeuwarden-based Gruppe need their rookies to gain confidence from combat experience. The inexperienced pilot began firing his 20 mm canons from a distance too far out of range to damage the B-17. The tail gunner responded to the long distance engagement with a burst from his own guns.

Suddenly the fighter pilot is surprised as a parachute rips out of the nose hatch jerking a flyer from the Fortress. The parachuting American flyer just misses the left side of his own tail plane as well as the German fighter. This event interrupts the rookie fighter pilot's concentration and he stops his attack. About the same time, the surprised tail gunner also stops firing his twin fifties as the canopy opens up, and like a big white balloon, floats away just under the fighter receding in the distance.

This departing flyer does not go unnoticed by the German citizenry, or their military observers.

Now the agitated second fighter moves into position to take up the fight and directs his fire into the vertical stabilizer, raking the tail and smashing the rear gunner's station. Parts of the debris from the 20mm cannon strike smash into the tail gunner's face fracturing his skull and temporarily blinding him in one eye.

The two pilots up front in the cockpit are not immune to the attacking fighters. A number of 20mm shell fragments pass through both the bulkheads separating the radio room from the waist of the ship and the bomb bay. With the sound of the shells striking the armor plating in the back of their seats, the pilot kicks his left rudder pedal while turning the control wheel in the same direction.

Just like that, their huge quarry has turned toward the southwest and drove into a large cumulus cloud. No doubt the two frustrated fighter pilots are incensed as their wounded prize, which should have been an easy victory, has evaded them. Now they skirt along beside the huge cloudbank, watching and waiting for the battered Fortress to emerge.

Meanwhile, the people down below watch the flyer hanging beneath his parachute as it drifts back toward the east at a good rate of speed. The Wehrmacht notes the parachutist's movement is back toward Hamburg. A number of the soldiers are rapidly racing their vehicles after him, hoping to be recognized for a heroic capture of an American flyer. The flyer drifts rapidly to the east and the soldiers giving chase are uncertain where to intercept him. A pair of German fighters come to their aid, following the flyer down, and pointing out his descending location. At last the flyer hits the ground hard, causing further injuries in addition to those suffered from his unusual nose hatch exit. He is quickly captured and taken to a hospital in Papenburg.

Crossing the Dutch border, the bomber has lost her cloud cover while the other four Boeings are rapidly moving off to the west. With nowhere to hide and the cloud cover gone, the bomber is spotted and the fighters race after her.

In the little Dutch village of Finsterwolde, stood the community schoolhouse near the old church. Far off in the distance toward Germany, a rumbling could be heard and the teacher assumes it must be early morning thunderstorms on this cloudy day of June 25, 1943. It is approaching 9:00 a.m., so she thinks it best to turn the children out early for their first recess. "Nothing worse than having all those kids indoors for the whole day", she reasons.

Enjoying an early recess, the students are busy burning off their excess energy. Two of the Nap brothers move to the north side of the school to listen to the wisdom of the older boys.

The rumbling begins again and now the sound is much closer. All discussion ceases. The boys gaze upward in tense silence, and in front of a huge wall cloud, they can see four large airplanes moving in their direction. One of the older students announces that they are American bombers. As the olive drab planes move off to the northwest, one of the students shouts that there is another bomber coming with two of her engines streaming wispy black smoke.

Suddenly, the big plane banks hard to her right and ten deafening and rapid explosions follow, coming from near the dike. All of the boys are mesmerized as they witness two fighters pursuing the lone bomber. The big four-engine Boeing is desperately trying to elude her attackers.

Near the center and on the port side of the big plane, a Messerschmitt Bf 109 is firing her cannons nonstop as if trying to cut the bomber in half. From near the same point in the bomber come numerous flashes streaking toward the fighter. The left waist gunner from Kentucky is a good shot and is intent on defending his struggling B-17F at all cost.

As the big plane continues moving off toward Emden, an orange flash is observed from the nose of the fighter. The witnesses are astonished to see the fighter roll upside down, in what appears to be a turn directly toward their school. With black smoke pouring from her engine, the 109 accelerates to unbelievable speed. The scream of the Messerschmitt cutting through the air can be heard for miles, and then there is one loud bang as she slams into the soft earth west of the school. The fighter completely entombs herself and her rookie pilot. They will finally be found 56 years later.

A few miles to the north, a Dutch fisherman, Meinto Oosterhuis is tending his nets when he notices the big bomber heading his direction. Suddenly a parachute blossoms out. Then a minute later two more parachutes appear as tiny balloons.

Now the fisherman can discern that the plane is under attack by German fighters. He continues watching as each fighter takes turns raking her with 20mm cannon fire.

The Fortress, with only one of her engines still producing power, has now lost her fight and is slowly spiraling downward. With the number 3 engine still at war power, the B-17 enters a spin, and then the fisherman notices a fourth parachute blossom out.

As the Dutchman watches, the spinning bomber explodes, falling in three large fiery sections. Each piece of the wreck comes crashing down near his boat. They settle into the inland sea shared by Holland and Germany, known locally as the Dollard.

One section, the fuselage with part of one wing is still burning. Near one of the buoys, the tail has created a notable wake, rushing against the incoming tide and up the "groote gat" (main channel) toward the Ems River.

Soon a speedboat appears, apparently in search of survivors. Near the burning fuselage they retrieve a seriously injured gunner. After a futile search for additional survivors, the five Germans in the speedboat roar off toward Emden with their wounded prisoner. Racing right into the downtown Emden docks, the flyer is quickly removed and transported to the Emden Marine hospital.

While the helpless flyer is being rushed into the hospital, he is slowly drifting toward unconsciousness. He can hear people shouting off in the distance. Their speech is garbled. "Why can't I understand them"? Then he sinks into unconsciousness.

When he comes to a little later in the German hospital, there are other flyers nearby that are in bad shape and some are dying. He tells the kind doctor his name, his hometown and about his new wife working at the PX back in the States. Slowly, the confused gunner with his fleeting thoughts of better days begins to fall into unconsciousness again. "Oh, if only I could be back in Sioux City, back at training camp, back with Marie", he thinks.

Hit by the defensive fire of *Miss Deal* the "Schwarze 10" of Uffz. Albert Oexle in her death dive. The image described by the witness is portrayed by the artist, Ab Jansen's excellent water color.

Chapter 2

Training

Jack Goetz's Training story

Jack Goetz was employed in a machine shop in Baltimore, Maryland when the war broke out. Although he wanted to enlist, his Mother would not allow it since he had a medical condition and was classified 3A. One day while at lunch he saw an ad in Life magazine showing an Air Corp flyer with a 50 caliber machine gun. He decided right then and there that was what he wanted to be, an aerial gunner in a B-17.

Sometime in June 1942 he was asked to take over a machine while a fellow employee went on vacation. He refused to operate a machine on which he had no training. After a dispute with the personnel department, he quit, citing that he was going to enter the service.

It was eighty miles to his home and the next Monday he entered the hospital and had his tonsils removed. He was sworn in on Wednesday. He was sent to Ft. Meade with all his stitches still in. The Army doctors were surprised when they found that he had just had his tonsils removed.

Jack was sent down to St. Petersburg and there he took his basic training. He volunteered for gunnery. At St. Pete there were not enough barracks, so most of the recruits were billeted in hotels.

While in basic, they had to experience high altitude low-pressure simulation. The chamber was depressurized to an equivalent altitude of 30,000 feet for four hours and then 25,000 feet for two hours. During this training, they asked for volunteers to test the effects of the loss of oxygen.

I volunteered and they told me to write the poem "Mary had a Little Lamb". They took off my oxygen mask and I started writing. I got about half way through the poem and fell asleep. They put my mask back on and I picked up writing the poem right where I left off. If I ever wanted to die, then cutting off the oxygen would be the easiest way to go; you just fall asleep".

Four out of twenty of Jack's fellow trainees got the bends during their time in the chamber and washed out of Army Air Corp basic training. Jack assumed that his next station would be for gunnery training at MacDill Field, which was across Tampa Bay. However, he was told that he had to first attend Aircraft and Engine Mechanics School: then, they would see about gunnery. So he was sent to Keesler field at Biloxi, Mississippi for A&M School for about 16 weeks. Next it was on to B-17 Specialist School at Boeing Field in Seattle for 8 weeks and finally on to gunnery school. Las Vegas, Nevada was where Jack landed for his gunnery training. He was somewhat surprised to learn that gunnery training was very rough. "All you heard was whistle blowing; we would start training at 4:30 in the morning and finish the day at 9:30 in the evening".

Gunnery training began with skeet shooting from the back of a pick up truck or a weapons carrier. Here, we learned to quickly react to the target, as you had no idea from which direction they were coming. Also, you learned to lead the targets while riding along at a pretty good clip.

The fifty-caliber training began with learning all of her parts and pieces and included assembly until you could do it while blindfolded. We studied ballistic and shot a lot of 30 and 50 caliber machine guns. After you learned your machine gun, then you would target practice where they would pull targets by tracked vehicles behind a barricade. You would shoot at the target, knock it over and it would come back up.

Next, we did our aerial flying for gunnery and one day there was a boy downstairs who had a whistle. Well, I had got some mail from home that day and this boy downstairs was blowing his whistle, and I yelled, "blow it out your a**". Suddenly, you could hear these quick slamming steps coming up the stairs and entered the commanding officer yelling who said that? When no one answered, he screamed again, "Who said that? Who said that? When I find out who said that, he graduates as a private, and if I don't find out who said that by 4 o'clock, everyone up here will pull extra duty the whole time you're here".

About 4 o'clock, 4 guys showed up from the commander's office, a staff sergeant, a buck sergeant, a corporal and a PFC. This PFC came up to me and said," Goetz, if you don't turn yourself in by 4 o'clock, I'm gonna turn you in". There was a boy standing beside me from Pennsylvania, a coal miner. He walked up to the PFC, looked at him and said, "I'm gonna tell you something PFC, if you ever talk or blow this off I'm gonna knock every tooth out of your mouth". Four o'clock came, nothing said, we pulled extra duty. They put the sergeant in charge and here's what he said to me; "Goetz, all I want to see out of you is your a—hole and elbows as you're picking up cigarette butts".

Once when we were scheduled for target practice in an AT 6, I asked the pilot to give me a nice ride after practice. The pilot said, "oh no, I can't do that". In the AT 6 the gunner stands in the back with the cockpit open, and when he uses up his ammo, he moves his gun up and down to signal the pilot that he is finished as the pilot is watching in his mirror. Suddenly, he puts the plane in a dive and rolls out upside down. Although, I am standing up and strapped in, it was the most terrifying ride of my life; I left my fingerprints in the steel grips of the .50 caliber. I could see in the mirror that the pilot was laughing his a** off, but I asked for it. I guess that was one of the most exhilarating rides of my life.

I had convinced two guys from basic named Miller to enter aerial gunnery school; one was from Boston and the other was from Tennessee. The Tennessee kid could not hit a bull in the a**. One day, he came to me and said he thought he was going to be washed out as he rarely made any hits. I asked him what color ammo he was using and he said *red, so I picked up a canister of red and so did the other gunner. This was on our next planned target shoot. When we landed his target had more holes than he had ammunition. So he passed.*

I was in Vegas about six weeks, and then we went back to Salt Lake City for a couple days for assignment to a Group. Here we were in a big building and they would call out names as they were assigning personnel to make up the crews. The Miller boys were called and assigned to a crew that went up to Spokane for their next training phase. Their story ended when their plane was taking off for their first flight, their B-17 crashed and exploded killing everyone on board.

One of The Miller boys that Goetz refers to may have been Lee Miller, who was killed when the B-17 *Scharazad* 42-3399 crashed on what is now known as Bomber Mountain in the Big Horn Mountains of Wyoming on 29 June 1943. Apparently one flyer survived the horrific crash near the ridge top at 12,887'. His remains were found propped up against a large boulder, nicely dressed, with his bible open, his wallet nearby and family pictures scattered about.

Finally, I was called up and I met Jacobs and the rest of the crew. After this initial assignment, we always flew together. Leaving Salt Lake we went up to Boise around the first of April or the last of March '43. This was the most boring part of our training, especially at high altitude. You might have twenty practice bombs on board. You fly over a target and if you hit the target, then you can see the flour make a cloud of white dust. We would drop one bomb at a time trying to improve the bombardier's skill. Boring... for all the gunners.

Sometimes, we would fly air to ground gunnery and we would shoot antelopes. The ball turret gunner was always the best at hitting the antelopes. Finally, they stopped that, as the upper brass got on our a** for shooting the wildlife. Every gunner had to fly and train at each gun station.

Most of our crew flew in the co-pilot's seat to get the feel of handling a B-17 in flight. I'm sure I got a couple of hours in the right seat.

Jack Goetz was the engineer on the Randolph Jacobs crew, which was one of the 384th first replacement crews. The Jacobs crew's training would have been considered rushed compared to the original crews. Due to the rapid demise of the 384th early crews, they never finished their third phase of training. The Group was desperate for new crews.

Goetz does not mention the testing for enemy aircraft identification. A lot of time was spent reviewing slides and models of enemy fighters. The Air Corps could not afford to have a bunch of "trigger happy" gunners shooting at allied fighters; although it did occasionally occur.

The Jacobs crew with their unknown training ship in Casper, Wyoming

Photo courtesy of Quentin Bland
Original crew left to right: Doy Cloud (ro), Robert Compton (tg), Larry Wager (wg), Eugene Boger (cp), Randolph "Moose" Jacobs (p), John Curtin (n), Jim Seibel (b), Donald Gorham (btg), Jack Goetz (wg), Aldo Gregori (ttg) (Donald Gorham at 6'1 and ½ inches may have been the Air corps tallest ball turret gunner)

On the next page is a picture of the Delton Wheat ship, 42-30048 *Flak Dancer*. Photo taken from *Miss Deal* 42-30049 in 1943 on a cross-country training mission shortly after the crews got their new Fortresses. Notice *Flak Dancer's* number 42-30048, which reflected that she was manufactured right before *Miss Deal* 42-30049. *Flak Dancer* was lost the day after *Miss Deal* was MIA.

After *Flak Dancers* belly landing in a wheat field near Laon, France, she was salvaged by the Luftwaffe and placed in KG 200. The Germans used captured B-17s in following and observing bomber formations and fighter training.

Photo of *Flak Dancer* courtesy of Ellen Corrigan

Six of the *Flak Dancer* crew evaded capture, two were killed in action and two spent the rest of the war in a German prisoner of war camp. The crews of *Miss Deal* 42-30049 and *Flak Dancer* 42-30048 became good friends during training and cross country missions.

Photo Courtesy of Ellen Corrigan

Bombardier school 1942 at either Victorville, CA or Selma, AL: Tom Corrigan, *Miss Deals* Bombardier on left. The other pictured bombardiers may have been assigned to the 384th one was nicknamed "Pinky".

John R. Way *Miss Deal's* only Pilot. Way was from Englewood, New Jersey and attended Mass at St. Cecilia along with Vince Lombardi. At St. John's he initially studied Divinity, where he graduated with a degree in accounting. He excelled in music and was employed by Glenn Miller working alongside the bandleader's bookkeeper.

Photo from Charles Crawford memorabilia
379th Gunners with their favorite Sgt., Bill Cain at Wendover Army Air Field. Standing: Crawford, Cain and Tesser. Kneeling: Mitchell, Smith and unknown. Note barracks have tarpaper exterior.

Photo by Tony Crawford
2009 Wendover Army Air Field barracks.

Photo from Charles Crawford's memorabilia.
The *Brinkman* crew photo taken at Wendover Army Air Field, February 1943.
Front Row: W.E. Homes (N), D.J. Andrews (B), W.H. Cochran (CP), W.F. Brinkman (P)
Back Row: A. Mitchell (BT), F. Murphy (TG), C.E. Crawford (RO), L. Tesser (RWG), R. Smith (LWG), C.F. Watkins (TT)

Train Rides
Per the book Shades Over Kimbolton: In February 1943, the entire 379th bomb Group packed up, and boarded a troop train for Sioux City, Iowa.   As the train pulled out, Major Walter P. "Duffy" Fulkerson, then assistant Group Ops officer, very graphically summed up Wendover by saying, "I've seen worse places, but for the life of me I can't remember where in hell they were".

The train ride to Sioux City, like most troop movements, was a long and tiresome affair. Most of the men spent the first few hours listlessly watching the scenery, reading or writing Letters, and then turned to the only real means of diversion----gambling.

A dozen poker games broke out in each car and two or three red-hot crap games held the interest of those not gambling. All through the long night, the games went on without respite.

One of the players was Charlie Crawford, Frank Murphy and Mike Arooth's training buddy, Elvin Doll. Rolling the dice was one of Doll's favorite games, especially if there was money on the table. Doll was Fortunate on this train ride, as he knew he could call on his three pals to spot him some needed cash just like the old days at Wendover and Gowen Field. He had always been good for the loans so you can bet he hung in there with the big boys when the pot was growing, that is, as long as his money held out.

Occasionally the faces would change, but still the rustling of bills, the click of dice and the chant of the players went on. It finally narrowed down to five or six men who bucked heads for the remainder of the journey and the amount of money, which changed hands often, mounted into the thousands.

After a couple of days while in western Nebraska, word spread about an approaching service stop to take on coal and water for the engine. It was rumored that it would be allowed for all personnel to disembark for a few minutes.

This is the description of the North Platte station by Lawrence Jones from Nacogdoches, Texas during his interview by Bob Greene. "There were probably five hundred military people on that train---field artillery, infantry, and air corps. After that long trip across the country, at five-thirty one afternoon we pulled into this place none of us knew anything about. We looked out the windows and there were these women talking to us, passing us sandwiches and everything. They said "Are you going to get off the train?" We said, "We don't know if we're allowed."   They said "We got it fixed---you can get off the train."   And so, he said they all did. "We were all in our uniforms when we walked into the train station …and there were these plank tables, loaded down with every kind of food you could imagine. Homemade cakes, pies, sandwiches, Coca Cola… We could not get over it. Out in the middle of nowhere, or at least to us it was the middle of nowhere, and it was getting toward dusk… this was like a miracle."*

This was known as the North Platte Canteen; here farmers from this part of western Nebraska supplied the food. The farmers brought milk, chicken, ham, etc. and their wives prepared it for the soldiers and they did it day after day after day. A few minutes after the trains were serviced, there would be two short blasts from the whistle, a signal that the train was about to depart, which resulted in a mad dash by the troops to load up on cookies, apples and the like before their scramble to re-board.

Most of the troops did realize that these people donated an enormous amount of their time, money and their ration stamps to support the North Platte Canteen. This facility reflected the love that this section of the U.S.A. had for the American G.I. It was estimated that these folks served over six million soldiers passing through North Platte, Nebraska.

*From the book <u>Once Upon a Town</u> by Bob Greene

Chapter 3

The Journey to the Unknown

After training and the train rides with the 379[th,] the crews move into their new quarters at Sioux City, Iowa. Soon the Brinkman crew was ordered out to the field to take a look at their brand new B-17. To Charlie and his crewmates, this was the most beautiful and baddest plane in the Air Corps. At first, they just stood around and admired her. She had graceful lines and there were four big engines, each capable of churning out 1,380 horsepower.

Before they could take delivery, the crew watched while she took her test flights. How easily she took to the sky, how quickly she climbed heavenward. She banked into her climbing turns, and just as quickly was back on the ground for more test runs and then a number of touch and goes. With everything all new and outfitted with all new equipment, this plane, like her crew, was part of their family. As the crew crawled on board to check her out, they couldn't help but notice that she even smelled new.

While Sioux City was their final place of training, it was where the crew really came together. Based in Iowa in the middle of winter, the 379[th,] could not practice formation flying in the normal dreadful weather. So the C.O. had no choice other than to direct his Bomb Group to make cross-country training flights down south and out west.

Some of the cross-country trips included a visit to Oklahoma City. Then they took a cross-country to Hamilton Field near San Francisco. On another cross-country trip the Group went to El Paso with an overnight stop. Then they flew to Bakersfield, California with an overnight in the famous old El Tejon hotel.

These trips were exhilarating to the men, as most had never been to California and the western states, nor to the South. Generally, wherever they were billeted they received passes and were exposed to the local sights and sounds. Here, the men began to realize that the Army made sure that as members of the Air Echelon, they were in a class of their own. The Army's brass was aware that the flyers manning the heavy bombers in the European Theatre were being decimated by Hitler's flak units and fighter Gruppes. Realizing that these new flyers were destined for vicious air battles with odds of never returning. The Generals had few complaints for extravagant training expenses.

Charlie and the *Brinkman* crew were given their final leaves and they rushed off telegrams of good Fortune to their loved ones back home. Most of the messages gave a general time that they could be expected. Charlie sent his telegram to his older sister in New York, which stated: DEAR GRACE I'LL BE HOME IN A COUPLE OF DAYS=CHARLES. This message went out on March 30, 1943 and his older sister was expected to notify the rest of the family. Just as curt, a few days later Charlie and the rest of the 379th aircrews got their telegrams from their C.O. to report back to their station. After a final farewell to family, friends and fiancé, Uncle Charlie and other members of the *Brinkman* crew returned to Sioux City.

Soon the ground crews were packing up and heading out by train to Camp Kilmer, New Jersey. Within a week after the ground crews have departed, the aircrews with their new B-17s depart for Maine. Unfortunately because of bad weather, the Group is forced down at Selfridge Field, north of Detroit.

Here an obviously ill Charles Crawford is directed to visit the field hospital by Billy Brinkman, his pilot. The next day, the crew learns that Charlie has been put in isolation as he has the mumps.

The aircrews depart Michigan without one of their crewmen, Charles Crawford, their radio operator. The young men making up the *Brinkman* crew have left one of their training buddies, a reliable crewmate and one of their family, as they move on toward their debarkation point in route to England.

After a bit over 2 weeks, Charles Crawford is sent back to Kearney Field. He is assigned to the radio room, back to practicing code. While at Kearney the 384th is being processed for overseas deployment. Soon the 384th personnel is not only getting all kinds of injections but new gear. Each crewman gets all new parachutes, "Mae West" (life preserver), flight clothing, and his personal oxygen mask.

Charlie is picked up by the *Way* crew as they have lost their ball turret gunner. He is welcomed to the crew and is also assigned the position as assistant radio operator. Here, he meets a number of crewmen, as there is a lot of free time between processing duties. He takes a liking to the Way crew, especially Feagin and the young waist gunner Raymond Dodge that the crew refers to as "Trigger".

Like the *Brinkman* crew, Charlie discovers the officers are cordial and are not into formality unless a couple of the "gung ho" pilots come around. One of Charlie's training friends verbally stated that he considered the animosity of the saluting officers as a "F… You" to the NCOs. Mike Arooth was quickly recognized as very street smart by his peers and they liked hanging out with this cunning little Arab.

The commanding officer, Budd Peaslee, is made aware that there are a couple of arrogant pilots in his outfit. So at one Group meeting he called his pilots down with all the crews concerning their manners. Here he referred to the pilots as "taxi drivers". In the same meeting, Peaslee told the pilots that the "guys in the back do all the work". Overall, each of the 379th and the 384th crews were a tight family knit team.

Soon the thirty-six B-17s from the 384th are all set to head out to Presque Isle, Maine. With the planes scheduled for takeoff at five-minute intervals, the flight line must have been an awesome sight and sound with the roar of one hundred forty-four big Wright cyclone engines. Slowly, the first B-17 lumbered into position, rolled down the runway, gently lifted off and upon reaching a few hundred feet, lost power in two engines. Returning to base with an embarrassed C.O. must have been quite a downer for the 350 flyers witnessing the old man bring his lead Fortress back in for engine repairs.

The 384th continued on without their Commander, arriving 1,700 miles later in Presque Isle, Maine. Finally, Budd Peaslee and his crew caught up with the 384th at Gander Bay, Newfoundland. Here the weather over the North Atlantic had stopped any aircraft from departing toward England. At this Canadian airfield there were over 200 airplanes parked for a number of days. Not just new bombers and their crews, but high priority freight desperately needed in the war effort.

Eventually, the weather was forecast as good enough for the planes to depart. While *Miss Deal* was taking her turn for takeoff, one of her engines would not develop full power.* She aborted her take off run and taxied back to a hardstand for repairs. She finally got off 2 days later with her new destination Prestwick, Scotland.

This part of the journey over the North Atlantic was uneventful until the following morning when all hands got their first look at a German submarine. As it slowly plowed through the rough Atlantic, the country gunners didn't know what to think seeing a boat that big. Feagin, a Kentucky Golden Gloves state champion, who before his entry into the Air Corps, was employed as a specialist loading fuel barges working the Ohio River, probably wasn't impressed.

The navigator got the approximate coordinates radioed into the British in Prestwick. By the time that *Miss Deal* and her crew spotted Ireland, the pilots were getting very concerned about their low fuel. After a number of rapid calculations, John Way decided "no problem" and to press on to the scheduled destination.

After touching down in Scotland, *Miss Deal* was met by a British escort vehicle and directed where to park. Some of the officers were called from the plane. This little entourage was hustled off to meet with an intelligence officer and others. Sherrer is grilled about how he got the coordinates of the German submarine. He gave them all the information that he had used such as air speed, wind speed, wind direction and reminded them that the overcast weather prevented use of the sextant. The problem was quickly discovered that *Miss Deal* had lost her tail wind along with her calculated ground speed. The Group of officers finally revealed to the Way contingent that the reported coordinates for the German submarine would have put her in the midst of a lake in Ireland. The meeting was closed with a statement that "anyone can make a mistake".

The pilots were directed to follow another escort vehicle to an area with hangars and shops where *Miss Deal* was to have her new engine checked out along with an inspection of all her systems. Since the 384th had already departed for their new Station near Grafton Underwood, the crew would be billeted at Prestwick for a few days. They were allowed passes each day and Charlie wrote his mother that he visited two Scottish towns.

As the *Miss Deal* crew is readying for departure, they realize that they are now about a week behind the rest of the 384th. Peaslee and his Group had already left for their new home at Station 106 near Grafton Underwood, when *Miss Deal* touched down at Prestwick airfield. Prior to the Group's departure for Grafton Underwood, the Commanding officer was informed that a plane would lead them to their new station.

17

Apparently, there were so many airfields in the Midlands that new crews were landing at the wrong airports.

Finally, John Way and crew make it to Grafton Underwood without incident and without a lead plane. The officers are shown to their new quarters while the enlisted men are guided to their 544th's NCO barracks.

Vernon Salmon, *Miss Deal's* crew chief, takes charge of Fortress 42-30049 and directs his ground crew to thoroughly check all systems on his plane. When *Miss Deal* is on her hardstand, she belongs to Vernon Salmon and it is his responsibility that she be placed on operational status as quickly as possible and only when the plane is ready per the "book".

When *Miss Deal's* Sergeants reach their new 544th bomb squad's quarters, there is a bit of celebration as the other crews thought they had ditched in the Atlantic on the "big hop". It was a learning time for Charlie as introductions were easy being part of a missing crew. To his surprise Charlie spots a dog in the barracks and gets to meet his owner.

There is another story here that a mysterious dog that had been with the 384th since Great Falls, Montana, had become quite adept at cautiously crossing roads designed for motorized traffic in the States. The story further states: "the dog, while making his rounds to different crews looking for handouts, did not realize that the vehicular traffic was in reverse" while in Gander Newfoundland. As a result, while looking in the wrong direction the dog paid the ultimate price. This story did not pass muster with the owner of the 384th's illegal mascot, or per other documents and photos.

Like Charlie I also was fortunate to meet Ray Gregori. Many years later at a 384th reunion in San Diego, and he told me the story about his dog, Delbert McNasty. Some of the most difficult issues were getting his dog overseas. He stated that he kept Delbert on their plane, the B-17F 42-30139, during the day while at Presque Isle, Gander and other airfields while they were in transit to their station in England. Delbert was happy on their B-17 as long as he was provided with a blanket, food and water. Sergeant Gregori would take Delbert out to do his business early in the morning and at night after dark.

After they got to England, Delbert was supplied with service records and even got his dog tags. At Grafton Underwood the official mascot had the run of the base. With Gregori and Delbert being in the 544th Bomb Squad, there is a written account of Delbert McNasty being present when the Morgue details were packing up the personal effects of the missing non-commissioned officers of the 544th on 25 June 1943.

A couple months later Delbert was indeed struck by a truck on base leaving a sad bunch of new friends. It seems almost fitting, as all the original crews of the 544th, with the exception of the Estes crew, had been lost. Now, Delbert could join all his old gunner buddies in eternity.

*Per a letter from Charles Crawford dated 26 May 1943 *Miss Deal* had problems with her # 3 engine during takeoff from Dow Field Bangor, Maine.

Although the Way crew is very late in catching up with their Bomb Group, they quickly are scheduled to get in on some training flights. This is necessary for the boys up front to get familiar with the lay of the English countryside. It is very important that the pilot and co-pilot re-sharpen their skills at tight formation flying.

Unfortunately, the Way crew was present when 16 of the 384th s B-17s were returning from a training flight, the co-pilot (Stephen Fabian) of the lead aircraft pointed out to the pilot that the approach to the west runway was incorrect. The pilot immediately began a go-around procedure resulting in a following Fortress pulling up into another B-17 (42-30036) and shearing off her tail. This accident brought home to all the Group's flyers just how unforgiving a simple mistake in flying can be. Although one of the planes was repairable the other crashed headfirst and was a total loss, with a loss of five lives. There were no injuries on the B-17 that landed safely. Naturally the pilot of the crashed Fortress was blamed for the mishap.

Photo of the crashed B-17F 42-30036 *Kowalski crew* lost on 12 June 1943.
Photo courtesy of Stan Bishop
For crew list see page xvi of the Appendices

It should be noted that Kowalski was co-pilot of the B-17 42-30037 in which Captain George W. Harris was the pilot of original crew number 68. Since Kowalski along with Eggers, Murphy and Blaise were from the same original crew and the co-pilot was not, then it is questionable if they were on a training mission. Also with Kowalski in charge of the Fortress number 42-30036, it is thought that he had been elected to "slow time" this ship to run in a new engine for the required one and one half hours. "Slow timing" nearly always involved a partial crew. It was not unusual when "slow timing" to keep the airfield in sight, as there was not a lot of trust in a ship which had a new engine installed. Also "slow timing" was flying with engines at much less than full power. The bombardier was probably acting as the engineer, standing behind the pilots keeping watch on the new engine and also the instruments during takeoff.

The Raid on Antwerp 22 June 1943

Ten days after the fatal crash of 42-30036 and the *Kowalski* crew, the 384th was directed by teletype that the planned mission for a raid on the Ford and General Motors plants in Antwerp, Belgium was to commence. The crews were well aware that something was up as on the previous day the clubs along with any other entertainment venues had been closed.

The 384th crews that were to take part in the Group's first raid were awakened at 0330 as over two hundred flyers were notified that they would be taking a trip across the channel. It wasn't as if any of the flyers had gotten much sleep that night because the ground crews had been running engines most of the night, not to mention the fuel wagons and armories were trucking all the ammo and bombs to each of the B-17s selected for the initial raid. A half hour after being roused awake, the flyers were greeted by a smiling "cookie" and his happy staff at the mess hall with fresh eggs on the "last supper" menu.

The two rookie Bomb Groups, the 381st and the 384th, were to perform a diversionary raid, while the main strike against Germany was the synthetic rubber plant at Huls. Most of the old hands that attacked the rubber plant in the Ruhr valley considered the Antwerp mission a "milk run".

This first raid for the newest two Bomb Groups was preplanned by the 8th Air Corp brass to acclimate the rookies to combat and confuse the Germans into directing their fighters toward the wrong Groups. With Squadrons of Typhoons and Thunderbolts (most of the flyers referred to them as "Jugs") escorting the bombers, it was hoped that German radar would assume there was a formidable attacking force.

The first mission of the 384th bomb Group was led by the commanding officer, Colonel Bud Peaslee. When Peaslee is leading the bomb Group it was a rare occurrence for any B-17s to abort their scheduled mission.

During the briefing, one of the pilots suddenly realized that his Grandmother was living in Antwerp. Fortunately, he did not know that she lived only a few blocks from the target; this information he kept to himself. There were twenty 384th Fortresses assigned to participate in this mission.

This left *Miss Deal* and the remaining crews, not selected as spares, sitting at Grafton Underwood. The following day the 384th was scheduled to attack the enemy fighter base at Bernay-St. Martin northwest of Paris, France. On this raid, 42-30049 was selected to fly as a spare. Unfortunately there were no aborts and upon reaching the channel, *Miss Deal* returns to base to be followed by the rest of the B-17s as the mission is cancelled due to the heavy under-cast.

Each participating B-17 for the Antwerp mission was bombed up with five each one thousand pounders. The Group took off at 6:19, which was a little late from their scheduled departure time (per Peaslee's memories the "H" hour was 0700). Then they learned, upon reaching the rendezvous point, that the 381st was a half hour late or perhaps the 384th was early (this confusion reflects a major mistake by someone). So around and around the 384th went. Looking down on Ridgewell, England, the 381st home base, the officers could observe the first B-17 lift off followed by twenty more. The 381st finally climbed up to the join up altitude of 12,000 feet, led by their famous Commander Col. Joseph Nazzaro, a West Point graduate and member of their football club. When the 381st linked up with the 384th, the two Groups climbed up to their bombing altitude of 23,000 feet headed for the coast and on to the target.

The Germans are watching (by radar) and waiting with their fighters on alert, armed and tanked up.

Upon reaching the channel, crews that are selected as spares must return to base as none of the Fortresses aborted this mission. These crews return to their hardstand where their crew chief and his cadre of mechanics prepare their B-17s for another mission and the armorers disarm the big planes.

Meanwhile, Peaslee and his band of raiders along with the B-17s from the 381st had met enemy fighters about halfway to the target without any escorts, as there was no synchronized meeting. Fortunately, there were only approximately sixty Focke Wulf Fw 190s that greeted the bombers with head on attacks. These attacks were very similar to what Peaslee had witnessed when he flew as an observer on the Wilhelmshaven raid on 11 June 1943.

When the two bomb Groups reached the flak fields near their target, the Germans had broken off their attacks. Although the weather was clear and the target was visible, it was estimated that only 5 percent of the bombs actually hit the targets. This inaccuracy might have been contributed to the bombardier's position in the B-17's nose, with her clear plastic bubble, as they witnessed the Germans attacking them head-on at a combined speed of five hundred miles per hour with their 20 mm cannons blazing. With the plants covering five hundred acres, five per cent bomb coverage seems questionable.

It should be noted that the ship 42-3231 *The Inferno* was leading the 545th Squadron to the target when suddenly the bomb bay doors sprung open frosting up the nose of the Fortress along with the Bombardier's sight glass. This probably resulted in many misses from this Squadron.

After releasing their bombs, the two Groups turned back toward England and were again attacked by the fighters from II/ JG 26. These attacks were made by Staffels or Squadrons consisting of nine to twelve fighters. The fighters would press their head-on attacks until the last seconds when they would quickly turn upside down pulling their fighters down and away. Just before the coast, most of the Fortresses guns were suddenly silent and the gunners could be overheard shouting on the intercoms describing the air battles as finally, the Typhoons and the Jugs showed up for the fight. And fight they did as they drove most of the enemy fighters away from their big brothers.

Two of the 384ths B-17s were lost on their return trip. The Oblinski ship was viciously attacked as she lost the formation and was about 9,000 feet lower than her assigned box position. At the debriefing, it was reported that, although three of her engines were on fire, the Focke Wulf's kept up their attack on the wounded ship until she exploded, spun down and crashed near Wilhelminadorp, Holland. Six of the crew were taken prisoner and four were listed as killed in action. The B-17 42-5853 was lost by the 384th that day, was piloted by Fred Disney, who ditched her about halfway across the channel. There were only three survivors recovered by the Germans, and the remaining crewmembers were listed as KIA. No doubt some died as a result of exposure to the cold waters of the channel, since no life rafts were spotted.

There were two 384th ships that followed the Oblinski and the Disney Fortresses down in an attempt assist in their defense. These two B-17s, realizing they could be of no help returned to the Group and back to base to face the ire of the Commander for breaking formation and the rule if a bomber lost the formation, she was on her own. These two gallant captains were threatened with court-martial in front of their peers, as Peaslee made his point to the officers. The 381st lost two ships to the II/JG26 Focke Wulfs while two others made their final crash landing at other English bases. Upon their return to Ridgewell, two crewmen that had been killed in their first air battle were removed from their severely shot up B-17s.

42-30016 *Iron Gut Gert* had received severe flak damage, and on her way home was jumped by fighters and crashed near Hoek, Holland. Charles Henry died in the crash and the Navigator, Lt. Griffith came down in the North Sea, drowned, and was never recovered. The rest of the crew was captured and spent the rest of the war in prison camp.

Soon after bombs away 42-30021 was struck by flak and quickly attacked. One wing came off crashing in the Dutch inland sea, Oosterschelde. Two of the crew managed to get out of the falling Fortress only to become POWs, while eight went down with their ship.

The Disney ship was escorted down below 9,000 feet by another 384th B-17, breaking 8th Air Corp rules after flak and fighter attacks. Realizing escorting Disney was proving fruitless, the Disney ship was abandoned. Unfortunately, the escort act may have actually encouraged some of the seven flyers to stay with the doomed ship as she crashed just off the enemy coast.

The Oblinski ship had similar problems as the Disney crew with another gallant B-17 escort. Unfortunately, both escorts paid dearly for their actions as they were also brutally attacked by fighters from II / JG26. Neither of the escorts made it to their home base, instead landing at the nearest British airfield as soon as crossing the channel.

MIA B-17s and their missing crews for the 22 June 1943 raid on Antwerp, Belgium can be found on page xix of the appendices.
For pilots load list of the Antwerp raid of 22 June 1943 see page xxiv of the Appendices

Chapter 4

St. Nazaire

After finishing gunnery and their individual phase training, the men were assigned to a particular crew that was named after the pilot in command. Many of the Fortresses would be later christened a name normally chosen by the pilot or one or two of the other crewmen. The assignment of the flyers to different ships resulted in the splitting up of friends that had come together during their initial phase training.

Three of Charlie's close friends through training were assigned to the *Tondelayo*. They were Mike Arooth, John Leary and Elvin Doll. Also, the *Brinkman* crew and the *Tondelayo* were both in the 527th Squadron of the 379th bomb Group. So, these friends did continue to visit.

Unfortunately for Charlie, his draw was not for the *Tondelayo*. This probably mattered little as the mumps redirected him to the *Way* crew with the 384th. This bomb Group was about a month behind the 379th.

The *Brinkman* crew was made up of 1st Lieutenant William F. Brinkman, the pilot from Pocahontas, Iowa. The co-pilot was William H. Cochran who was from Hagerstown, Maryland. The navigator, William E. Homes was from Phoenix, Arizona. The bombardier, Donald J. Andrews came from Muskegon, Michigan.
My Uncle Charles E. Crawford was the original radio operator and due to illness was replaced by William A. Carver from Farmersville, Texas. The ship's engineer and top turret gunner was Clarence F. Watkins from Loring, Montana. The two waist-gunners were Robert E Todd from New Orleans, Louisiana and Ralph J Smith from Des Moines, Iowa. The ball turret gunner was Alfred H. Mitchell from Lyndhurst, New Jersey. The tail gunner was Frank Murphy Jr. from Benavola, Alabama. This was the make-up of the Brinkman crew on her fatal raid of 11 June 1943.

28 March 1942 St. Nazaire
After the fall of France, St Nazaire proved an excellent location for one of Hitler's submarine bases. Quickly, the docks were improved and heavy concrete structures were built to hide and protect the Kriegsmarines' rapidly expanding U-boat fleet. These structures were termed "sub pens" and afforded excellent protection for the submarines and the mechanics when they were in for maintenance and repairs.

Once the Army Air Corp began arriving in England in sufficient numbers, Churchill and the British Bomber Command began pushing for the 8th Army Air Corp to deploy their bombers against the German submarine bases. The subs were simply destroying supplies and armament in quantities, which many believed were inadequate to supply and defend the Crown.

It had already been shown that the continuing bombing of the heavily defended St. Nazaire Submarine Pens did little damage to the port facilities, while practically wiping the town off the map.

Early in the morning of the 28th of March 1942 a flotilla of small gunboats were escorting an old American destroyer that had been rechristened "The Campbeltown" by the British. The old naval force bypassed the channel and headed straight in toward the St. Nazaire port and the Normandie dock. Unfortunately, the coastal batteries and flak stations had been tipped off by an alert German patrol boat, with her winking signals. Most of the small British gunboats were lost during the raid as a result of the vicious attacks by the shore batteries. The old Destroyer herself was successfully driven right upon the big dock. Unknown to the Germans, the Campbeltown was laden with explosives, which were hidden with delayed fusing. The following day, a Sunday, saw many of the Nazi big brass parading down the dock with their wives and girlfriends showing off the captured British destroyer. Suddenly, a massive explosion destroyed the dock, to such an extent that it was not serviceable again until 1952. The visiting Nazis, families and friends that were marveling at the old "Campbeltown" disappeared. This naval action consisted of 611 men, of these 169 were killed.

A similar sized attack by B-17s would have normally included 61 Fortresses from three bomb Groups, with an equivalent loss of 17 ships. Not a single air raid against any of the sub pens could come close to the destruction of this naval raid.

During this naval raid, Charlie and his old friend from Alabama, Dub Wright, were stationed at Sheppard Field, Texas. Per a letter home there were fifteen thousand Air Corp cadets at Sheppard and only six airplanes. Odds of making a pilot seemed very slim.

29 May 1943 St. Nazaire, France

One of the latter raids on St. Nazaire, as the AAF brass was beginning to see that attacking the German submarine pens, with their heavy concrete roof structures, was akin to attacking the enemy with ping-pong balls. The British, however, needed these raids to continue for morale purposes, if nothing else.

Unfortunately, the next two 8th AAF raids were attacks on the submarine docks at Wilhelmshaven (11 June 1943) and the submarine slips at Bremen and Kiel** (13 June 1943) with a loss of thirty nine B-17s, two hundred twenty six flyers killed and ninety one prisoners of war.

Charlie's old crew (*Brinkman*) along with twenty three other 379th bomb Group B-17s were scheduled to attack the St. Nazaire submarine pens. This five and one half hour raid would be their first target after arriving at their new base in Kimbolton just ten days prior.

*The Normandie dock was used to service all kinds of German ships and the only Atlantic dock capable of servicing their great battleship *Tirpitz*

The attacking Forts were bombed up with two each two thousand pound bombs. The size of the bombs was an indication of an attempt to at least inflict some kind of damage on the sub-pen or the related structures.

The schedule called for the Brinkman ship to be in the same formation with the *Tondelayo*, and her original pilot Simones. The crews had already heard about St. Nazaire, as it was referred to as "Flak City".

The high flying bombers were crossing the English Channel flying SSE toward the Brest Peninsular of France. After passing west of Guernsey, the Wing began a slight turn east then passing near St-Brieuc, and on to the I P point of Blain, France. Here a ninety-degree turn would point the formation toward the target.

Approximately half way to the English coast one of the B-17 aborts, then before the coast a second one turns back toward home. Near Guernsey, a third Fortress aborts and 3 Focke Wulfs are turning to make pursuit, but all 379th aborted ships returned to base.

Soon after crossing the French coast, the fighter escorts near their range limit, turn back for home, leaving the B-17s to fend for themselves.

The crews were now approaching the culmination of all their training for the chance of aerial combat, but first they must run the gauntlet of the heaviest concentration of flak in France.

Some of the crewmen would not be able to fire a single round in combat, as their Fortresses would become a German flak crew's victory, which would be indicated by a stripe around the barrel of their cannons.

Most all of the ships were able to deliver their bombs on or near the target. The heaviest damage appeared to have been inflicted to buildings alongside the wharf.

Leaving the target, the accuracy of the St. Nazaire flak units began to take their tolls. First a 305th Fortress was hit just at "bombs away", at an altitude of 27,700 feet. The aircraft went out of control and crashed just west of the target, killing nine with only one crewman surviving, the tail gunner who was able to get out of the spinning craft.

A second B-17, *The Concho Clipper*, the lead ship, which was piloted by Lt. Colonel J. Russell of the 351st bomb Group was hit by an 88 mm shell in the ball turret just after bombs away. This hit also killed the radio operator and both waist gunners. The hopeless, burning Fortress with two engines out was used for target practice, before being finished off by German Focke Wulf Fw 190s.

Next, a 303rd bomb Group B-17 damaged by flak, which was quickly attacked by fighters. This sent the Fortress *Yardbird* crashing down into the French farmland, killing two of her crew. The co-pilot, Thomas Vaughn was likely killed by shrapnel from a flak burst and the engineer mortally wounded. The engineer, Paul Prescott was removed to a Paris hospital where he died from his wounds on the 4th of June 1943.

The first 379th to go down in combat was B-17 number 42-29773 piloted by Captain John Hall, the commanding officer of the 526th bomb Squadron. The loss of all the gunners plus the radio operator can be attributed to the accuracy of the St. Nazaire flak crews. After bailing out, copilot Willard Thomas is acknowledged by two smiling and waving Focke Wulf pilots. The French farmland near the village of Kerdavid rapidly approaches and Thomas' landing is met by over a hundred curious citizens. Moments later three German soldiers step out of the crowd to place him under arrest.

About fifty kilometers further north, a second 379th bomber was damaged by flak and loses in her battle with fighters. After eight of the crew bailed out, Lt. Arthur Hale crash-landed Fortress 43-3113 near Pontivy. Fortunately, the entire crew survived resulting in their spending the rest of the war in a German POW camp.

The last B-17 to go down in France that participated in the 29 May 1943 St. Nazaire raid was a 305th bomb Group ship. She was shot up by fighters, resulting in the loss of one engine and her breaking into. Pilot Marshall Peterson and his crew managed to escape with the exception of the right waist gunner. Some of the crew, while in their parachutes, witnessed their own ship 42-29531 crash twelve miles southwest of St-Brieuc.

A 379th Fortress whiched crashed on her return from the St. Nazaire raid was *Lady Godiva*. She went down due to severe flak damage and crashed in the English Channel one mile north of Saint-Quay-Portrieux. All her crewmen survived. Two of the lucky flyers were assisted by the local French resistance network in evading capture.

The final raider to go down was ship number 42-29742. This 305th bomb Group B-17 did not quite make it back to England, as she suffered heavy flak damage and lost her left waist gunner. The *Stevenson* crew ditched with nine of her crew rescued.

About the time St. Nazaire was under attack, three other bomb Groups were attacking the Naval Storage Depot at Rennes, France. The 94th, 95th and 96th bomb Groups each lost two B-17s. Of these six Forts, thirty flyers made the ultimate sacrifice, while twenty-four were captured and carted off to prison camp.

There were seven very lucky American flyers on the Rennes raid, as they bailed out and evaded capture. Eventually they made it back to their bases to learn firsthand that their participation in air combat was over. The Allies could not risk the capture of a former evader, who might reveal the identity of those aiding their escape, thus losing undercover escape routes.

The Kriegsmarine had eight big experienced flak batteries surrounding the harbor at St. Nazaire. Any enemy aircraft entering this naval repair area was in danger of being lost before they had time to escape from this prime target.

The German Flak guns fired antiaircraft shells at enemy aircraft. The most common flak-gun was various models of the 8.8cm (88s) modified for high muzzle velocity. Flak shells were produced in 1941. They weighed approximately twenty pounds and could be set to explode at various altitudes blasting shrapnel in all directions. Flak probably took down more B-17 than fighters or damaged them so extensively that they became easy targets for enemy fighters.

Every B-17 that made the target and was lost on the St. Nazaire raid of 29 May 1943 was hit by flak and would have been an easy target for the German fighters.

Barrel of German 88 flak gun with 19 victory stripes

Luftwaffe flak emplacement with soldier proudly posing in front of his cannon with kill rings.

Photos from Tony Crawford's collection

German soldiers posing in front of their large flak gun.

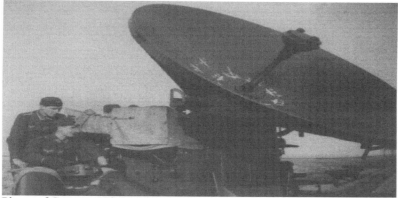
Photo of German radar station courtesy of Jos Stock
German Radar 1943/1944

Small Kriegsmarine flak cannon firing with soldier on left using range-finder. This cannon is located along a Western Front seashore.
Photos of flak stations from Tony Crawford's collection

Luftwaffe Flak Unit Personnel with one of their 8.8 cm cannons in the background.
Photo from Tony Crawford's collection

MIA B-17s and their missing crews for the 29 May 1943 raid on St. Nazaire, France can be found on page xvi and xvii of the appendices.

Chapter 5

The Wilhelmshaven Raid

The Bremen/Wilhelmshaven mission was originally scheduled for an early morning lift off on 11 June 1943. All crews were up early, only to be told that the raid had been scrubbed. When an early mission was cancelled most of the crews headed back to their bunks for some good rest or letter writing.

Later that morning around 10:30, the crews were again roused for briefings. The 384th commanding officer, Budd Peaslee, and four of his key officers had arrived at Molesworth the prior evening, as they had been requested by the brass at High Wycombe to fly as observers with the 303rd bomb Group on the next raid, which turned out to be the Bremen mission. This would be their first taste of WWII combat in B-17s with an experienced Group nicknamed "Hell's Angels".

The 303rd was the first bomb Group to bomb occupied Europe and she received her nickname "Hells Angels" from aircraft 41-24577. This was the first 8th Air Force B-17 to complete twenty-five missions. The honor was bestowed on 14 May 1943 a few days before the 384th reached England. The 384th Deputy Commander, Major Seldon McMillin flew as co-pilot on the ship 41-23605 "Knockout Dropper" with pilot in command Captain Jack Roller. They were assigned the lead ship in the low Squadron.

The primary target was to be the shipyard of "The German Ship and Machine Building Company", in Bremen. Due to weather, the primary target was bypassed with the formations turning toward Wilhelmshaven, the secondary target.

Leading the formations was Colonel Chuck Marion of the 303rd bomb Group. The 379th, was airborne and away from Kimbolton by 1444 while the last ship from the 306th was airborne from Thurleigh at 1440. The 8th Air Corp planners scheduled the timing of each bomb Group's departure.

It was a nice day at Kimbolton as the 379th Fortresses began their take offs. The gunners in the back of 42-3148 gathered around the open waist ports during taxi. Following Group procedure the boys in the cockpit timed the previous Fortresses thirty second takeoff run. The pilot likely turned toward Cochran, his copilot, who would have nodded that all engines and their instruments were a go. Releasing the brakes while all four engines were at full power, the heavily loaded B-17 slowly began her run. The roar from the four big Wright Cyclone engines made the most experienced flyer pause and gaze toward the big Boeing. While standing by the waist gun stations the four gunners waved at the men watching the Forts take to the air. The flyers felt their pride grow as the ground crews and even the executive officers up on the control tower waved back.

Watkins, the engineer in the top turret standing behind the pilots, calls out the airspeed as Brinkman's B-17 accelerates. With his Fortress racing down the runway Brinkman hears the number one hundred and he eases back on the wheel. At one hundred and ten miles per hour the ship is airborne and accelerating rapidly toward her climb out speed. Reaching one hundred and twenty her gear is up and locked.

At one hundred and forty miles per hour, the pilots start their first ninety degree turn as they work their B-17 to assembly altitude. With their route in hand the navigator keeps the pilots abreast of their waypoints and on course.

Prior to reaching twelve thousand feet, Andrews was directed to arm the bombs. Once in the bomb bay the bombardier removed the pins from the arming vanes mounted on the nose of each bomb. Returning to his station, he secured the pins as evidence that their bombs were armed. By now all the gunners have donned their masks and connected to their oxygen outlet. With 50 percent cloud cover, the gunners get an occasional good view of the North Sea and the distant coast of Holland on their right.

The journey toward Bremen is a comfortable ride for all the young flyers on their way toward their target. With the 379th forming up behind their Group leader, the crews catch glimpses of other Groups of B-17s forming up into a growing Wing. Most of the rookie crews probably have a nice confident feeling knowing they are traveling with over two hundred and fifty B-17's to Northwest Germany.

With towering cumulus clouds, the Brinkman's tail gunner is probably reminded of funerals back in Alabama. The preacher would occasionally quote the 23rd Psalm: "Yea though, I walk through the valley of the shadow of death, I will fear no evil." Frank Murphy Jr. has never had a problem with controlling his fear per his old buddy Chester Graham from Benevola. "Frank was always quick to defend himself no matter how big the other boy was". Chester continued, "Frank carried his lunch to school in a syrup can and bent up a good number of buckets hitting the bullies upside the head".

Meanwhile the 379th Group leader directs his four commanders to bring their squadrons of B-17s into a tight formation. On this mission the 379th has launched thirty-one Fortresses within the Wing of two hundred and fifty-two ships. The "Brinkman" crew can see the other B-17s as the Groups merge. The tail-gunner, Frank Murphy Jr. has an excellent view of the "box formations" following his ship.

The formations begin heading northeast toward the North Sea as all groups join-up with the mission leader, the 303rd Bomb Group. Slowly the B-17s gained their required altitude and the various groups and squadrons form their defensive box formations.

Approaching the Island of Heligoland, Brinkman had to throttle back his Fortress as other lead ships were slowing down. Fortunately, he heard his Group leader's warnings that the Wing was slowing and turning to the secondary target, Wilhelmshaven.

In reality, Col. Marion's B-17 took two strikes in her engines from flak while over the island of Heligoland. With his plane decelerating significantly and little warning, the Groups following the leader had to take violent evasive action to avoid mid-air collisions. This scattered the lead Groups, and the formations never got reorganized.

This occurred while the Wing was well north of the German coast and added additional stress to Brinkman and his reassigned old B-17. This ship was not as comfortable to Brinkman and Cochran as 42-29892, which they had received new in Sioux City. They had flown her over from the states and taken her on the St. Nazaire raid. Although somewhat disappointed, the Brinkman officers could keep an eye on their old Fortress "892" as she was hauling their Squadron leader and they were flying on her right wing.

Approaching the German barrier islands, the Brinkman crew witnessed black puffs of smoke indicating that the flak stations on the Frisian Islands were attempting to engage the Wing. As the formations turn toward the IP or the inital point of the bomb run, the fighters came into view. The top turret gunner Watkins warned his gunners that fighters were on their right and racing past their Squadron.

The strength of the enemy fighter opposition was formidable. It was estimated that approximately two hundred enemy fighters took part in the action including Fw 190s, Bf 109s and Ju 88s. Even the German night fighters, the Bf 110's, were reported at debriefing as attacking the Fortresses.

Within the next few minutes the fighters could be seen banking into the front of the formations. Quickly the fighters began their head-on attacks in an attempt to break up and scatter the formations. The attackers were Focke Wulf Fw 190s and Messerschmitt Bf 109s. The Brinkman crew, while watching their sister ships under attack, may have felt Lady Luck was with them.

The officers and the turret gunners of the crews under attack were probably terrified by the fighters blitzing head-on. These men observed the bright orange flashes from the 20 mm cannons of each fighter that came charging in toward the formation's leading Fortresses.

At this point in the War, even the most experienced German Ace was fearful of attacking a formation of Fortresses alone from any quarter other than head-on, as the combined firepower of thirty-one B-17s was awesome. An attacking fighter could expect to see a minimum of ten per cent of a Group's fifty calibers firing at him when he moved closer than the thousand yard range of the formation's guns.

Before reaching the initial point (IP) where the bombardier, Don Andrews would take over control of the B-17. Watkins, the top turret gunner was able to get off some good shots with his twin fifties at the incoming fighters. While Alfred Mitchell, the ball turret gunner, got an excellent view of the fighters as they went under the lead bombers upside down.

Although the Brinkman ship was not under attack, there was plenty of excitement from the gunners shouting their warnings on the ten-station intercom. The officers could feel the vibrations of their Fortress from the firing of the heavy machine guns as the fighters flashed through the formation. The firing of the machine guns probably did little if any damage to the distant fighters. The shouting from the various gunners was interrupted with the attacking enemy fighters. With the gunners trying to engage the German fighters, a sudden a calm swept over the big Boeing's intercom.

The combined speed of the fighters meeting the bomber formations was in excess of five hundred miles per hour. This allowed the gunners in back of the ship only a quick glimpse of the streaking fighters. Every gunner wanted to score a claim on one of the German planes and be honored with a Swastika painted next to his gun station on the exterior of his B-17. Unfortunately, the speed of the frontal attacking fighters made a gunners victory close to impossible.

Even the gunners in the back of the Brinkman ship that managed to get off a few rounds at the upside down fighters, noticed they were streaming a bit of black smoke as they sped away. These gunners were ignorant of the oil burned with the fighters' stressed engines under maximum power. This led to a number of shouts on the intercom of hits on the fighters, which the gunners took for a score either as damage or a kill.

Entering the flak fields, the German fighters broke off their attacks thus allowing the antiaircraft crews their turn to attempt an undisputed victory over the B-17s. With scattered puffs of smoke surrounding the Brinkman Fortress, the flak was not near as intense as what was encountered on the St. Nazaire raid. On that mission hundreds of pieces of harmless shrapnel rained down on their ship from the flak exploding above. No doubt Frank Murphy Jr. recalled his days back in Alabama when a storm went through Benevola with the noise of the sleet falling on the tin roof of their old home.

Brinkman turned control of his B-17 over to Don Andrews his bombardier after he reached the initial point. The bombardier immediately switches to the open position the bomb bay doors. This activates the electrically driven jack-screws and opens the big doors. Now on the bomb run Andrews must find the target as his pilot holds their Fortress to the required bombing altitude. Once the lead bombardier releases his bombs all the bombers within that particular Group would normally drop their bombs.

Taking the cue from the lead bombardier, Andrews releases his timed string of high explosive bombs. The Brinkman crew feels an upward lurch as bombs away is announced. Then, four long jackscrews would start spinning and pulling the bomb bay doors shut.

With the bomb bay doors closing the pilot Billy Brinkman re-takes control of the Fortress. Now it was back thru the flak and homeward bound.

At this time, there was relief that the mission was half over, but then the fear returned as the crews knew the fighters were waiting for the formations to leave the flak fields.

Leaving the flak fields, Bill Cochran, the copilot, unhooks his seat belts indicating to Brinkman that he is heading down to the bomb bay. In the meantime, a Staffel of Focke Wulfs from Hosum, Germany have been ordered to intercept the American bombers that are retreating from Wilhelmshaven. The Focke Wulfs are racing south across the North Sea.

Departing Leeuwarden airfield, a Schwarm of Messerschmitt Bf 110 night fighters from NJG 1 have also been ordered to intercept the departing Fortresses. These twin-engine, twin tailed fighters are climbing to the B-17's altitude. Streaking to the northeast their interception point is near the Ostefriesland Islands.

Cochran has been flying now for over six stressful hours and needs to visit the boys' bathroom: the bomb bay. After feeling much relived, he returned to the flight deck where he was watching for fighters. After he had climbed back into his seat, he noticed a number of Focke Wulfs had started a frontal attack directly on their ship.

Unknown to the officers, this Staffel of Focke Wulf fighters had departed from Hosum. With this base northwest of Kiel, it is apparent that these fighters were not released by the German controllers until it was certain that Kiel was not the target. These fighters also gave chase to the departing Groups as the B-17s moved out over the North Sea on their homeward route.

The following is an excerpt from a letter from LT. W. H. Cochran in 2003.
"On our plane, it is surprising that any of us survived. We were having head-on fighter attacks. As they came through, they would roll and be on their backs to pull down rapidly after they got their last shots off. You had little chance to shoot at them going away. One Fw 190 was halfway through his roll when he collided with our aircraft. His wing cut through the nose of our plane and back through much of the fuselage. The impact was like an explosion and I was thrown through the windshield or canopy. I had unfastened my seat belt moments before and hadn't had time to refasten it. Otherwise I would have been trapped in the wreckage and gone down with the plane. Lt. Homes was at the right nose gun and missed being struck by the Fw 190 wing by inches. He was injured by the flying debris but managed to claw his way out of the remains of the nose. The other lucky survivor was the German pilot who was thrown out or got out of his plane. The fighter pilot and Lt. Homes were picked up by the same ambulance and taken to the Marx medical facility. Unfortunately, the Focke Wulf pilot didn't speak English to tell Lt. Homes whether his controls were shot out or just what had happened".

The survivors parachuted down one km north of the Luftwaffe base near Marx, Germany. One account stated that the right wing and one engine broke off of the fuselage. Carl Stewart, left waist gunner, and Joseph Biernacki, tail gunner on the B-17F 42-5382 *The Witches Tit* from the 303rd Bomb Group, witnessed the head-on collision between the Focke Wulf and the Brinkman ship. They reported that the enemy fighter collided with the B-17 knocking the nose and cockpit off of the Fortress and then watching as she went down spinning in flames. No one was seen to get out.

The crash of the Brinkman ship ended the war for this crew and left eight men dead and Cochran and Homes as POWs. The injured Navigator, Lt. Homes was taken to the naval hospital at Sanderbusch.

The pilot of the Focke Wulf was Hans-Geong Guthenke from 7 JG/11. On 12 May 1944, his career as a fighter pilot ended after a serious injury from another head-on crash with a B-17 on the Leipzing raid. Witnesses claimed the Fw 190 attacked an unknown raider head-on and they stated that the left wing had come off of the B-17. The uncontrollable Boeing reared up like a "war horse" directly in front of Guthenke's flight path. The Focke Wulf slammed into the ship vertical right wing severely injuring the fighter pilot and ending his career in the Luftwaffe.

The Wilhelmshaven raid saw the loss of eight Fortresses. Six of the eight were from one Squadron, the 527th from the 379th Bomb Group. All of these lost flyers came from the same Squadron, and were either acquaintances or friends. Thanks to the mumps my Uncle Charles was not with his old Brinkman crew. His illness delayed his eternal destiny to another day.

The fighter attacks were so intense on the 379th Fortress 42-5809 *Mary Jane* that she barely made it back to the English coast, landing at Coltishall with her pilot wounded in his right ankle and foot. The engineer was wounded in the face, both legs and feet, while the tail gunner was wounded in his left forearm and left leg. The right waist gunner received wounds in his right heel, right arm and right buttock. With three gunners and her pilot wounded, *Mary Jane* and her crew continued the fight until the enemy fighters either ran out of ammo or reached their fuel range. The following day 379th personnel inspected *Mary Jane* and were astounded at the damage from all the 20 mm strikes and declared her unflyable and her only worth was salvage.

Dangerous Dan
On the 11 June 1943 Wilhelmshaven raid, the 379th Fortress *Dangerous Dan* 42-29891, was returning home when she was attacked by a lone enemy fighter. She caught a burst of shells from a Focke Wulf's 20 mm cannon striking the cockpit. Fragments from one exploding shell knocked Bersinger, the co-pilot unconscious. While, another bullet struck the pilot Jones in the mouth passing on through his shoulder. With both pilots completely helpless the top turret gunner engineer, Cliff Erickson took over the controls and guided *Dangerous Dan* back to England. During her approach to Kimbolton the Navigator fired a flare notifying the other Fortresses to give way as there were wounded on *Dangerous Dan*. Most everyone at the base after hearing the radio operator description of the carnage in the cockpit and who was at the controls were well out of the way of any path the B-17 might take. To everyone's pleasant surprise Erickson brought *Dangerous Dan* down. Although the landing certainly was nowhere near a greased touchdown but neither did he ground loop the big bird.

A German Fighter Pilot's story of the Wilhelmshaven Raid*
The German night fighters based in Leeuwarden, Holland were directed to intercept and destroy the B-17s heading back to England after the raid on Wilhelmshaven. Uffz. George Pfeiffer would only have been concerned with defending a predetermined quadrant against British bombers during their night raids against the Reich. As wingman to Oblt. Sigmund, Pfeiffer and the other members of the Schwarm, lifted off and climbed rapidly toward the American bombers, which had already moved past the coastline and

were flying over the North Sea. The Fortresses and their crews were heading toward their bases in England with great anticipation that in another few minutes this mission will be in the hands of the two officers in the cockpit.

Unbeknown to the B-17 crews are the Schwarm of Bf 110s from NJG 1 (night fighters) giving chase as they are rapidly closing from northern Holland. There is little safety to be had heading home while over the North Sea, as these cold waters are unforgiving to the flyer without a raft.

The Schwarm of twin engine Night-fighters were designed to intercept the British bombers attacking at night. These Messerschmitts were set up with radar to search out and destroy invaders at night. Why were the Night-fighters being directed up to confront these American B-17s in daylight? The thought of engaging a Flying Fortress other than at night was frightening, with an attack suicidal. At that time the B-17s were considered nearly invincible.

In Pfeiffer's own words he recalls this episode: "Adjusting the pitch of the propellers for additional speed and a last glance at the canon light indicators. Having been switched on, the canons are loaded and armed.

I am closing rapidly on the port side of a B-17 that I find perfect for my flight path. Keeping the target in my sights becomes a challenge as the entire bomber Squadron suddenly descends rapidly as if trying to evade our attack. Thus I am forced to re-correct my angle of attack on my target, which slows my closing rate.

This interruption of my plan of attack concerns me that my 110 will now be the target to all the Fortresses' aerial gunners. Instead of my fast hit and run attack, I now fear that my reduced speed may be my last flight.

I am able to regain my closing rate when suddenly I am in range of my target. I fire a few bursts only to be confronted by numerous American gunners spewing tracers at me like madmen.

The olive drab bomber looms larger and larger as I patiently hold my fire because the range is not close enough for my nose cannon and the two wing cannons to effectively make their mark. I had to give all my attention to my rapid closing rate and hold my fire until the Fortress enveloped my gun-sight to have a chance of victory. Now…. my cannons should find their mark as I squeezed the trigger firing all my cannons in one long burst.

One second later we had torn past as we went underneath the huge bomber. I stopped firing and immediately put my 110 in a vertical dive to quickly get out of range of the American gunners. The maneuver, to detach oneself quickly from the enemy, proved not only difficult, but also fatal for many of my fellow night fighter pilots. Slow to turn their fighters away from the Fortresses presented their ships up as targets to scores of the B-17 gunners.

Breathing again I throttled back and pulled out of our dive as we were out of range and began our climb for a second attack. As to hits, I had not noticed any damage to my target.

When we looked down below, we could hardly believe our eyes: For the rear tail section of my Boeing, suddenly came off. At the same time, five parachutes blossomed up as the crew had stepped out. The main fuselage of the dying Fortress now out of control, stood vertically with all four propellers still spinning as if trying to climb back to rejoin her sister ships. Then she went into a spin falling into the North Sea.

Over the radio came a sudden short announcement that the operation had ended and we were instructed to return to our base at Leeuwarden.

We were still somewhat stressed from our daylight fight with the Americans and I realized later that I must have made a rather hard landing. Then after rolling out and taxiing to our hardstand, we were greeted by Oblt. Sigmund, who had come over to congratulate me on my victory. "You don't get a Boeing easily", he thought as he smiled, while being a bit embarrassed, as he had missed his target. I have always appreciated this kind gesture from my superior officer.

We had always liked one another and posthumously I can with sincerity say that, "He was a good man".

Messerschmitt Me-110 with Opel Blitz service truck.
Photo from Tony Crawford collection
*The Pfeiffer story was a gift from Ab Jansen to Tony Crawford.
Karl-Georg Pfeiffer Bf 110G-4 (night fighter) was shot down on 25 June 1943 Hamburg raid near Abbenes, Netherlands. Pfeiffer is credited with destroying 7 British bombers at night and one B-17 during daylight in his Luftwaffe career.

The Brinkman crash site was approximately one kilometer north of the airfield at Marx, Germany. Notice the large number of German soldiers enjoying some time away from their base, along with looking for a souvenir from the B-17.

Photo courtesy of Olaf Timmermann

Photo of Brinkman
Courtesy of Kyle Brinkman

Photo of Andrews courtesy of Andrew Family

Photo courtesy of Kyle Brinkman
The original B-17 trainer used by Billy Brinkman

Photo courtesy of Betty Banks
(L-R)Brothers Leonard and Frank Murphy Jr

39

The initial resting place for the 8 members KIA from the Brinkman crew

Photo courtesy of Olaf Timmermann

Bad Zwischenahn Cemetery at Bad Zwischenahn, Germany, west of Bremen.

Photo courtesy of Olaf Timmermann

At the time of the Brinkman crash, Allied airmen were given military funerals. Hermann Goring, a WWI German pilot, considered the Luftwaffe and her enemy airmen as honorable combatants or modern day knights thus deserving a military funeral.

The Pilot Lt. William F. (Billy) Brinkman final resting place is beside his Mother and Father in Clinton-Garfield Cemetery, Pocahontas, Iowa.
The Bombardier 2nd Lt. Donald J. Andrews and the Ball Turret Gunner Alfred H. Mitchell are buried in the American Cemetery in Ardennes, Belgium.
After the end of the war, Frank Murphy the Tail Gunner, William Carver the Radio Operator and Charlie's replacement, Robert Todd Right Waist Gunner and Ralph Smith the Left Waist Gunner were re-interred in a mass grave at Jefferson Barracks, Missouri. Clarence Watkins' remains were interred at Fort Snelling National Cemetery, South Minneapolis, Minnesota.
Crew list for the MIA Wilhelmshaven B-17s can be found on pages xviii and xix of the appendices

The disaster of the Kiel raid of 13 June 1943

The leader of the Kiel Raid convinced the 8th Air Corp brass to forego the box formations and attack the target with Squadrons of the bombers wing tip to wing tip. The leader was Brigadier General Nathan B. Forrest III. Forrest was the grandson of the Confederate Lieutenant General Nathan Bedford Forrest, a famous cavalry leader. This experiment cost Forrest his life along with one hundred sixty seven other flyers and thirty B-17s. While leading the formation, the Fortress 42-30164 from the 95th Bomb Group crashed in the Baltic Sea. After the number 4 engine was apparently struck by flak she began losing power and smoking. Leaving the formation she was quickly attacked by fighters before crashing in the Baltic Sea. This B-17 carried a crew of 12 flyers, which included General Forrest, two navigators and an observer. Ten of the crew perished in the crash. After this raid the 8th AAF stayed with the defensive firepower using the box formation.

Luftwaffe officer inspects remains of 42-29940 after she attacked the submarine yards at Kiel.

Photos courtesy of Olaf Timmermann
Remains of the B-17F 42-29940 lying southwest of Neumunster believed to be the victim of a German aerial bomb. The two noted crew lists for the Kiel raid can be found on page xix of the appendices.

Chapter 6

The Briefing

25 June 1943: The First Hamburg Raid

The combat crews had been rousted and were having breakfast before 2:30 a.m. The main delicacies of the combat breakfast were fresh eggs and bacon, which other Groups had nicknamed the "last supper". Since the combat crews for the day were the only men on base allowed fresh eggs, their meal was the envy of the officers and ground crews.

After breakfast, they would have boarded trucks outside the mess hall, which delivered them to the briefing. The two targets for the second mission of the 384th were revealed at the early morning briefing as: the Blohm & Voss Shipyards* and the nearby submarine pens in Hamburg. At one end of the large assembly hall, a curtain was pulled back revealing a large wall map of East Anglica, the North Sea, and Northern Germany. When the officers realized that the target was to be Hamburg, a large cheer went up.

This was the kind of mission the Group had been hoping for, an opportunity to strike deep into Germany such as Hitler's submarine shipyard. Across the map there was a red string, which was stretched from Grafton Underwood to Hamburg. The route headed up across the North Sea toward Norway, and at approximately the halfway point, there was about a ninety degree turn leading straight to the Elbe River estuary. Twenty kilometers beyond Cruxhaven, another right turn to the I P** at Bremervorde, then a ninety degree turn toward the Elbe, the docks and the heavy industry of Hamburg.

This was the track that the formation was supposed to fly. So naturally, the navigators were busy taking notes along with the pilots and bombardiers. The briefing continued when the meteorologist stepped forward to report that there would be good weather at the formation altitude and at the target. The weatherman then reported that the winds at 25,000 feet above base would be fifty five miles per hour at two hundred sixty degrees. At the target the wind direction would change slightly to two hundred seventy degrees and decrease to forty five miles per hour.

The officers were given numerous amounts of additional information that they must note, including formation positions, radio codes, IP position, latest known flak station locations, reconnaissance photographs of the target, bombing elevations, etc., etc. After all the various Group officers had completed their portion of the briefing, each of the crews officers then synchronized their watches, as mission points were to be based on time.

At this point in the 384th history, the gunners may have had a separate briefing reviewing the latest recommended escape and aversion tactics, German interrogation protocol, and the maximum ammo to load on board. Also discussed were the latest German fighter tactics for attacking the Fortresses and how to defend against these attacks. The gunners were told what enemy fighters they could expect along the planned route.

After the briefings, a few minutes were allotted for meeting with their Chaplains. Here a Group might be kneeling and others with their heads bowed in prayer.

While standing around waiting for their trucks, one couldn't help but notice the flash from a zippo here and there plus the glow of numerous burning cigarettes.

After the briefings and the meetings with the Chaplains, the crews would have picked up their machine guns, parachutes and other equipment and then were trucked to their Squadron's hard stands.

As the crews approached their individual planes, they knew that they only had a maximum of sixty minutes to get all their equipment in order before liftoff. Here, each crew member would have been greeted by their four mechanics and the crew chief, along with the sound of the gasoline generator purring away, inside near the tail. Each Fortress had a yellow glow coming from inside, as all the interior lights would have been turned on by the ground crews, who had been working all night.

In the meantime, the ground crew would have already fueled each B-17 with up to 2,750 gallons of high-octane gasoline. The Armoires would have secured ten 500 pound bombs to the racks and installed a fuse and fuse wire in each bomb. It was not unusual for these men to write in chalk on each bomb messages to Hitler and his higher ups. These bombs were often referred to as airmail. Fueling and bombing-up were the most dangerous preflight operations performed on the big bombers.

The ground crews should be complete or nearing completion of their final checks plus they would have already "walked each propeller through", thus clearing any excess oil from each cylinder of the big Wasp radial engines. The engines would have been started and shut down with all the instruments and gauges for each system checked and rechecked.

The gunners would go through the motions of removing the wrapping rags and stripping the grease from their 50 caliber machine guns, then the guns would have been properly mounted at the gunner's station. The gunners would then check their ammo boxes and belts, which would have been placed at each station by the Armoires. Next, they would take and feed a belt of ammo into the appropriate feed guide ready to chamber the first bullet.

The turret operators would check the turrets for any missing or out of place components. The radio operator would check that all their equipment was functional, although he would not dare test any transmission, as "the enemy is listening". Then the crew would take a pee break, before putting on their high altitude electric suits.

Their parachutes are then stored in their appropriate location. The ball turret gunner would have hung his chute on the back of the radio room wall (bulk head), while the tail gunner would usually hang his chute near the rear hatch. The waist gunners and the rest of the crew would usually keep their chutes and mae-wests or life vests on until completion of the mission. Their carbine in its scabbard*** is hung on the radio room bulkhead wall adjacent to the ball turret gunner's parachute.

In the case of *Miss Deal*, John Way, (pilot) who was looked up to by his crew of sergeants, would have been performing the walk-around with Vernon Salmon, his crew chief. Together, they would check everything from flight control surfaces to the landing gear to satisfy each that the ship was battle ready.

Once Way had accepted the ship, he would have signed off on form 1A, that *Miss Deal* was mission ready. It was not unusual for the Captain to gather his men together in a huddle to discuss the mission and give them encouragement before loading. John Way was a good man and a good leader, having studied Divinity at St. John's. He was well thought of by his instructors as the pilot that carried out his orders and directions to a "T".

On this day the navigator assigned to *Miss Deal* was Bob Jansen from the *Yankee Power House*. Jansen probably had a calming effect on Charlie and his crewmates as he was older than the other officers for *Miss Deal*. He met with the crew and told them about the target.****

After the crew boarded *Miss Deal*, a new co-pilot was brought over in a jeep. He hopped out, hustled over to the waist hatch, and climbed in, greeting the gunners in back, then nodding to Ed Gadomski, the radio operator, along with Charlie, who was standing near the radio desk. Passing through the two bulkhead doors of the radio room, the co-pilot crossed the bomb bay catwalk. Here, he had to squeeze himself between the two racks of five hundred pound bombs before reaching the ships ladder to the flight deck. He saluted the engineer as he reached the right hand seat. After getting situated, he asked John Way. "Where are we going"? Then, he turned and introduced himself to the engineer Bill Hill, as Stephen Fabian, the co-pilot from the Halseth ship. Fabian stated that he no sooner had gotten belted in that Way had already begun the startup procedure. With the electric starter slowly spinning the propeller on the number one engine, a puff of smoke was whipped back from the engine exhaust indicating to an observer that the B-17 was coming to life.

Although the weather was heavy mist with light rain, the Fortresses with their navigation lights burning, began their movement to take their positions for takeoff. With *Miss Deal* in the high Squadron she was assigned the thirtenth slot for lift off.

Lead crew for the 384th Group for the first Hamburg raid was assigned to Maj. Seldon L. McMillin, the Deputy Group Commander. McMillin was a big man from Texarkana, Texas, where his family was in the road building business.

McMillin, was in the lead B-17 42-5850 for this raid. This ship was normally in the hands of Lt. James W. Smith, but on this mission, he would be the co-pilot. Also on board the lead ship was the Group navigator Cpt. James H. Foister.

44

Considering the weather, practically every pilot assigned to the first Hamburg raid was stunned when they witnessed that the green flare was fired from the control tower. This was evidenced by the number of 384th crews that aborted the mission; eleven.

As the ships received their signal for the leader to begin his takeoff roll, there were two crewmen just returning to base. Hearing the rumble of 19 B-17s preparing for takeoff, Walter Harvey and Dick Sherrer (*Miss Deal's* co-pilot and navigator) rushed up to the fence near the flight line. Not knowing that there was a mission scheduled for 25 June, they were returning from a good time at a tea dance.

Suddenly, they were stunned as they witnessed their ship, the *Miss Deal's* blinding landing lights come on as she takes her position on the runway. There was their crew and ship heading off to battle without them.

As *Miss Deal* took her turn on the runway, John Way set her brakes waiting for their time to start the takeoff run (timing is everything for a safe climb out to altitude in weather for a Group of B-17s). John Way applies full power to all four engines, while confirming that the flaps are at the correct angle, all propellers are properly set for takeoff and all engine gauges are reading normal. Both pilots keep an eye on the instruments, as their Fortress needs to operate perfectly to lift off with a full fuel load and two and a half tons of bombs, not to mention all the extra ammo that the gunners may have sneaked on board.

Prior to the takeoff roll, Charlie moved into the waist adjacent to one of the gun ports to get a good view of the base, perhaps give a wave to some of the boys watching the Group lift off. He had no interest in crawling into the ball with the tarmac rushing past during takeoff. Soon after liftoff with nothing but clouds to view, he moves into a sitting position with Dodge, Feagin and Westlake with their backs against the radio room bulkhead. Gadomski remains at his station monitoring the radio equipment. Charlie and the other gunners stay against the bulkhead for a few minutes.

As *Miss Deal* begins her takeoff roll, Bill Hill, the engineer, is responsible for calling out the airspeed to the pilots during the acceleration to liftoff. While in the back the gunners feel the occasional soft bounce as their heavily laden Fortress accelerates. Reaching one hundred miles per hour, the B-17 is airborne and within a minute her speed is past one forty with her gear up and locked. Climbing on instruments John Way nudges *Miss Deal* to one hundred fifty miles per hour. The ride is now smooth with all her engines steadily pulling the big ship toward her predetermined altitude while the pilot keeps her on her climb out course. The steady drone of *Miss Deal's* four big engines in sync is reassuring to her rookie crew. During the early morning climb to target altitude, the gunners have the sensation of an impending battle. There is grim determination on their faces to defend their ship against all comers.

While approaching twelve thousand feet, *Miss Deal's* pilot, John Way reminded Tom Corrigan, the bombardier, to arm the bombs. Corrigan stepped into the bomb bay removing the pins from the fuses. Returning to his station, he secured the pins as proof the bombs were armed when dropped.

Prior to reaching twelve thousand feet, the gunners move to their stations and put on their oxygen masks. Also they were recently reminded at the briefing that gunners absent from their station, was an undefended Fortress. They were also told that they should expect to see enemy fighters after they leave the coast.

As for Charlie, he is assisted by Raymond Dodge the right waist gunner into the ball. Sliding into his station, he straddles the bullet proof circular viewing/aiming window. Once in the ball, Dodge verified that the ball turret door latches were secured in the closed position. The waist gunner then assured that the clutch driving the ball was engaged.

Raising his guns to a horizontal position, Charlie gets a view of the marker beacon located on the aft of the main fuselage. Rotating the turret 180 degrees, he is facing forward and has a good view of the bottom arc of the four propellers. After a call over the intercom, the radio operator learns that Charlie and all of *Miss Deal's* gunners are at their stations.

Fortunately, Way and Fabian keep one hundred percent of their attention to their work and there were no collisions, considering the dreadful weather during the climb out. Fabian, the co-pilot reflected that during the climb to altitude, he and Way witnessed three B-17s returning to base. Two of the aborting Fortresses just missed colliding with the climbing *Miss Deal*. One of the descending B-17s had crossed in front of the Way ship. When *Miss Deal* went through the slip stream of the returning Fortress, there was a sudden jarring and slamming noise crossing through the disturbed wake. Way notified his crew through the intercom the cause of all the noise.

As for Bill Harvey and his navigator, the next thing they knew they were confronted by the Squadron Operations Officer where they learned that their crew is on the mission and replacements had to be found for both of them. Soon Harvey and Sherrer were at attention in the Group Commanders office as they were berated for missing the mission and received the threat of court martial. Quickly, Harvey explained that they were neither told nor had any idea there was to be a mission that day.

Later that day, instead of staying in their barracks as directed, they watched with some of the other officers, as the crews were returning, only to realize that *Miss Deal* did not return.

Harvey and Sherrer were given the sad task of packing up the kit of *Miss Deal's* Captain, John Way along with her bombardier, Tom Corrigan who did not return from the Hamburg raid. This kit was returned to the grieving families in the U.S. and by the following morning a new replacement crew would be on base. The same scenario would also have occurred in the enlisted flyers barracks.

As to Charlie and his friends, their kits were also packed up; the MIA's possessions would have eventually been sent back to their mourning families. The difference here was that it was noted that Delbert McNasty, the Group's canine mascot, was in attendance with the morgue detail during this sad job at Charlie's and his crewmate's quarters.

Delbert's owner, Ray Gregori, the tail gunner on *Vertical Shaft* reflected at a 384th reunion in San Diego that he and Charlie Crawford, along with *Miss Deal's* gunners all bunked together at Grafton Underwood. What was interesting to Ray was how Charlie and some of the other gunners took a liking to Delbert. He mused that he thought his dog made them feel comfortable and perhaps a little homesick.

Ray Gregori was awarded the Silver Star for his actions on the raid of 12 August 1943 against the synthetic fuel plant in Gelsenkircheen, Germany. As tail gunner Gregori was severely wounded fifteen minutes prior to reaching the target while defending his station. An exploding 20 mm shell from an attacking enemy fighter should have incapacitated the tail gunner. Instead he continued to fend off the fighters never complaining. On the return from the target one of the gunners discovered Ray's condition, still at his station.

After Gregori was hospitalized following his injuries defending the B-17 *Pistol Packin Mamma*, Delbert probably disappeared after losing touch with his master. The day after the Gelsenkircheen raid, an unknown flyer occupied the hospitalized Gregori's bunk.

Photo courtesy of 384th bombgroup.com
B-17F-90-BO 42-30142 *Pistol Packin Mamma* SU*L 384th Bomb Group 544th Bomb Squad

303rd Bomb Group chart of the 25 June 43 Hamburg raid

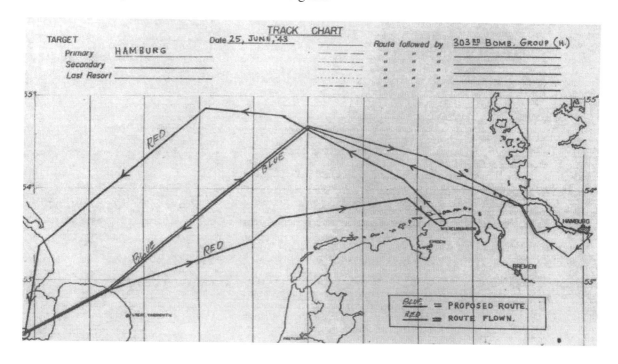

Hook on device for carbine scabbard taken from 42-30049
Miss Deal by a Dollard fisherman.

*Blohm & Voss was noted for the construction of the battleship Bismarck. Also Blohm & Voss built 238 submarines and had started 17 others before it was closed. The yard was also noted for the assembly and outfitting for XXI electro submarines. By February 1945 and prior to the end of hostilities, approximately twenty thousand people were working at the yard. The Submarine pens were constructed of reinforced concrete with a roof thickness of 12 feet.

**I P Means Initial Point. This is the point at where the pilot made his final turn toward the target and relinquished control to the bombardier. In the case of *Miss Deal* the bombardier could not find the target due to heavy cloud cover.

***Brass hook on device for carbine scabbard carried on early B-17's (reportedly taken from *Miss Deal* by a fisherman) a gift by the writer Jan Stegmeijier.

Per William Dixon, of the 100th bomb Group, carbines were standard issues for B-17s until mid-1943 when 45 caliber automatics were issued and all carbines were turned in.

****In a letter written by Robert Janson, the navigator assigned to *Miss Deal* for the Hamburg raid, he stated that he did not have time to meet the men, only time to tell them that the target was Hamburg.

The Target   U-Boat Bunker Hamburg

Photo from Tony Crawford's collection

Chapter 7

We Broke on Top

After the 384th broke on top, *Miss Deal* 42-30049, was throttled up to war power in order to catch up and move in close to form up with the 384th lead formation. The Group leader, McMillin was pilot in command of ship 42-5850. This Fortress would have been the lead ship with a Fortress on his right wing and a second one on his left wing. Behind McMillin and out of the way of his two wingmen would have been a fourth ship also with two wingmen, the total ships scheduled for the lead formation was six. *Miss Deal* was selected to be "tail end Charlie" in the high formation (above and slightly to the right of the lead formation). Nuttall, the deputy flight leader was to command seven ships in the high Squadron. Unfortunately, he and four of his other B-17's had aborted from the high formation, leaving only Way and the Estes crews. The low formation, which was below and slightly behind and left of the lead formation, saw her leader fail to even take off and five of his crews abort the Hamburg mission. Thus the scheduled low formation had only one crew participate in the raid. This was George Riches of the 545th Squadron, who was assigned *Yankee Powerhouse* 42-30143, a ship from the 544th Squadron.

Only eight 384th B-17s participated in the first Hamburg raid. Two-thirds of the scheduled crews aborted the 384th Group. There was now only one formation, which rendered the Group defensively inept, as the "defensive box" required three or more Squadrons.

The eight Fortresses, with their tail wind and at an altitude of 25,000 feet, were racing toward their target at a ground speed of approximately two hundred and eighty miles per hour. This kind of speed was a great advantage for getting the big Boeings past the fighters and on the target unscathed.

McMillin and his ragged band of raiders, thanks to their tail wind, have knocked over a half-hour off of their time to target. *Miss Deal's* navigator, Bob Janson has spotted the island of Heligoland and proudly notified the two pilots that they were rapidly approaching the target thanks to the tailwind and their elevation. With fair visibility Janson is able to spot critical landmarks and keep Way tracking toward the target.

Miss Deal and the other 384th B-17s make a sweeping right turn with a heading toward the Elbe River. In less than five minutes they are moving past Scharhorn. Cruxhaven is in sight as the cloud cover is again approaching one hundred per cent. As the pilots begin their turn to the east and toward the I.P. point, they have pushed their throttles to "war power".

Somewhere in the area Southwest of Hamburg, a Staffel of German fighters that were vectored by their ground controllers, has caught up with this small, scattered Squadron of Fortresses. The Luftwaffe radar net has been tracking the raiders since they left England. Numerous fighter Gruppes from Holland, Germany and France have been called to defend the northwest quadrant of the Fatherland against the approaching Boeings.

Prior to encountering the first ring of flak batteries, McMillin and his scrappy pack of raiders are probably spotted by the Heligoland fighters. The first air battle begins for the 384th leader. Head-on attacks ensue on the leader's Fortress before she reaches the I.P. The only two gunners that are able to effectively combat the fighters attacking head-on are the top turret gunner, Robert Buckley, and the ball turret gunner, Lynn Jones.

The attacking Bf 109s rake the ship from the right wing to the cockpit area. The fighters knock out the #3 engine, which lost oil pressure, before seizing up with the propeller flat to the direction of her flight. The #4 or right outboard engine was struck in the master rod with the loss of pitch control to the far right propeller. Unfortunately, Buckley, the engineer, is struck in the face by an exploding 20mm shell and mortally wounded while defending his B-17.

The fighters break off their attacks as the B-17s enter the flak fields around Hamburg. The batteries, like the fighters, have been notified of the approaching bombers and given their elevations. With this information, the gunners set their big 88 shells to explode at the prescribed altitude.

The Group's lead bombardier, Francis Meyers, claimed to have found and bombed the target. Other returning crews also claimed to have bombed Hamburg. *Miss Deal*, could not find the target. When Corrigan notified his pilot that the target was completely obscured by the cloud cover, Lt. Way ordered his navigator: "get us a heading for another bomb run". Now it is becoming clear to the other officers that Way fully intends to deliver his bomb load onto the shipyard or take a one-in-a-thousand shot drop that would damage the sub pens or dislodge one of the gates.

With her engines being whipped for all their power, *Miss Deal* banks onto the I.P. for her second bomb run. The 88s continue their barrage at the two B-17s, while the bombardiers search for the target.

Now the Way crew is tempting fate by remaining in the flak fields. Approaching the heavy industries adjacent to the Elbe River, the B-17s are now being targeted by the Kriegsmarine shore batteries. They raise their radar-directed cannons to compete with the Luftwaffe batteries for victory stripes and commendations for the month of June 1943.

The Germans pause from their work as the air raid sirens sound. Twenty minutes earlier the "Luftschutspolizei", or air raid police, began warning the businesses and people of Hamburg that an air raid was eminent. Those that did not heed the initial warnings are now rushing to the nearest concrete bunker. They discover that only those living or working nearby will find room, as all bunkers quickly fill up. If the sirens are not enough warning, then the cannon fire is. Recalling summer thunderstorms, the sounds from heavy cannons alert the citizens. They are well aware that something dangerous is flying above Hamburg.

Fear spreads through the people locked out of the overcrowded bunkers. There is no escape from the sound of wailing sirens and the un-abating noise from the firing cannons. Elza Litzas, a Hungarian, visiting Hamburg relations ran to the bunker nearest her cousin's home, only to reach the main doorway too late. The heavy steel doors were slammed closed, crushing two fingers and permanently disfiguring her right hand. In unbearable pain she collapses against the doors, crying uncontrollably. An old man who also reaches the bunker too late, tries to comfort Mrs. Litzas as he attempts to stop the bleeding.

Disappointed for the second time, John Way turns *Miss Deal* on a westerly course. He has overheard the Group leader notifying his Forts that each pilot is on his own. Realizing that another run on the "socked in" Hamburg is useless, he asks the navigator, Bob Janson, for a heading toward Emden. In the back of his mind he realizes that the shortest way home is west. Knowing that McMillin is a wise old pilot, he decides that if his ship has terminal problems, then west is the shortest and quickest route home -- that is, after dropping off his load of high explosives at Emden.

The bombardier in each retreating B-17 has switched his bomb-bay doors to close. The four long, spinning jackscrews make the sixty-plus revolutions sealing the big doors tight.

Leaving the primary targets, the tailwind has changed to a headwind; this distinct disadvantage affects the retreating Fortresses flying west, dropping their withdrawal speed significantly. It is estimated that the Group leader's ground speed is well under 100 miles per hour thanks to this headwind, a shut-down engine and a wind-milling propeller.

With *Miss Deal* moving away from Hamburg, the Way crew suddenly feel their ship lurch as she is struck by flak in the ball turret. She stumbles again, this time she is struck on the far right engine. John Way asks his engineer, Bill Hill, for a damage report. Returning from the waist, Hill notifies his pilot that the ball has been smashed and his wounded gunner, Crawford, has been moved into the radio room. The burning # 4 engine has been shut down along with her un-feathered propeller creating a drag on the Fortress.

After Charlie Crawford was pulled out of the ball, moved into the radio room and chuted-up, he collapses from loss of blood and oxygen. Charlie is then propped up against the right wall adjacent to the waist/radio room bulkhead. The radio operator, Gadomski, has little time to attend to Charlie's wounds or contend with his lack of oxygen, as he must assist in defending the dorsal area and keep the radio operational.

Gadomski continues his job of monitoring all personnel, plus concerns himself about the condition of his wounded assistant. With *Miss Deal* still on her westward route, Gadomski probably begins to think about the best exit from his station if she is struck again. With a full bomb load, about the only way out is through the waist hatch or one of the waist gun ports. God help them if they take a shot from an 88 in the bomb bay.

Two flak-damaged Fortresses are falling back along with the Group leader's shot-up B-17. The westbound *Miss Deal* and the *Yankee Powerhouse* are approaching Bremen.

Continuing west to an area near Oldenburg, *Yankee Powerhouse* is met by a Staffel of German fighters in route to Hamburg. The Staffel of fighters is probably from the Soesterberg area and is being vectored by the Luftwaffe ground controllers to intercept hostile aircraft approaching Hamburg.

The George Riches' crew were suddenly met head-on by nine enemy fighters. The swarm of attacking Germans quickly overwhelm the *Yankee Powerhouse's* gunners with their 20mm firepower. The attacks come from practically all directions after the initial head-on attack kills the co-pilot. The pilot is the victim of the same strike when an exploding 20 mm practically takes off his right arm. Fortunately, Riches was able to issue the bail-out order while holding his ship straight and level as the crew began to exit. With the ship burning, the tail gunner, Stanley Martin and right waist gunner, William Waller remain at their stations, doggedly defending their B-17 as she is cut to pieces by the unrelenting fighters.

The exploding Fortress comes down near Oldenburg with four of her crew trapped in the wreckage. The mortally wounded American flyers are removed from the wreckage and on the 30th of June 1943 are given full military honors with a Luftwaffe funeral detail at the New Cemetery in Oldenburg, Germany. Lt. George W. Riches was posthumously awarded the Silver Star.

Somewhere between Hamburg and Nieuweschans, Holland, the clouds break up and the fury of numerous fighter attacks begin. *Miss Deal*, alone like the injured deer, tries to escape by fleeing into the clouds. When she reappears the vicious German wolves are waiting and the furious attacks resume.

It is in this area that the right waist gunner, "Young Dodge", had already heard the warnings from their new tail gunner of the impending attacks. A pair of German fighters approaches far off from the north. Now, in the distance, with a backdrop of an enormous wall of clouds, Dodge can see them bank their planes in his direction. It is "Young Dodge's" turn to warn the crew of the rapidly approaching fighters coming in their direction at 3 o'clock high.

Dodge aligns his sights with the lead fighter, holding his fire until the German is within the range of his single machine gun. Soon enough he is firing along with Bill Hill, the top turret gunner. In a flash, the two enemy fighters streak past.

Hill spins his turret to the right, firing his twin fifties at the two fighters receding to the south. With faint trails of black smoke from their stressed 2,000 horsepower V-12 Daimler Benz engines, the Messerschmitts roll into a banked turn back toward Hamburg.

Now the top turret gunner Bill Hill comes across the intercom. He tells his fellow crewmembers that the fighters are continuing their turns and are approaching *Miss Deal* from the 6 o'clock low position. He encourages the tail gunner with a shout, "GET EM Westlake, GET EM".

In the meantime Dodge is feeling a horrible pain in both hands and wrists. Looking down as his gun is torn from his hands; he can see an enormous amount of blood pouring from his jacket sleeves. His gloves dangle strangely from his wrists. With a wave of nausea he realizes that his hands, have been almost completely torn off from the exploding twenty-millimeter shell.

Standing at his gun-port, Dodge drops to his knees and waits for his final minutes to pass, praying that his pain will cease. Recalling his days as a child back in "good old Wisconsin" he remembers his mother's love. Only three years ago, he was fifteen and Mama had bought him a .22 caliber rifle. His usual target was a rabbit for supper and Ray could really put them on the table. He remembers the pride reflected in his little brothers' eyes as they all walked to school together… how they looked up to him, listened to him and heeded his directions.

He turns to his right, into a sitting position and waits. He is watching Red at the other waist position taking a few shots and he can still hear the new tail gunner insistently hammering away with his twin fifties. He can see a number of holes in the side, roof and floor of *Miss Deal*. Maybe she will get us home, back to Wisconsin, back to Mama and Daddy. Maybe, just maybe. Somewhere between Oldenburg and the Dollard bay, *Miss Deal* slips into her last good cloud cover.

Meanwhile, in the cockpit an argument has broken out among the officers concerning abandoning *Miss Deal*, jettisoning her bomb load, and the struggle to keep flying while the valiant gunners are slowly losing the battle with the fighters.

During one of the fighter attacks, probably from the tail, Fabian, the copilot, vividly recalls the sound of bullets hitting the armor plate on the back of his seat. William Hill, the engineer, also heard ricocheting bullets or shrapnel and brings to their attention that the Captain has been wounded.

In the nose, Janson and Corrigan are observing the increasing inferno of the adjacent engines. Quite suddenly, Janson comes to the realization that John Way intends to either bomb Emden and get back to England, or fly this ship into the ground trying.

Without any further words, Janson releases the nose hatch and steps out.

Stepping into the wind-stream slams the navigator into the hatch jamb. Pushing out and away from the jamb while pulling his chute's "D" ring snaps Janson free from *Miss Deal*. The injured flyer is now making his painful descent enveloped in clouds. Landing hard Lieutenant Janson experiences additional injuries as German troops quickly capture the American. After he is transported to a Papenburg hospital for treatment, Janson learns that after recovery Luftwaffe guards will be his escort to Frankfurt for interrogation.

Prior to Janson's exit from *Miss Deal*, the tail gunner was engaging a Focke Wulf Fw 190. "As he banked away from my position, I noticed a parachute open below (later on in prison camp I learned that it was our navigator). I couldn't watch him, as I was busy again with fighters".

Westlake continued his narrative, "Another single engine fighter swung in directly behind us and was headed straight for me. I began firing at the fighter as he was closing rapidly; I noticed what looked like orange balls of fire flashing from the fighter… when suddenly, part of the tail exploded sending shrapnel into my face and forehead. I thought for a moment that I had lost an eye as I was temporarily blinded. Fortunately, it was just that my own blood had filled one eye".

"By then my guns were empty and we were really burning. I called the pilot and told him I was wounded, could not see and asked for permission to bail out."

Miss Deal burning but still eluding her pursuers, continues her blind track in cloud cover without a navigator. Before she crossed over the Dutch frontier, two more fighters based out of Leeuwarden, Netherlands, are vectored toward her with orders to shoot her down.

The bombardier, Corrigan, has heard the tail gunner's request to bail out due to injury, and decides to check on the gunners. After walking the catwalk and squeezing between the racks of bombs, he entered the radio room. He finds Gadomski at his radio station, pointing toward the floor near the waist door. Looking in that direction, he recognizes Charles Crawford lying in a pool of blood. Stepping over Crawford, he peers briefly into the waist and immediately turns and heads back.

Corrigan can hardly control himself, after seeing the team of four, severely wounded gunners in the back of the ship. Quickly, he retraces his steps back through the radio room and the bomb bay. He scurries up the ship's ladder to the flight deck. Pushing Hill, the top turret gunner aside, Corrigan demands that Way salvo the bombs so that the crew can bail out.

Then Corrigan notices that their engineer has a bloodied face, cuts apparently from flying plexi-glass. Hill points toward where his two top-turret fifties should project and Corrigan realizes that one of the gun barrels has been shot off, possibly from the recent fighter attacks that they encountered after leaving Hamburg.

Meanwhile another pair of Messerschmitts are rapidly closing on *Miss Deal*. Also the big naval guns of the Kriegsmarine shore batteries that guard the Dollard have been made aware of her track by the radar station at Fiemel. This same radar station is tracking another Group of B-17s approaching from Rysum.

Way refuses to act on Corrigan's demand; instead he intends to stay the course. There were shouts from Hill: "Drop the bombs so we can get out of here".

Copilot Fabian is incensed at Way's refusal to acknowledge the crew's demands. Realizing that the raid on Emden is futile, Fabian reaches across Way and activates the emergency red bomb release. Then he informs Way, "I am leaving this ball of fire". The bomb bay doors slam open, and *Miss Deal* gave a big lurch as her two-and-a-half ton payload of bombs is released.

Hurriedly, Fabian gets down the ship's ladder, nervously crossing the open bomb bay's catwalk, and finds the three gunners together near the right waist gun station. After he shouts, "Let's get the chutes on and get out of here", one of the dying gunners responds to him, "Go on leave us alone". Realizing the gunners are not going to get out of the burning plane, Fabian turns to his left and heads for the bomb bay. Returning through the radio room, the copilot dives out of the plane through the bomb bay. Next, Hill, the ship's engineer, goes back to the radio room and directs Gadomski to leave Crawford and jump.

Corrigan notes that he went once more into the radio room and found Crawford wounded and non-responsive. After surveying the waist of the ship, he believed that all the gunners were dead. Returning to the bomb bay and crossing the cat walk, the bombardier meets Way coming down the ships ladder. Way pats Corrigan on the shoulder telling him and pointing for him to go and with a firm hand presses him toward the open bomb bay. As Corrigan begins his fall, he hits one of the ball turret's gun barrels with his right leg. After his chute opens, he passes out. Upon dropping into the Dollard, he comes to his senses and removes his parachute. He is quickly picked up by a German launch.

The bombs hurtled down toward an area probably to the north and west of Nieuweschans, Holland. Here, a group of farm workers take notice of the scream of the falling bombs and run for cover -- with the exception of Jan Hendrick Schuur, his son and Klas Alles. These three men were killed as a result of the concussion from an exploding, five-hundred pound bomb.

The elementary school at Finsterwolde had just dismissed the students for recess around 9:00 a.m. One young student named Roel Nap was playing on the south side of the school when one of his older brothers comes rushing up to him, demanding that he follow him to the opposite side of the school to witness an air battle. What he sees from there is a Messerschmitt Bf 109 G6 from Leeuwarden making a 9 o'clock attack on *Miss Deal*. He can also discern tracers coming from the left waist of the B-17.

Unknown to Albert Oexle, the rookie Bf 109 pilot, he has attacked *Miss Deal* at the only area of the Fortress where a gunner, although wounded, still man's his station. A sudden, vicious battle erupts between Albert Oexle and Red Feagin, *Miss Deal's* left waist gunner.

All of this occurs after the tail-gunner, Westlake, has released the hatch near the tail in preparing to bail out. Looking to his left, he notices the right waist gunner motioning him with his head to come forward. As Westlake works his way around the tail wheel and up to the waist, he realizes that both of Dodge's hands are nearly shot off, "hanging from his arms by their tendons".

He sees Charlie lying in the radio room. Realizing that Dodge needs his help, Westlake moves across the ship to open the waist hatch and assist "young Dodge" out of *Miss Deal*. Then, he noticed that the left waist gunner, Red Feagin, although wounded, was still manning his gun position. Suddenly, Feagin began firing his fifty-caliber non-stop. Just as Westlake reaches for the hatch release, an incoming twenty-millimeter from Albert Oexle's 109 strikes the doorjamb of the waist hatch. The exploding shell deforms the jamb and locks the door and jamb together. The same exploding shell further wounds Westlake in both legs.

Now Westlake cannot open the hatch, nor is he any help to the others, as he cannot stand. Although the bomb bay is open, the only hope for these men is the wounded pilot, who is coming through the radio room door into the waist. At this point, the pilot has to decide to either drag Charlie to the bomb bay, push him out, pulling his ripcord in hopes that the Germans will give him aid, or continue on toward the waist.

Since *Miss Deal* is flying on autopilot and with only one engine, she is no doubt an inviting target for the Dollard flak stations. It will be reported by the copilot, that after he jumped, he last saw the burning *Miss Deal* with debris coming off her, and then he fell into a layer of heavy clouds. Opening his chute, he was suddenly jerked upright. Breaking out of the clouds, Fabian witnessed three Focke Wulf Fw 190s bearing down on him. Believing that he was going to be another strafed flyer, he prayed for divine intervention. Suddenly, the three fighters streaked past wagging their wings in a salute.

With the checkered pattern of small farms rushing up, Fabian tries to relax as he lands in a large field. Luckily, he comes down rolling on the soft earth of a freshly plowed cabbage patch. While lying on the ground, he hears the sharp crack of a firearm as dirt flies against his face. Quickly coming to attention with his arms raised in surrender, Fabian momentarily traveled back in time more than two decades. Confronted by an elderly German in his WWI uniform, wearing a spiked helmet and carrying an old Mauser rifle, a second shot in the air brings *Miss Deal's* copilot back to reality.

Meanwhile, when Way reached the waist, he saw three of his gunners, Feagin, Dodge and Westlake huddled against the right waist wall. Unfortunately, Way and his three gunners have run out of time as *Miss Deal* explodes. With the tail breaking off from the fuselage in the area near the waist, all the gunners are blown out or thrown from the spinning ship with the exception of Crawford. The ball turret gunner, is lying in the radio room in the strongest section of the ship.

Westlake's recollection of being blown out of *Miss Deal*:
"The next memory was of a loud explosion and I am falling. I passed out, then came to with my chin hitting the "D" ring on my parachute. I thought; "Oh I know what that is and I pulled it, opening my chute. I passed out then I came to again; I was in the water. I looked around and there was someone yelling at me asking me for my knife, that he can't get his chute off. So I answered him and told him I had lost my knife and that even my

pants had been blown off. *Miss Deal* was lying in the water about 75 to 100 yards from us and she was still burning. After maybe twenty or thirty minutes, that young man just slipped under the water. He never cried out - he just quietly went under."

"Pretty soon five old Germans arrived in a launch and pulled me aboard. They noticed that I was looking around in the water and realized that one of the crew had drowned. We searched for other survivors but there were none. I was transferred to a truck and taken to the German marine hospital in Emden. There I found out that I had forty-eight pieces of shrapnel in me from the waist down, a fractured skull and a broken wrist. After two months, I had recovered enough that I was sent to prison camp."

A terrified young boy, Roel Nap, witnessed the death dive of Oexle's Bf 109 as she came screaming down just to the west of his school, where she not only crashed with one loud bang, but with such speed that she was swallowed up by the soft earth. She was found 56 years later by the dedicated research of Lenny Schrik, of Veendam, Holland.

Prior to the crash of the German fighter, Nap's brothers had seen four flyers parachute from *Miss Deal*. Roel learned from his father that after the big bomber broke apart, two additional parachutes were seen by Dutch citizens to land in the Dollard. These four flyers were probably Corrigan, Gadomski, Hill and Fabian. As to the two additional parachutes, one would have been Westlake and the other was probably the pilot, John Way, who had been in the waist trying to help his gunners out of *Miss Deal*.

The Luftwaffe is rapidly assembling many of the flyers at a staging area near Emden. Here the bombardier, Corrigan, meets up with *Miss Deal's* copilot Fabian and is asked "Did we hit anything?" To which Corrigan answers "Naw, nothing".

Jack Schmitt, the copilot of the B-17 *Boozeness* 42-3023, barefoot and soaking wet, is escorted to the "Hauptmann" in charge of the assemblage. Fabian can overhear the rapid exchange in German between the second Lieutenant and the shouting irate "Hauptmann". After some heated words from the German leader, the now humble Schmitt, is escorted by a sergeant to visit with Fabian. When the sergeant leaves the two flyers alone, Schmitt explains to his fellow copilot that he had tried to escape by swimming the Ems River to Holland. Perhaps fortunately, he was captured by the Kriegsmarine who picked him up in a launch. Otherwise he probably would have drowned, as Holland was a good distance from Germany via the Ems.

Schmitt also confides to Fabian that his family was originally from Germany and the Hauptman (Captain) made it known to the other Germans in his unit how he despised German-Americans fighting for the enemy. Finally, Schmitt inquires to Fabian if he would either give him his shoes or his flight boots, he would be forever grateful. Later in prison camp, Fabian wishes that he had kept the warm boots and given Schmitt his oxfords.

While *Miss Deal* was losing her battle with fighters, the Group's Deputy Commander of the 384th raiders, Selden McMillin, was struggling to get his Fortress back to England. Staying hidden in the clouds on a direct westerly track was impossible with the clearing weather. McMillin's B-17, had two un-feathered propellers which were creating too much drag for the two remaining engines to overcome. With a ground speed well under one hundred miles per hour and the continuous loss of altitude, McMillin made the decision to put his Boeing down in Holland. The bail-out order was given and once the crew had exited, the Fortress crash-landed near Smalbroek.

The son of a local farmer raced to the crashed plane and observed: "A pilot who was still moving, then quiet". He had obviously seen the mortally wounded engineer, Robert H. Buckley, struggling to leave his station. Meanwhile a number of the Dutch citizenry watched the burning Fortress from a safe distance. The surviving nine crewmembers were rounded up by the Luftwaffe and carted off to Oberursel near Frankfurt for interrogation. Eventually the McMillin crew ended up at a Polish prison camp known as Stalag III.

Miss Deal's navigator, Bob Janson was assigned to the same camp after recovering from his injuries. Less than two months after his arrival at Stalag III, Janson is shipped out of Germany by train. Eventually he crossed the Pyrenees and wound up in Lisbon, Portugal. Here he boarded the Swedish liner *Gripsholm* as part of an exchange of German and American prisoners of war.

The crew of *Miss Deal* that survived the Hamburg raid spent their first day and night at Jever airfield. Here they were initially interviewed with proper documentation executed and personal effects recorded and filed. On 26 June 1943 the prisoners were sent to the prisoner of war facility in Oberursel near Frankfurt along with their documentation and personal effects. The professional interrogation at this post was designed to gather intelligence from all Allied POWs. Following interrogation, their final stop was prison camp. Bob Janson was the exception, needing approximately six months to recover from his injuries before his short stint as a POW.

After recovering from his injuries, Westlake was released from the Marine Hospital in Emden to the Luftwaffe. He and several other recuperated flyers left the Emden hospital and were marched by German soldiers to the nearest railway station. After walking several miles, Westlake was attacked by an old lady with a garden rake. Fortunately, the guards came to his rescue.

During his time at the Emden hospital, Westlake was threatened by an orderly from Hamburg. The German told the recovering tail gunner that if he lost any of his relatives in the Hamburg raids, then he would kill him. After the garden rake incident Westlake was beginning to think that perhaps his luck had gone from bad to worse.

The train ride from Emden to Frankfurt must have been interesting and perhaps even a little enjoyable compared to their Emden stay. When Westlake and his new pals arrived at Frankfurt, they came in contact with a large number of flyers that were shot down on the Schweinfurt raid. Of these flyers some were from the 384th Bomb Group. Here, Westlake learned that his old crew (Cuddeback) was lost on the Villacoublay raid of 26 June 1943.

A few days after interrogation, Westlake, along with a large Group of the Schweinfurt Regensburg raiders and others, were put on a train for prison camp in Krems, Austria. One night while en-route, their train stopped and was waiting on a siding. A woman came over to the train and started talking to one of the prisoners; they were speaking in Polish. One of the guards warned her to stop talking and get away from the train. She immediately began berating the guard and then returned to her conversation with the prisoner. Once again she was ordered to stop her conversation; however, this time when she started her berating, the guard shot her dead.

Shortly after this, the prisoners were relieved to reach prison camp and their new home. Now life would be a struggle as most of the prisoners nearly starved to death. Thanks to the Red Cross for their care packages plus the meager rations supplied by the Germans most of the flyers survived prison camp.

At his barracks Westlake was put in charge of cutting and dividing the daily ration of bread. Food was so scarce that even the crumbs were saved. When it snowed the men had a treat: a bowl of snow with bread crumbs sprinkled on top.

The following information was gleaned from official German documents: A B-17 bomber was shot down by fighters and flak at 9:09 a.m. and crashed in the Dollard. Also, the German naval observing station in Emden reported on 25 June 1943, a burning airplane at 220 degrees fell into the Dollard. This would have been the approximate angle of where *Miss Deal* was found from central Emden. Other records indicated: It was around 9:00 a.m. when German fighters were attacking a number of damaged and retreating B-17s over Lower Saxony, Germany and the Groningen area of northern Holland.

While *Miss Deal* and the "McMillin" B-17 were fighting for their lives, they came near a number of 379th B-17s in the same predicament. Six of these struggling Fortresses were intercepted by as many as 70 enemy fighters from Holland and the Ruhr area rushing to defend their country from the American bombers.

One 379th B-17 the Quade ship 42-5839 was lost near Oldenburg at 0915. This crash location and time leads one to believe that she had joined up with McMillin and his band of 384th raiders in attacking Hamburg. Unfortunately the 379th and the 384th Boeings met vicious Germans hellbent on destroying any enemy airplane flying over the "Fatherland".

Also farther west another 379th B-17 was shot down 4 miles northwest of Friesoythe, Germany. This B-17 F 42-29892 was originally assigned to Billy Brinkman. It is interesting to note that this Fortress, piloted by Douglas Groom from the 527th Squadron, crashed less than five miles from Bad Zwischenahn, where 8 members of the Brinkman crew were interred. Her crash site was approximately 14 miles east of the wreck of *Miss Deal,* which lay in the Dollard with another original Brinkman crewman, Charles Crawford. None of the 379th Fortresses lost on 25 June 1943 were able to escape German air space.

Photo of two German fighter pilots with floral gifts credited with destruction of the B-17 with remains of the bomber smoldering near Oldenburg, and political officials eager for publicity.

Same two fighter pilots surrounded by the ladies

Photos of pilots courtesy of Olaf Timmermann
School boys surrounding the German fighter pilots credited with downing a B-17 on 25 June 1943.

German photographs of flyers wading out of the Dollard or the Waddenzee. The waiting German soldiers place the flyers under arrest and then they are shipped off for interrogation, and on to prison camp. Following four photos from Tony Crawford's collection

Above photo from Tony Crawford's collection

Pushback of a Messerschmitt Bf 109; perhaps in the forest surrounding Jever airfield.

Two Cocker Spaniel mascots: one representing the German fighter Gruppe 8/JG 1 and the other from the American 384th Bomb Group. Two planes from these units dueled to the end both crashing within minutes and less than 10 miles apart.

Photo courtesy of Lenny Schrik.

The Staffel mascot for 8./JG I, "Brendy" sitting atop "Black 10" a Bf 109 G-6, this German fighter unit was based at Leeuwarden during the 25 June 43 Hamburg raid.

Photo courtesy of Quinten Bland

Delbert McNasty posing with the Sierens crew in front of the B-17F 42-30046 *Merrie Hell*. Nine members of the Sierens crew perished when *Merrie Hell* was lost on the Gelsenkirchen raid. This was the same raid that saw Ray Gregori severely wounded. Gregori was hospitalized leaving his pal Delbert facing a stranger in his master's bunk. McNasty disappeared following Gregori's hospitalization.

Unteroffizier Albert Oexle of the 9. Staffel of III./JG 1, based at Leeuwarden, Northern Holland.

ALBERT OEXLE
UFFZ.
20.1.21 † 25.6.43

CB
14-342

Photos courtesy of Lenny Schrik.

Above, a photo of Albert Oexle, a rookie fighter pilot who lost his fight with *Miss Deal*. Believing the struggling bomber would be his first victory, he attacked her at 9 o'clock midship, only to fall victim to the left waist gunner William Feagin's fifty caliber. Air battle and crash of th.e Bf 109G was witnessed by Roel Nap. Albert Oexle final resting place is at the German War Cemetery Ysselsteyn in Southern Holland

Photo courtesy of Olaf Timmermann
German salvage workers with what is believed to be remains of the B-17 *Yankee Powerhouse* loaded on
their truck and wagons.

MIA 25 June 1943 the *Yankee Powerhouse* 42-30143 crashed near Oldenburg, Germany.
George Riches was assigned the *Yankee Powerhouse* for the first Hamburg Raid as his ship 42-5849
"Hell's Belles II" was under repairs following the 22 June 1943 raid on Antwerp, Belgium.

Strato Sam painted by a Walt Disney artist after manufacture at Burbank, California. The "Quade Ship".

Photo courtesy of Olaf Timmermann
Lost on 25 June 1943 at 0915 hours following viscous attacks by German fighters.
9 KIA one POW. Crash site approximately 13 kilometers east of Oldenburg, Germany.

Bombardier Tom Corrigan with his Fortress *Miss Deal* 42-30049 at Sioux City.
Photo courtesy of Ellen Corrigan

MIA 25 June 1943 Crashed in the Dollard, Near Emden, Germany
Luftwaffe pilot claims 25 June 1943 in Dollard area:
Gruppenkomandeur Hptm. Emil-Rudolph Schnoor 1.JG/1 S.E. Groningen 9:10
Lt. Heinert 3/JG11 12 Km S.W. Emden 9:02

Photos courtesy of A.A. Jansen

B-17F-25-VE SO*M 42-5850 "The McMillin Ship" 384 Bomb Group, 544 Bomb Squad

Top photo taken shortly after the crash with Dutch boys watching the burning B-17 on 25 June 43.
Bottom photo of the remains of the Fortress along with soldiers, and politicians.

Major Selden L. McMillin was the Group Commander for the first Hamburg raid. After crash landing his B-17 near Smalbroek, Holland, McMillin and eight of his crew were taken prisoner. While at Stalag III he sent a post card to Colonel Bud Peaslee, the 384th commanding officer with the phrase "Keep the Show on the Road", which became the 384th motto. He was also made one of the POW leaders. As the U.S. Army was approaching the prison camp, McMillin was directed by a German General to meet with General Patton and establish the area of Stalag III as a free zone. Patton stated that it would be free the following morning at 0900. When American troops occupied the area, McMillin witnessed an Army Lieutenant with his 45 caliber under the chin of an old German guard who had been very helpful to all the POWs. All the prisoners referred to the old guard as Woody because of his wooden eye. The Lieutenant was threatening to kill old Woody when McMillin, all 120 pounds of him dove headlong into the officer. After much explaining to the superior officers, the old guard was treated with dignity.

Major Selden L. McMillin

Photo courtesy of James Traylor and the 384th bombGroup.com

Noted MIA B-17s and crew lists on 25 June 1943 can be found on pages xx and xxi of the appendices

Chapter 8

The *Avenger's* last raid

The Palmer crew was in the 360th bomb Squad of the 303rd bomb Group, which was based at Molesworth, England. On the 25 June 1943 Hamburg mission, the 303rd dispatched twenty- five aircraft, with one B-17 returning early because one side of the main landing gear would not retract. There were two other aborts with no reason noted.

The 303rd Hamburg mission report stated that the cloud cover was 10/10 and most aircraft abandoned their mission and salvoed their bombs in the vicinity of the Friesian islands. However, at least two of the returning aircraft attacked the Bremen area. It is believed by the writer that in actuality five aircraft attacked Bremen and these included the Palmer crew the *Avenger* 42-5390, the Mack crew *The Witches Tit* 42-5382 and the Stallings crew *Quinine-The Bitter Dose* 42-5468. These three ships were all from the 360th bomb Squadron.

While flying at 24,000 feet the 303rd like most Groups were lost. Following bombs away the *Avenger* was flying on the left side of the formation that was moving away from the target in a westerly direction. The fighter attacks were sudden and head-on. One of the attacking Messerschmitts took out her number 3 engine, and a following strike ignited the oxygen and the hydraulic oil reservoir setting off an inferno behind the pilots.

The pack of 109s that had turned on the wounded Fortress began taking turns on raking her with 20mm cannon fire. The 21-year-old pilot, Joe Palmer and the 22-year-old copilot, Bob Sheldon were in control of the *Avenger*. They were considered "old hands," as this was their eleventh mission with the 303rd.

With a raging fire just behind their stations, they never had a chance to grab the fire extinguisher before another Bf 109 swept in with heavy fire hitting the windshield. Both of these young men were killed instantly. The navigator noticed that the formation had turned to the north while they were steadily moving west and away from their sister ships. A confused Claude Kieffer, the navigator, called to the pilot and asked, "what's going on Joe?" There was no answer from the cockpit as they continued their westerly direction. The German fighters kept up the attacks until the battered and burning ship went into a roll and entered a spin.

The navigator and the bombardier were well aware that they were in serious trouble with the engine just to their right, on fire and the bomb bay ablaze. Opening the nose hatch, they both jumped.

In the back of the ship all hell had broken loose as exploding 20 mm shells were ripping the waist apart. The gunners moved into the radio room to bail out thru the bomb bay. Opening the door from the radio room to the bomb bay, the flyers were confronted by an inferno. About this time the ship rolled and went into a spin. The centrifugal force trapped everyone in back. Fortunately for the tail gunner and the photographer, the tail snapped off. The photographer was near the tail when it broke off and he either threw himself out or was thrown out. Likewise the tail gunner, Alva Hodges, was able to open the tail hatch and jump as the tail momentarily stopped spinning. Hodges came down in the village of Termunten landing on a steep pitched slate roofed Dutch home.

After gathering up his chute, an older lady hearing all the noise on her roof opened her door and invited the young flyer in. While serving the shaking American tea, there came a knock on the door. Opening her door she was confronted by a big German soldier with his Mauser "Karabiner" at his side demanding that she bring her guest out. At this point in the conversation, she politely but sternly told the German that they were having tea and her guest was not going anywhere until after they had finished. The German waited.

H. Groenhagen, a farmer from Borgsweer, Holland was working in his hay field on the 25th of June in 1943. Mr. Groenhagen had just finished loading his wagon with hay, which was being drawn by his two big Friesian horses.

Hearing the whine of stressed engines and the rhythmic bang from 20 mm cannons, he looked up and east toward Emden. He witnessed a large four motor airplane moving west across the Dollard. There were four fighters attacking the big plane when suddenly the burning Fortress turned in his direction. Nearing the area above Termunten, Holland the plane suddenly exploded. Groenhagen stated that the nose/cockpit section along with the fuselage and tail section had blown apart in the explosion. With the exception of the tail, the wreckage came hurtling toward him. Running for his life, he dived into a nearby ditch for cover. There was such a gust of wind created by the crash that all the hay was blown off his wagon. Then he had to run to catch his horses and calm them down as they had panicked from all the commotion. He quickly went as close as he dared to the cockpit, which crashed about 100 feet from him and was still burning. There was nothing he could do for the boys trapped in the wreckage. Later the Germans brought three of the four POW's and made them observe what was left of their plane and their dead crewmates. This was very traumatic for the three crewmen as they were crying and weeping uncontrollably. The exact location of where the wrecked sections came to rest remained burned into Mr. Groenhagen's mind the rest of his life.

The following day Mr. Groenhagen was part of an enormous crowd from all the nearby communities to attend the funeral. Although the Germans gave full military honors at the funeral, they were unappreciative at the size of the crowd. After the minister had spoken and offered a prayer in English, the mayor placed flowers at the graves of the fallen Americans. Then a German officer stood before the graves and spoke bitterly "enemies we were once and now we are friends" and with that he flung a bouquet of flowers on the graves and stormed off.

This story ends with a letter from a Dutch woman to the family of Burl Owens, the ball turret gunner. Miss Nannen witnessed the crash and attended the funeral for the victims.

Dear Owens,

I want to write you some details about Burl M. Owen, No. 18109164. It was Friday June 25 1943 at 9 A.M. I saw planes approaching from a westerly direction bound for Emden, I believe, a German city across from here. As they returned I saw a plane on fire in the sky. It was a dreadful sight. Parts were blown off the burning plane. Near my house lay the tail. Suddenly the plane fell and landed in a stretch of land. The disaster was terrible. Seven young men were killed there. Far from their family, far from home. Two of them who had been in the cockpit were charred. The five others were mutilated but not burnt. All were mutilated at the head, a couple had broken arms. Their parachutes lay beside them. I don't understand why they do not jump.
At the time the seven bodies were put in coffins and were taken to the church. All of us were quite overcome by what had happened. The entire village joined in mourning. Next day the burial took place in the churchyard. The organ played and thus the seven flyers were interred in a common grave. All of us were present. The mayor spoke and the minister offered a prayer in English. After the ceremony I went home quite overcome. Poor boys who had to lose their young lives here far from their relatives. We have taken flowers to their graves. Flowers were also planted on their graves. All we could do. A couple of months ago, the bodies were exhumed and were taken to a central cemetery for American soldiers killed in battle. Perhaps you already knew that.
I hope that you receive this letter and that you will be able to have it translated.

With kind regards,
Miss A.J. Nannen
A 16 Termunten, Holland

Mr. H. Groenhagen standing in the Borgsweer Church Cemetery pointing out the location of the initial graves for those killed in the crash of the *Avenger* on 25 June 1943. Mr. Groenhagen witnessed the explosion of the B-17 and was missed by approximately 100 feet of being struck by the falling cockpit.

B-17F-50-BO 42-5390 PU*L the *Avenger*   303Bomb Group, 360Bomb Squad
All of Palmer's crew that were KIA final place of rest is in the American Cemetery at Margraten.
MIA 25 June 1943 Crashed at Borgsweer, Holland at 0915.
Avenger's crew list can be found on page xxi of the appendices.
Photo courtesy of Jan Stegmeijer

Focke Wulfe Fw 190 posing with her proud pilot
Photo from Tony Crawford's collection

Chapter 9

Bombs on Holland

Throughout the night and early morning of 25 June 1943 the ground crews of the 1st and 4th Wings have been readying their bombers for an attack on northwest Germany. Sleep has been elusive for many of the aircrew members selected to participate in the mission. There is no way to completely block out the sounds of the rumbling engines which are continuously started, shutdown, and restarted.

Soon enough the flyers from the selected crews are awakened. They are notified that their early morning breakfast is being prepared and they are expected for a scheduled briefing.

Following the briefing and meetings with the Chaplains, the crews load personal equipment along with their fifty caliber guns as they climb aboard trucks. They are then transported to their assigned Fortresses' hardstands. While a heavy mist gradually becomes a light rain, each flight crewmember is welcomed by their ground crew. Each crewman is responsible for final assembly of his guns, feeding the ammo belts through the guides, storing flak jackets and helmets for quick access.

An hour later a green flare is the notification that the mission is a go and the pilots are to start their engines. The Group leader is followed to the runway by the lead Squadron. As a general rule, the high Squadron is first to takeoff with the low Squadron last. This orderly departure gives the B-17s with the most altitude an orderly and clear climbing path.

Over the British Midlands thirteen Bomb Groups are lifting off and climbing to altitude. Their destinations are various industrial and military targets in Hamburg. All the Groups experience difficulty in forming up at their assigned altitude due to the overcast. After leaving the coast the visibility problems continue. The Groups that climb above the heaviest overcast are in a haze, which is compounded by the contrails.

The observers have difficulty spotting all their B-17s. Likewise, the trailing Fortresses can only spot a few of their sister ships. Many of the bombers are not even certain which Group they are in.

Shortly after 0800 the raiders begin turning toward Germany. Some of the Groups are separated but press on toward their assigned target. A large number of the Boeings are approaching the Frisian Islands. A few of the 4th Wing bombers are headed straight into the gauntlet of the fighters from Jagdgeschwader 1 or 1st Wing.

The unlucky Group on the spear point is the "Bloody 100th". For three crews this will be their first and only taste of combat. Of the thirty flyers in this first encounter only five will survive. No doubt many succumbed to the frigid waters of the North Sea.

The German Adversaries

The woods surrounding Jever hides over forty Bf 109s. Many of these single engine fighters were armed and fueled in the early morning of 25 June 1943. The Luftwaffe radar net was aware of a growing contingent of airplanes in the south east of England.

Many of the pilots have been over indulging in strong drink since the early morning. Now it is after 7:00 am and the controllers are notifying the flyers with the clear minds as well as the hungover pilots to prepare for flight.

Unknown to this Gruppe of pilots one hundred and sixty-seven B-17s are flying across the North Sea; their destination, Hamburg.

The *Black Men* (ground crews) have assured operations that their 109s are fueled, armed and ready for flight. While the pilots approach their fighters, the ground crews swarm around their plane performing last minute checks. The pilots are given a visual once over that all their personal equipment is in order. This includes life vest, parachute, helmet, goggles, oxygen mask and bandoliers of flares. The pilot is quickly assisted into the cockpit and securely harnessed into his seat.

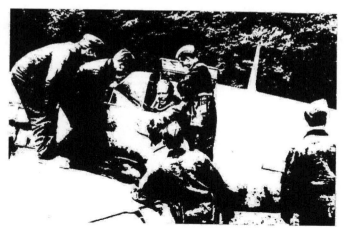

Hptm Alexander Von Winterfeld surrounded by his *Black Men*

these ground crewmembers admired their heroic Captain

The controllers confirm by radio that each fighter is ready. The command to start engines and begin the operation is given.

One by one the line of mottled grey fighters with their *Balkenkreuz* symbols turn into the taxiway and begin their movements toward the runway. The *Black Men* have moved away from their hardstand to a safe remote viewing area.

The ground crews excitedly wave with their caps high in the air as their fighter races past. Gently lifting off one by one the pilots retract their landing gear. Now the accelerating planes cross the threshold near the end of the runway. With the two thousand horsepower Daimler Benz engine near maximum power the pilot gently pulls back on the stick of the hyper sensitive fighter. It is probable that all the base personnel with the exception of the hospital staff proudly watch as each racing fighter rears up into a climbing attitude; rapidly disappearing into the overcast.

This same activity is occurring at fighter bases over northwest Germany from the Ruhr valley to Heligoland. A number of Luftwaffe bases in northern Holland are sending fighters off to join the battle. Over two hundred of Germany's aerial knights are racing to duel with America's flying Fortresses. A looming contest that will involve approximately two thousand combatants in a continuing struggle for air superiority. A running battle that will stretch from Hamburg in northwest Germany and west across Holland. This deadly contest will end somewhere over the North Sea.

Ten minutes after liftoff from Jever the fighters attack the first American raiders at 0835. This battle erupts approximately twenty kilometers north of the German island of Wangerooge with the loss of the first B-17 in another ten minutes.

Ten victories are claimed by the Luftwaffe pilots within thirty kilometers of the Ostfriesland barrier islands.

Many of the lost Fortresses from the 379th, the 305th, and the 306th Bomb Groups have turned south in hopes of finding Hamburg. With no visual reference points a good target of opportunity becomes the objective. Moving across northwestern Germany many bombers have missedWilhelmshaven, Bremen, Emden and Oldenburg. Apparently the weather is near 10/10 with few openings in the undercast.

As the Fortresses approach the Oldenburg Papenburg area they are met by the German fighters from the Soesterberg, and Ruhr valley areas. Fighters from the coastal Gruppes are also giving chase. There are a large number of Staffels from both Jaggeschwader I and II working to clear the bombers from northwest German air space. Unfortunately six 379th Fortresses are quickly overwhelmed and sent crashing down to the German farmland.

A few minutes later five westbound Fortresses from the 384th Bomb Group fly over this area on a direct track for England.

The 379th entered Germany near Wilhelmshaven per a statement from Jack Schmitt, the copilot on *Boozeness* 42-3023.

After the bomb run and approximately twenty-five miles west and south of their target of opportunity, the B-17 *Boozeness* was attacked. Flying high at 28,000 feet the pilot Simones had his Fortress above most of the weather.

The left waist gunner warned that fighters were approaching from eight o'clock. The tail received numerous 20 mm strikes as the Messrschmitts tore past. There were no more communications from the tail gunner, Norman Schoolcraft.

For another ten minutes the Germans continue their attack. The left waist and the ball turret were the next target. The left waist gunner, Norbert Meyer receives the brunt of this pass as he is sprayed from his face to his legs by exploding 20 mm shell fragments. The right waist gunner, Fredrick Hartt had to physically move Meyer to a sitting position. As Meyer kept pulling his oxygen mask down and pointing out his waist window. Was Meyer trying to point out more approaching fighters off in the distance?

Meanwhile the radio operator, Gerald Metthe went back into the waist to help Hartt get Joseph Noonan out of the ball. About this time another attacking Messerschmitt delivered a 20 mm strike into the top turret. The gunner engineer received a second strike and collapsed in the top turret.

The bailout order is given just as Metthe had rolled the ball up to where Noonan can get out of his station. Before Noonan can get his chute on, *Boozeness* went into a spin. The copilot, Jack Schmitt was followed by the pilot Thomas Simones to the nose hatch when their Fortress exploded. Schmitt escaped through the nose hatch while Simones is too late. The Navigator, Harold Aebischer, the bombardier, Thornton Baker, the radio operator and the right waist gunner are blown from the B-17. All of these flyers were able to open their chutes and safely make it down.

Jack Schmitt, while coming down in his chute witnesses, the exploding *Boozeness* and the falling debris. Schmitt attempted to escape by swimming the Ems River. Schmitt and four of his crewmates were arrested by the local police with assistance from area farmers.

Just east of the Simones crash site, the rampaging Germans score their second victory over a 379th Boeing. This B-17 is cut to pieces near Dingstede, Germany. The pilot, Kenneth Quade and eight of his fellow crewmates perish following an attack which set the oxygen system on fire. Following the bale-out order, the navigator successfully exited out of Fortress number 42-5839. Like the five members of the Simones crew, nine members of the Quade crew were given a military funeral. They were interred on 30 June 1943 at the New Cemetery in Oldenburg, Germany.

Near the Dingstede crash site is the town of Friesoythe. Here Gruppen Adjutant Olt. Friedrich Hardt from III/JGI who is piloting a Bf 109 G6 crashes after a fatal encounter with a B-17. It is possible that Hardt shot down the *Yankee Powerhouse* 42-30143 near Oldenburg and then had his fatal encounter with the Quade B-17.

Between the Simones and the Quade crash site is the German village of Neu Arenburg, Germany. This small town saw the crash of the Douglas Groom B-17 after encounters with a Staffel of German fighters. The Groom ship 42-29892 broke up with five of her crew surviving.

The B-17 42-29864 was heading for the Dutch border when she was attacked by Focke Wulfs. The pilot, Courtney Browne gave the bail-out order too late as only two of his crew were able to escape the B-17 before she exploded.

It is interesting to note that both the Courtney Browne crew and the Thomas Simones crews who were KIA were all buried in the Lingen/Ems cemetery.

On a parallel line with and two hundred miles east of Amsterdam is the German town of Quakenbruck. This is in the area where the B-17F 42-30107 *Black Magic* lost her battle with fighters. The little village of Wieste is recorded as the crash site. Both turret gunners, Winston Tinker and Wilbur Koloen were killed by 20mm gunfire. They were initially interred in the Quakenbruck Cemetery. The rest of the crew successfully bailed out and spent the rest of the war in prison camp.

The 379th Fortress 42-30165 piloted by Paul Hartman was shot down near Sogel after losing her battle with German fighters. The radio operator, James Blick and the right waist gunner, Harold Schrader were both killed by the attacking fighter. Schrader's remains were never recovered.

With the disorganized and scattered Groups turning west, the Fortress 42-29499 *Ma MA Chang* was struck in her number one engine by friendly fire. This incident by a gunner from a sister ship forced this Fort to leave the formations protective fire power near the Dutch border. Falling back, she was quickly attacked by German fighters.

Ma Ma Chang's crash as described by Dutch citizens and recorded by Ab. Jansen: *One of them* (the flyers) *descended near Vriescheloo; the man was injured. A local clergyman, Ds. Ph Jac. Greeven, was only able to exchange a few words with the American. His fervent assurance "we are friends" only brought a faint smile on the man's face, grey and contorted with pain. A short time later, a Dutch police officer, who was known as a good patriot, arrived by bicycle. He had a collapsible stretcher with him. Insofar as an eyewitness could remember, the injured man was taken to the public elementary school of Vriescheloo on this stretcher. There he was picked up by the Germans and moved to the hospital at Winschoten.*

The aircraft circled around above Oude-Pekela/Winschoten/Zuirderveen, which suggested that it may have been flying on auto-pilot. According to an eyewitness in Blijham, the aircraft flew at a low altitude over the village. "One of the pilots stood upon the wing. The circles became smaller and smaller". According to another eyewitness who saw it happening: "It was frightening". The aircraft steadily lost altitude and finally came down in a potato field in which it gouged a wide track with a length of some 100-150 meters; before striking a cinder dike along the Gockinga-wijk (a canal now filled in). As a result of its crash-landing speed, the aircraft then cartwheeled and then came to rest on its back in a cornfield on the other side of the canal. The engines were torn from the wings and flung forward, (they were found five meters behind and 600 meters further on). The plane then caught fire and was totally destroyed.

It did not take long before lots of people went to the place where the aircraft had come down. Two members of the crew landed by chute near the crash site. According to various eyewitnesses, at least one of these crewmen, whilst floating down hanging on to the silk, was strafed by a German fighter aircraft. With its deadly work done – it turned and flew away. After about five minutes, the parachute with its now lifeless body floated down to earth coming to rest in a cornfield in the vicinity of Kenterslaan-Tjabbesstreek, about 2 km east of Oude Pekela. Soon a crowd assembled around the dead man who was lying in the young corn. Later that day the body, was taken to Oude Pekela and buried. (Other information asserts that the American died in the Academic Hospital in Groningen).

According to a statement of the Dutch Red Cross, the dead man was Sergeant George Harles from Rigsby, Georgia. When we researched into these events many years after the war, it appeared that this airman was unknown in the Washington D.C. archives. In 1979 when volume I of "SPOREN AAN DE HEMEL" was published, we had not established the airman's identity.

Another crewman landed unhurt on the land of the Smit brothers at the Winschoterweg Nr. 7 at Oude Pekela. He was captured by a member of the pro-German NSB party, a certain Jacob Braam Ruben, at the time garage-proprietor at Oude-Pekela. The American was temporarily locked up in the water tower.

A 306th Bomb Group B-17 referred to as "DFC" approached the Dutch border after dropping out of her formation. Having lost two engines due to mechanical failure she was attacked by German fighters. The pilot Thomas Logan gave the bailout order and the crew quickly began their exit. The radio operator, Albert Schwartz was the only fatality. The Fortress came down near the historic Dutch Fort, Bourtrange. This historic structure was built during The Eighty Years' War along the only road between Groningen and Germany.

With other lost Fortresses under attack and in retreat, then likely the first observed village was considered a target of opportunity. Thus unloading five thousand pounds of bombs was considered a most expedient decision. Unfortunately, however, the village of Bellingwolde was located in Holland and not Germany.

A description of this fiasco as written by the noted historian Ab. Jansen: *It was about nine o' clock in the morning when one of the loose American formations was attacked by German fighters while over the Dutch side of the Dutch/German border, Bellingwolde, a village with most of its buildings built along a central street. Eyewitnesses speak of 15 or 20 Allied aircraft, "but there could have been many more as it was cloudy". It is not clear whether they had abandoned their mission and were on their way back to their home bases. Locally, it was believed that the fighters had taken off from a new aerodrome in the Munsterland, as a consequence of which the Americans were completely surprised. (No confirmation of this assumption has been found.) We fail to know whether the American formation changed its course as a result of these attacks or that it had already abandoned the planned mission beforehand.*

Anyway, it is also highly probable that the 'Yanks' felt hard-pressed and were possibly under the impression that they were already over Germany. The entire formation dropped its bombs just over the picturesque Groningen village. With a dreadful whine the bombs rained down. Though the greater part of the explosives fell on both sides of the extended village, the consequences were bad enough. "It was if the world perished", somebody related later.

In the village there was hardly one window left intact, tiles were swept in rows from the roofs and many houses, especially those on the Northern side of the town. The big water tower suffered heavy damage, considering that the water pump was torn from its socket and was found later on a roof. A sixty meter long garden in the village center, belonging to Mr. Bulten, the Cartwright, was transformed into a moonscape by three bombs, which produced a trio of five meter deep craters.

Near the Werkhuislaan (since renamed Lindelaan) some seven bombs had come down, causing heavy damage to the house of the Kruise family. Not a tile remained in place and in the loft, "a cart, full of mould" was found". Mrs. Kruise, who had fled into the bedroom, was found later by the neighbors: she was lying between two bedsteads, stunned but unhurt. Mr. Kruise, who had been working on the tramline near the municipal hall on the main road, abandoned his work. Together with his colleagues he made a helter-skelter escape between houses and through a ditch. He had just sought cover between two houses when a bomb hit the place where they had been at work moments before. Parts of the tramlines fell on top of the house next to which he had lain down; right above his head a piece of tramline was hanging in a roof gutter. He only received a slight head injury

There were a number of other people who escaped death by the narrowest margin, like Mrs. Trientje Takens-Edens, the wife of a labourer and mother of a three-year old daughter, who was living in the Leete, about one kilometer from the Dutch/German border. She relates: "I was alone at home with my little girl. Our dog was on its chain and was behaving very nervously, when far in the distance in Germany, a rumbling became audible. One moment it could be heard distinctly, whilst another moment, it seemed to be much farther away. Our little girl used to go to our neighbor's. Because the explosions were sounding louder and louder, I called out to the child, but when I did not get any reply, I took it that she was with the neighbor. When I went there I saw the girl through the window of the living room. Our neighbor called out to me "come in, it might be dangerous."

I entered the living room, which was situated in such a manner that I could not see our own house and yard. The explosions came nearer and nearer. All of a sudden there was a dreadful blast, crash, bang and the neighbor cried out, "Oh gosh, I believe they will destroy us!" After that the detonations seemed to abate and after a time did not hear anything more. "So" I said to our neighbor, "let's go to our house again – by now the danger will be over."

When I went outside with my little daughter, I could not immediately see our house, as my view was restricted by their fence and outer door. When I came around the corner I could not believe my eyes: Our house had been razed to the ground! The bed covering, torn to ribbons, was hanging in the trees. Our dog, lying at his chain at a distance of some six meters from the house was alright. The animal didn't even have a scratch. So my little girl and I escaped certain death in a miraculous way.

A bomb fell in the front garden of the beautiful residence of the local physician, Doctor F. van der Laan. He recalls: "On the north facing façade of our house, about three meters from the front door, a 'whopper' of 500 kg, as they said, had fallen right in front of the flight of steps to the garden, exploded and blasted a hole in the ground with a depth of some four meters. The entry door for the patients had blown inside, just at the moment that a middle-aged woman was about to leave. She saw the door tumbling down and just managed to jump backwards. In her fear, she fled down to the cellar and hardly had she arrived there when a full pantry cupboard crashed on the cellar floor just behind her heels. Quite taken aback, she was able to escape from the cellar through a small window. In the waiting room, a panic had broken out; the people fled through the garage out to the garden and hid in shallow ditches nearby. Bombs were hailing down, the detonations followed one another in an almost indescribable fast rate; it seemed as if the whole event lasted for hours, whereas everything took place within a few minutes.

When the aircraft had disappeared, we walked back to our house where we found enormous chaos in the place, where so recently, I had held a consulting hour. The house had become unfit for habitation. Sand and mud were lying half a meter thick on the roof, from which all tiles had gone. It was a solid and well-built house, yet the entire north wall had been pushed inside about 20 cm. All windows were smashed, the ante-room window had disappeared, the dispensary was strewn with broken glass and medicaments. Before I could take stock, people came running from all sides, calling for my help for the wounded. To my surprise, there were only two people dead (later the number rose to three) and two people seriously injured, despite, as it later was established, a total of over one thousand bombs having fallen! A fifty year old woman, had been injured by many glass splinters. For some years afterwards, larger and smaller fragments would continue to be expelled by her body".

Victims
One of the bombs had fallen close to the house of the family of H. Koens, in which, at that moment, only the seven-year old Tjabina (nicknamed "Bienie") was lying ill in bed. From the ravaged ruin to which, within a few seconds, the house had been reduced, her small lifeless body was removed from the debris of the Koens home. While behind the house, stood the perambulator containing the Koens' youngest child, who only months-old, was miraculously unhurt.

The second victim was the barge man, Nies de Jonge (33) of the steep-stern Dutch inland water barge "Treintje" moored in the Boelo-Tijdens canal, near the Rhederbrug (a bridge). Whilst observing the activity in the sky above, he had been blown from the deck by the blast from a bomb exploding on the canal bank. He fell into the canal and drowned.

A third victim was Heiko Diddens, locally known as "Old Mr. Diddens", who lived on the Hoofdstraatweg. He had just woken up. Together with his lady companion and housekeeper, Tonnie Mulder (27), he was standing in the bedroom when they suddenly felt the house shaking under their feet. Of what then happened, Miss Mulder had no recollection. When she regained consciousness, she was lying in the hospital at Winschoten.

What had happened? A bomb had struck the house, passing through the roof, went right through the bedroom and then drilled itself through the living room below. It proceeded right down through the cellar and come to a stop four meters beneath the house's foundation. Due to a faulty fuse, the bomb was a dud and did not explode. However, Miss. Mulder and Mr. Diddens had dropped through the breach and fell through the living room ceiling and floor following the path of the bomb right down into the cellar. They were freed a short time later by their fellow villagers who had rushed to their aid. Miss Mulder survived from this misadventure, after receiving numerous contusions and lacerations, which required about a six weeks hospital stay. Fortunately she returned to Bellingwolde in good condition, almost fully recovered. The elderly Mr. Diddens had been less fortunate. His chest had been crushed by a heavy beam, and one of his legs was shattered. A few hours afterward he died in the hospital.

With the raiders continuing their retreat, other Dutch villages appeared to the bombardiers. Later it became apparent that these towns with their canals were assumed to be German towns. Whatever the excuse the mistakes were costly in lives and property as noted by Ab Jansen continuing commentary, from his book, **A Hard Lesson Learned.**

That day bombs not only fell at Bellingwolde, but high-explosive bombs were also dropped to the west and northwest of the village, at Blijham, at Beerta and still further to the north, as far as Finsterwolde.

In nearby Oudeschans the terror-stricken school children had sought cover underneath their desks, whilst others ran out of the school in a panic. They were, however, stopped by a woman passer-by who, by her resolute action, probably saved their lives. One bomb drilled itself into the road (now known as Molenweg), right in front of house no. 14, in which a grocery store was located. The premises were almost entirely destroyed.

In the Bult, a hamlet to the northwest of Oudeschans consisting of two farms and a house, an estimated 25 to 30 bombs fell. The inhabitants fled into their cellars. When they later emerged, they saw several mounds of earth on the land, these being the rims of bomb craters. Fortunately the buildings had not been hit and no lives were lost.

In the neighborhood of Blijham, several (approximately 15) bombs fell – of which the majority came down near the outer dike. Geert Baas (39,) a labourer, who was working in the fields, was killed.

In Beerta there were two fatal casualties Cornelius Feikens (60) whose small house was completely destroyed, and shop assistant Richte Rosevink (17) whose body was found opposite where Feikens house had stood. He must have been passing by when the bomb fell.

Finsterwolde and the region further to the north got their share of high explosives. Here too, some people lost their lives in the Carel Coenraadpolder, northeast of Finsterwolde, who were weeding fields. When the racket in the air increased, most of them sought cover against the bank of a ditch, with the exception of Jan Hendrik Schuur (54), his son, bearing the same name (22) and Klaas Alles (42), who calmly continued working. Presumably, they thought it would not be too bad. Fate proved them wrong; as a bomb fell very near to the area where the three men were at work. Schuur and his son were killed on the spot. Alles was seriously wounded. Doctors in the hospital tried to save his life, amputating one of his legs, but it was to no avail. Five days later he succumbed to the injuries he had sustained.

When evaluating all the materials available to us, it appears that the formation entered Dutch airspace on a course that was north-northwest, and then made a slight turn in a northern direction. An eyewitness at Vriescheloo, who could see the aircraft through a gap in the clouds, speaks of a "Group of at least 20 aircraft," which flew in a northwesterly direction. The accuracy of this information is confirmed by the bomb scatter-pattern, stretching from Bellingwolde, skirting along Blijham, Beerta and Finsterwolde.

Should the formation have flown longitudinally over the village (Bellingwolde), the jettison may have caused a far greater disaster. The bombs from the "tail" of the series fell into the Carel Coenraadpolder and possibly further to the north, even into the Dollard.

The destruction and carnage wrought on the innocent Dutch towns and villages finally ends with the Fortresses moving out over the North Sea. The last encounter noted from intercepted German radio transmission was at 1000. At this time most all the retreating Fortresses are over the North Sea and on their way back to base. As might be expected the returning crews are experiencing clearing weather

Chapter 10

A German Ace

A German Fighter Ace Takes on Fortresses from the 100ᵗʰ BG on 25 June 1943

Heinz Knoke, an ace German fighter pilot, and his comrades have been on a drinking binge until daylight on 25 June 1943. After only a couple of hours sleep, he is awakened by the telephone that there is a concentration of enemy aircraft in sector Dora-Dora. After having breakfast Knoke tries to shake his hangover and pull himself together by running up and down the runway with his dog. Unlike most American pilots who over-indulge in liquor try to overcome the effects by inhaling pure oxygen for a few minutes.

When Knoke and his fellow pilots are ordered to stand by for an alert, it is a signal to dress for flight, which includes flying suit, fur boots, and life jacket. Next the pilots stroll over to their fighters where they find their mechanics and ground crew waiting. After being assisted into the cockpit and with fastening his harness, the German pilot puts on his helmet.

When the commanding officer inquires of each pilot by ground telephone of their readiness, it is assumed that the American target is Wilhelmshaven. The fighters take off in flights, with a total of Forty-four planes airborne at 8:11 a.m. They pass through the first cloud layer at six thousand feet and can see farmland below at breaks in the clouds. At fifteen thousand feet another cloud layer is encountered. After passing through twenty thousand feet, the fighters expect to see the bombers. Instead they witness beautiful cloud formations as described by Heinz Knoke: *We fly between cumulus clouds. High above us spreads* a *third layer of ice clouds. We fly through valleys and caverns, across gigantic mountains of clouds. Our planes seem absurdly small, dwarfed by this majestic background.*

Finally Knoke and his fellow pilots did find the bombers three thousand feet below and proceed in their attacks as the B-17s are grouped in formations of twos, threes, fours and some are alone. This lack of proper massed formation is perfect for the fighters, as this leaves the Fortresses practically defenseless. This is also reflected in the loss of eighteen B-17s for this raid.

The weather was so bad during takeoff and climb out that one hundred and eight out of two hundred and seventy-five Fortresses aborted the mission. Most of the attacking B-17 crews could not locate their Group formations, and as a result only two of the 384ᵗʰ returning Fortresses claimed to have found and bombed the target. However, the B-17 42-5850, with Group leader Seldon McMillin on board, found and hit the target while the B-17 42-30049 *Miss Deal* located the target area but the bombardier could not see the docks, ship yards, or submarine pens, after twice circling the target area. Departing the Hamburg area with a full bomb load, John Way had requested that the navigator give him a heading for the secondary target, Emden.

Knoke continues with his story of defending northern Germany against the B-17s on 25 June 1943 as he begins his attack from three thousand feet above the enemy. *Peeling off, we go down diving. "After them," the chase is on. It is a perfect surprise. Our attack throws the Americans into a state of utter confusion. They dodge turn and dive for cover in the clouds as they try to get away from us. It is impossible to estimate how many of them there are. It is as if a beehive was overturned. We call out to each other the best firing positions by radio.*

In pairs our pilots attack the individual groups of Fortresses. As my wingman today, I have a young Sergeant with me for the first time. This is his first experience of air combat. There is a good chance that it may be also his first victory, if he keeps his head. I select two isolated heavy bombers flying wing tip to wing tip, and we go down to attack them from the rear. "Dolling, you take the one on the left".
I call to the Sergeant; but he keeps flying away off to the right and does not heed my call. "Close in, man! Other side—over to the left! Get in and attack!"

I open fire at short range. My cannon shells land beautifully in the center of the fuselage. The rear gunner persistently returns my fire. I calmly close in, guns blazing. Holes appear in my right wing as I am hit. That bastard of a rear gunner! He will not leave me alone—must have a lot of guts. Closer still I keep on blasting away at the Fortress, concentrating on the rear turret. It disintegrates under the salvos from my cannon. More high explosive puts the dorsal turret out of action also.

We are between clouds, in a deep ravine, with milky walls towering high on both sides. It is a glorious picture. Dolling still keeps flying obstinately in his position to my right, calmly watching the shooting. Why does he not go after the second heavy bomber? I lose my temper with him now: Attack, you bloody fool, attack!
He still makes no move.

Woomf! Woomf! Woomf!
I am under heavy fire from the side. It comes from the right side turret of the second Fortress. I am in a position close alongside. The dorsal gunner also blazes away at me with his twin guns. Tracers pass close by my head.
Woomf! I feel another hit. We pass through wisps of cloud. My window fogs up, so I slide open the side window.

My Fortress is on fire along the back and in the left inside engine. Still the two gunners in the second Fortress keep on blazing away at me. They are only 100 feet away. I continue firing at my victim. The bastard has got to go down, even if it means my own neck. I remain 150 to 200 feet behind his tail. The fire now spreads to his right wing. I drop the stick for a moment and try to attract the attention of Dolling by waving and pointing to the second Fortress. There is a sudden flash in front of my eyes, and I feel my waving hand slammed violently against the right side of the aircraft. Alarmed, I reach for the stick, but drop it again immediately. My right glove is in shreds, with blood trickling out. I do not feel any pain.

Once again I grasp the stick with my injured hand, line up the sights on my opponent, and empty the magazine in one long burst. At long last the Fortress goes down, falling in the clouds like a flaming torch. I go down after it, following as far as the sea. There, all that is left of the heavy bomber is a large patch of oil burning on the surface.

By now my hand is starting to hurt; I take the stick in my left hand and find it smeared with blood. Shreds of flesh hang from the torn glove.

I lost my bearings some time ago during the shooting above the clouds. Heading south, however, I am bound to reach land somewhere. It is a miracle that my engine has not been hit. By a stroke of good luck the gunners on that Fortress were not good marksmen. The pain in my hand is getting worse. I am losing a lot of blood. My flying suit looks as if I had been wallowing in a slaughterhouse.

How far out to sea can I be? Minutes drag by and still there is no sight of that damned coastline. I begin to have a peculiar hot, sickly sort of feeling: must be getting light-headed.

An island looms up ahead: Norderney. Only seven or eight minutes more, and then I can land. The time seems interminable. Finally, I am over Jever.

In spite of the throbbing pain in my hand, I dive low over the flight dispersal point and announce my success with a victory roll. The mechanics wave their hands and caps, as delighted as children. And now I need both hands for landing. I grit my teeth. My right hand is completely numb. My ground-crew chief is horrified at the sight of my hand and the blood over my flying suit. The mechanics swarm around my aircraft. The chief has been wounded!

Knoke is taken to the hospital where one finger is partially amputated and given a tetanus injection. He returned to flying after a couple of weeks of recuperation, although combat was not allowed until 28 July 1943. On the 25th of July the Fortresses returned and successfully raided Hamburg with high explosive five hundred pounders. Unfortunately, of the seven attacking B-17s from Charlie's 544th Squadron, only one ship returns.

Knoke took a four passenger Messerschmitt Taifum and flew over Hamburg, where over one hundred thousand Germans citizens lost their lives as a result of the British using incendiary bombs on the night raid of 25 July 1943. He reported that the smoke from the fires was some ten to twenty miles wide drifting out over the Baltic. Thus, for the bomber crews, they will now be faced with a more determined Luftwaffe defending their homeland.

Heinz Knoke flew over two hundred missions with thirty-three victories. He was shot down many times, always returning to fight again in overtaxed and inferior German fighters. His injuries finally grounded him from flying and probably saved his life.

The crew lists for the two B-17s lost from the 100th Bomb Group are on page xx of the Appendices.

Chapter 11

SECRET DOCUMENTS

The following secret documents have been declassified and reflect the enemy radio transmissions of the Luftwaffe in their battle against the American raiders. Also included are summaries of the raids by the 1st Wing. They were reprinted herewith to reflect the cost of ordering this mission to proceed knowing that the weather would be the initial challenge to the crews. All of the training for the nine Bombardment Groups of the 1st Wing was not sufficient to organize and maintain 149 of the attacking B-17s in their defensive formations. Fortresses participating in the 25 June 1943 Hamburg raid were Fortunate if ½ dozen could maintain visual contact. At this point in the war, the German fighters were continually directed to their adversaries by radio because their ground control was tracking all their hostilities by radar. The flak stations were likewise alerted when enemy aircraft entered their area of responsibility. At the end of the day, the smart pilots had not only recognized the futility of the mission dictated by the Brass, but aborted to fly a future mission where they could see and destroy their target.

Mission No. 67 from VIII Bomber Command Selected Secret Documents

The 1st Wing included B17s from 9 bomb Groups attacking. They included the 91st, 92nd, the 303rd, the 305th, the 306th, the 351st, the 379th, the 381st, and the 384th.

With 197 aircraft dispatched, 48 B17s failed to bomb: 16 for mechanical and equipment failure, 2 for personnel failure, 21 because of adverse weather, 3 were spares and returned as scheduled, and 6 were missing believed to be lost before bombing. *

Encounters: 1st Wing: Strong opposition was encountered. 100-150 e/a reported to have made attacks from 0825 to 0945 hrs. while formation was over enemy territory, with attacks being broken off because of bad weather over the North Sea on return route. The majority of e/a were Me-109s and Fw-190s, with a few Ju-88s, Me-110s, Me-210s and one Do-217. Attacks were moderate to intense with e/a flying off the wings of the formation, apparently waiting for stragglers. Attacks were concentrated on low formations with most coming from the nose 10 to 2 o'clock, high and level. Frontal attacks were made with 4-6 e/a coming in one behind the other, dropping down from above to gather speed, leveling off at about 1,000-1,200 ft. ahead executing a half-roll as they closed to about 600 ft., and then breaking off attack by passing down and under the formation. Several attacks were reported from 5 to 7 o'clock level with the same system of half-roll and break away by diving down and under. Occasionally a Group of 2 to 6 e/a would attack abreast, fly through the formation with the apparent effort of breaking it up. Air-to-air bombing was again reported with fair accuracy as to height. Bombs were dropped in strings of 4 to 12.

---

* The total number of missing B-17s from the 1st Wing for mission 67 was 15.

Markings noted: Fw-190s blue and silver with yellow noses, some fuselages blue with carefully camouflaged crosses on silver bellies, yellow tails and red noses and some with white cowlings resembling P-47s; Me-109s, some silver and some black, black crosses on silver bodies, some with checkerboard tail markings, some grey and green in color, and others with white stripes painted on tail and yellow crosses in center of white circle on fuselage; Ju-88s, yellow nose, yellow on bottom of fuselage and light blue on top of fuselage, some were all black and others all dun color; Me-210s, all black.

One Ju-88 and one Me-210 were observed to fire cannon broadside. 20mm side guns were reported to fire horizontally. One crew reported a Fw 190 with a heavy cannon, 30mm or heavier, bolted under fuselage and engine. This cannon was used rather accurately on another formation.

FLAK: 1st Wing: Moderate to meager, flak generally inaccurate, was reported at altitudes varying from 14,000 to 27,500 ft. A.A. installations were believed to be observed at Emden, Bremen, Heligoland, near Wardenburg, mouth of the Elbe river, Friedrichskoog, Cruxhaven, Langeooge, Wilhelmshaven, Scharhorn, Norderney, and Oldenburg. Positions were generally uncertain due to heavy clouds. One a/c states it encountered very accurate and intense automatic weapon fire, and one Group believed A.A. was radio directed.

As usual it is unfortunate that those de-briefed did not include the crews that were lost. Flak was reported by one of the surviving crewmembers of *Miss Deal*. The Bombardier, Tom Corrigan aptly described the flak after leaving the obscured target. Flak hit us, first it set # 4 engine on fire, and smashed the ball turret. We fell back and then the 190s came in.

FIGHTER SUPPORT: 1 Squadron of Spitfires and 1 Squadron of Typhoons were detailed to give withdrawal cover from a point about 100 miles out from Cromer. 20 returning bombers were sighted about 10-15 miles from the English coast. A diversionary attack on Western Holland by 12 Bostons of 2 Groups supported by 10 Squadrons of Spitfires was abandoned near the Dutch Coast because of 10/10 cloud cover at 7000 ft. 8 Squadrons of P-47s carried out uneventful sweeps over the Dutch Coast.

OBSERVATION: 1st Wing: A heavily camouflaged B-17 was seen flying with formation over the Elbe Estuary. Its color was lighter than our a/c and windows of waist gun positions were closed. It disappeared after 2 or 3 minutes. A single engine black e/a with square Wings, round cowling and low Wing, trailed about 1500 yards behind the formation for over an hour as though observing. No shots were fired. A Me-109 appeared to issue flame and smoke from a jet 1½ ft. from fuselage on left Wing, and after diving as if hit, flame was extinguished and attack resumed. One pilot reported seeing 12 objects about 6 feet square and flat, falling like leaves in front at 11 o'clock low. No explosions were noted. Single shells were reported fired about 1500 yards astern, flashing on leaving e/a and exploding like flak in the formation. Aerial bombs were reported to be 25-30 lbs. weight.

ENEMY TACTICS:

Mission HAMBURG – BREMEN. Date 25.6.43.

Time over Target.	No. of a/c	Seen
Approx: 0930	275 Fortresses	100-150

Withdrawl	Time up	
Cover for	1024	9 Sp.
Fortresses	1030	9 Typhoons

German Fighter Reaction

Jafue Peuteche Bucht.

Heligoland Staffel	) Fuge 7	10 aircraft
T/E Jever	)	14 aircraft
Naval Fighters	)	6aircraft
1 Gruppe from Jever	) Fuge 16	30 aircraft
	)	
1 Staffel from Oldenburg	)	10 aircraft

Jafue Holland/Ruhr

Leeuwarden Area	10 aircraft
Soesterberg Area	40 aircraft
Peelan Area	10 aircraft
S. Holland Area	10 aircraft
	140

German Fighter Action:

As on past occasions the amount of traffic intercepted on Fuge 16 was too slight to allow any confident estimate to be made of the No.of a/c put up from the Deutsche Bucht. R/T was intercepted on 2 VHF frequencies but no callings were heard: It is possible that they represented a Gruppe from Jever and a Staffel from Oldenburg. About 30 a/c operated on Fuge 7: 10 from the Heligoland Staffel: some 14 twin-engined day fighters from Jever, and Naval Fighters, possibly a Schwarm on convoy work. Seven Staffeln reacted from Jafue Holland/Ruhr operating chiefly in the Ems estuary/Gronigen area.

German fighters from the Deutsche Bucht intercepted the Fortresses in the Juist area on their way in and held on until they were west of Borkum and on their homeward route.

The defenses at Jever first announced raiders at 0817, probably north of Nordeney. Those were the Fortresses detailed to attack Bremen. At 0822 the height was estimated at 20,000 ft. and at 0825 as 23,000 ft. The Heligoland Staffel probably reached the Nordeney area and engaged about 0925. Twin-engined fighters from Jever vectored due North at 0831 may have been in contact shortly afterwards. At 0834 the Fortresses turned south and flew overland in the Jever Oldenburg area.

Some of this formation probably turned on a N.W. course some five minutes later because at 0858, a ship on convoy 30 km. north of Juist signaled to its fighter escort that it had sighted 20 hostilities. There was no other reflection of the attack on the convoy. The rest of the formation may have taken a more westerly route home.

At 0842 the Fortresses raiding Hamburg were signaled some 60 km. north of Norderney and tracked toward Heligoland. It seems likely that the majority of the fighters were sent northwards to deal with this new raid. It is not possible to follow the course of the raiders in detail. Some were still in the Heligoland area at 0907, while others were plotted at this time over an area stretching from the Ems estuary to Vegsack flying westwards on their homeward course. The Heligoland Staffel landed at 0912, but twin-engined fighters were still pursuing the withdrawing raiders in the Borkum area at 0927.
They were recalled two minutes later, as pilots only had enough petrol left for 15 minutes flight and control recognized that further pursuit was useless. The Gruppe from Jever operating on VHF was first heard at 0825. They attacked at 0835 although no R/T was heard after 0834; they presumably held on until they had reached the limit of their endurance. The only two intercepts from A/C in the Oldenburg area were not illuminating. A pilot informed control at 0908 that he was flying alone at 20,000 feet. It seems reasonable however to assume that at least one Staffel from this area attempted interception.

At 0817 a Staffel from Leeuwarden (Jafue Holland/Ruhr) was sent to intercept in the Langeoog area. It reached this area at 0848, but it is not clear whether contact was made. Pilots were vectored back to base at 0926. 4 A/C from a unit of NJG 3 at Vechta were intercepted in the Heligoland/Oldenburg area from 0856 – 0925.

Jafue Holland/Ruhr concentrated his main effort on intercepting the Fortresses on their homeward route in the Ems estuary/Groningen area. 4 Staffeln from the Soesterberg area were vectored on a N.E. on a course from 0833/0847.

Three minutes later when flying at 31,000 feet. German pilots sighted hostiles in the Leer area and in ensuing combats one FW 190 was shot down at 0906.

Nothing was heard after 0908 when one pilot complained of petrol shortage.

A Staffel from Doelen was also sent to this area from 0836 – 0847, but it is not clear from the broken R/T intercepts whether contact was made.

A Staffel from S. Holland Controlled from Gilze Rijen was vectored N.E. at 0841.

At 0855 when a/c were 50 km. S.E. of Leeuwarden, hostilities were reported to be ahead on the starboard side, but there is no evidence that German pilots sighted the raiders.

Air–Sea-Rescue searches were carried out in an area N. of Norden to Scharhorn from 0956 – 1255.

German Air-Raid Warnings: Nothing intercepted.

German Aircraft Reporting System: Nothing intercepted.

Intercepted German Radio Transmission

0819	3.670 NC/S	Hostiles N. Norderney.
0822		Hostiles at 19,500 feet W. Norderney.
0824		Hostiles at 19,500 feet 22 miles N. Schiermonnikoog, partly in the clouds.
0832		Hostiles at 22,500 feet N of Wangerooge, the German A/C were due south of them at this time.
0836		One A/C had to land because of engine trouble or damaged engine.
0837		Hostiles in Langroog/Emden area.
0841	40.0 NC/S	Position of German A/C 25 miles SSE Gronigen, hostiles in Wilhelmshaven/Emden area.
0842	3.670	New Hostiles reported N Langroog.
0843		Old formation flying slightly higher than the above in the direction Schiermonnikoog.
0845		Hostiles 15 miles N. Spiekeroog.
0845	42.0	Position of German A/C S. Gronigen.
0848	42.2	Position of German A/C 10 miles N. Langeoog.
0848	3.670	Hostiles 16 miles NE Spiekeroog, height unknown.
0849		Height of hostiles 24,000 feet.
0849		Hostiles 17 miles NW Scharhorn.
0856	39.7	Position of A/C 10 miles NNE Heppol (?)
0859		Hostiles to starboard ahead. Position as last message.
0856	3.375	Hostiles 9-15 miles S Heligoland.
0856		Hostiles 30 miles N. Norderney.
0858		A ship reported hostiles 25 miles N. Borkum.
0900		Ship reported 20 hostiles in sight, position 27 miles N. Borkum.
0901	38.9	German A/C position 20 miles W Heligoland, A/C warned of

		hostiles below.
0903	40.0	Position of A/C 20 miles S. Emden
0905	38.9	Position of A/C 35 miles N. Borkum
0905	40.0	…190 shot down (=Fw 190?)
0906		German A/C 37 miles NW Schiermonnikoog
0908	3.670	Hostiles 23 miles SW Heligoland and over the Island at 22,500 to 26,000 feet
0909	3.375	Hostiles in Emden/Oldenburg area
0912		Position of German A/C Oldenburg area
0915		Position of A/C 12 miles NNW Bremerhaven
0916	3.670	(German) D/F position of A/C SSW Wilhelmshaven
0917	3.375	One A/C 20 miles S. Bremerhaven, and one A/C 7 miles SE Wangerooge
0925		Hostiles too far away, A/C ordered to return to base
0929	3.670	The "last hostile" reported about 50 kms. Ahead of A/C, still at 22,500 to 26,000 feet. A/C said he could only fly for 15 minutes more so G/S ordered A/C to return to base.
1011		A/C ordered to search in Norderney – Wangerooge area.

It is obvious after reading the below comments of the 25 June 1943 raids, that the 8th Army Air Corps learned a lesson after receiving heavy criticism, from military leaders as well as politicians back home.

Comments on Report of Raid:

1st Wing. Target: Hamburg.

1[st]Wing

1. As noted in the Comments and Recommendations in the Air Division report of this mission, weather was the deciding factor in the non-success of this mission. The First Air Division plan to have the Group Commanding Officer or Group Air Executive of the Group leading the Division formation fly in the lead A/C is sound. It is realized that it was possible that too much emphasis may have been placed on reaching the target at all times. Experienced personnel must lead these formations and must also feel free to abandon a mission whenever they deem it advisable to do so.

2. The errors in execution of this mission have been brought to the attention of all concerned on previous occasions. However, it must be realized that events such as occurred on this mission arise with great rapidity and, due to the large size of the formations with which we are forced to operate, it is oftentimes very difficult to carry out a decision to abandon a mission the moment such a decision is made. Groups may be forced out of position by weather or other circumstances and the leader must allow these units time with which they may regain their formation position before initiating any action directed toward a return of the mission.

3. Air Division and Combat Wing Commanders must impress combat crews with the fact that there are many factors which may affect a mission, and which may make it a success or failure. Weather is one of the greatest factors, and, due to its characteristics in our zone of operations, is often so variable that our forecasts and analysis may be wrong. A cloud just large enough to obscure the target – which is drifting with an unknown speed, may obscure the target at the critical time on the bombing run. We miss the target, and aircraft and crews are lost without obvious profit. But there is a profit in every operation we make. Air war is governed by many variables, and to win the decision we cannot wait for perfect days, we must press home the attack, and sometimes gamble. Every operation inflicts some damage on the enemy: his morale, his fuel supply, his reserve of men and aircraft, all suffer a certain degree of attrition with every attack. We hope for, but should not count on, every mission being a 100% success.

Finally, it should be noted that winds near the target at 25,000 feet were forecast to be 45 mph at 270 degrees with a temperature –25 degrees celsius.

Chapter 12

Schweinfurt Regensburg Raids

What a grand plan: Send two armadas of the highly touted B-17s to targets deep into Germany. Attack the coastal area with a diversionary raid of B-24s. P-47 escorts would get the raiders inside the German frontier with Belgium and Holland and past a good number of German fighters. Then upon reaching Frankfurt, the two Wings would split apart with LeMay's Wing turning southeast towards Regensburg and Williams continuing to the east and Schweinfurt.

With all their historical data the planners at High Wycombe still considered the one hundred and fifty mile per hour B-17 and her eleven 50-caliber machine guns equal to the German fighters in combat. Actually the Fortress was considered superior when the box formation was adhered to. These formations would bring a lot of firepower on an attacker. Perhaps up to thirty or more 50-caliber machine guns. This firepower was offset by one simple tactic. Attack the four engine bombers head-on. The only gunners that could get a few good shots off would be the top-turret. If the frontal attack was low then the ball-turret might get in a good strike.

The 8th Air Corp was well aware that the speed of the German fighters made them a very difficult target for the B-17 gunners. Also once the fighters 20 mm cannons were in range, strikes from the exploding shells would wreak havoc on the engines and all of the Fortresses' systems. The carnage wreaked on the crew of a B-17 could be mortal to all.

As to the weather, it would have behooved all the crews participating in the raids of 17 August 1943 if Eaker and LeMay had studied the reports of the raid of 25 June 1943. The weather was devastating concerning the assembly of the Groups. Finding the targets. Attacking the innocent towns and villages of Holland as targets of opportunity.

The 8th leadership studied the proposed tactic of Brigadier General Nathan Bedford Forrest III. Instead of using the box formations, Forrest led his Armada of B-17s with Squadrons in a wing to wing raid on the Kiel shipyards. This disastrous mission occurred on 13 June 1943. It was obvious that Forrest wished for an overwhelming lightning attack on the enemy as did his Confederate Grandfather with his Calvary. However the young Forrest was flying 150 mile per hour Boeings and not the high-speed ground attack P-47s. LeMay and the top brass reinstated the box formation after Forrest's disastrous raid.

The Schweinfurt raid was originally scheduled for 10 August 1943. Prior to liftoff the raid was cancelled because of weather. The scuttlebutt among the flyers was the Germans with their network of British spies were well aware of the planned missions. Perhaps the British with their secret code machines became aware of the Reich's plans to waylay the raiders.

With the fickle weather and the generally poor allied weather forecast on the Germans side, even the best-laid plans often go awry. Instead of two Armadas of B-17s splitting the German fighter defenses, the 8th Air Corp was unable to get the Schweinfurt raiders in the air per their schedule. The Schweinfurt Wing finally departed the coast of England around 1315, a good six hours behind the Regensburg raiders. Even the force of over one thousand British fighters that was designed to give the bombers a safe sendoff were out of sync and wound up being of little help. However, P-47s from the 56 Fighter Group shot down a number of German fighters while losing three of their Jugs.

A few spitfires manage to escort the B-17s to the coast and wag their wings in a salute or farewell, leaving all the lumbering Fortresses on Hitler's doorstep. Now, with the German fighters ready again after their pursuit of LeMay's Regensburg raiders, the Fortresses would learn the meaning of running the gauntlet. The attacks began near Antwerp and did not let up until Schweinfurt. Even the return trip was no milk run as again the Luftwaffe re-armed and re-fueled their fighters.

There were numerous fighters that had recently arrived from the Eastern front to assist in defending their homeland from the American bombers. Of these, were scores of aces strengthening the Luftwaffe Gruppes. They had heard plenty of stories about the B-17s and like all bold fighter pilots they wanted a Fortress in their victory column.

The Regensburg raiders led by Colonel Curtis LeMay took off at 0645 on 17 August 1943. The target was the Messerschmitt plants in the Regensburg area of Southern Germany. Following the raid the 3rd Bomb Division was to fly on to bases in North Africa.

The Germans that were assigned to monitor the Army Air Corps radio communications notified the Luftwaffe at 0730 that numerous signals were being intercepted. The Germans determined that a large contingent of airplanes was assembling in the vicinity of Great Yarmouth. Quickly the German fighter Gruppes were notified that a raid was pending.

A German's Victory over A Regensburg B-17
LeMay's raiders were initially intercepted near Antwerp, Belgium. The Luftwaffe fighter Gruppe JG 26 made first contact and witnessed the bombers' escorts turn back near the Belgian border.

Gruppe III/JG1 from Leeuwarden based fighters caught up with LeMay's Wing in the Aachen area and vicious combat with the Regensburg raiders ensued. Robert Olejink the Gruppe commander selected a 95th Bomb Group raider bringing up the rear of the 366th Squadron. The B-17 42-30283 *Mason's Morons* was on her 19th mission and the crew was well aware that two Messerschmitt Bf 109s were stalking their ship. The tail gunner Robert Bickford, the engineer Richard Carter, and the ball turret gunner Herschel Beane were issuing warnings over the intercom. The American bombers were approaching Saarbrucken and moving to the southeast.

With his cannons armed, the lead fighter sweeps in from the 7 o'clock low position. Approaching within three hundred yards of the target, the pilot throttles back to keep from overrunning his quarry. The tail gunner notices the telltale sign as a slight amount of black smoke whiffs from the slowing fighter. Bickford is quick to engage the decelerating 109. With little apparent damage to either plane, a second pass is attempted. Both the fighter pilot and the tail gunner are confounded as the fighter appears undamaged and the bomber is still holding her position. Now, the 109 pilot is beginning to have concern for his own health as the B-17 gunners continue to blaze away.

After the fighter's third pass, the Fortress with one engine pouring black smoke begins to lose her formation. Fortunately, the growing distance from the other bombers is encouraging to the fighter pilot. Suddenly, the bomber salvos her bombs, in her struggle to either regain her position in the Squadron formation or give the crew an easy exit.

With the Fortress gradually becoming engulfed in flames the German is further emboldened and makes his final attack. Now the B-17 has lost her battle. As the pilot empties his cannons, he witnesses the tail hatch fly off and sail underneath his fighter. The burning wings break off one by one as they follow the falling fuselage and a shower of burning debris crashing in woods near Darmstadt.

After prison camp, Mason reported that the number two engine was shot out of commission and was feathered. Fortunately, the entire crew survived and spent the rest of the war in a POW camp.

Dear Mom 42-30389 QE*Z 94th Bomb Group,
331st Bomb Squadron MIA Schweinfurt/Regensburg

Photo Courtesy Olaf Timmermann

Above photo are the remains of *Dear Mom* after a vicious attack by German Fw 190s on her way to Regensburg. The right side of the nose and cockpit of 42-30389 was raked with 20 mm cannon fire killing all the officers and the top turret gunner. The ball turret gunner was the only Sergeant in the back of the ship that failed to exit before she exploded.

Peg of My Heart 42-30315 Damaged by flak and fighters after her raid on Regensburg 17 August 1943. She was forced down near Berne, Switzerland. Notice salvage work is underway.

42-30315 B-17F-95-BO CC*S *Peg of My Heart* 390th Bomb Group, 569th Bomb Squad MIA 17Aug 43

Photo Courtesy Olaf Timmermann

El Rauncho's **Raid on Schweinfurt**

The Schweinfurt raid was originally scheduled for 10 August 1943. All the 384th selected ships bombed and fueled up. The tower fired a red flare indicating the raid was cancelled. The executive officer was notified that the Germans had all their fighters in the vicinity of the route fueled and armed. Somehow the enemy was well aware that their ball bearing plant was targeted for attack.

When the raiders took off on the 17th of August 1943, the Germans again had the details of the Schweinfurt raid. With escorts turning back after entering Dutch airspace, the individual B-17s in the participating Groups could only hope that they would be lucky on their four hour run to the target.

The *El Rauncho* 42-29728 was an early B-17F, which meant she was manufactured prior to the installation of the extra fuel tanks. These tanks were installed in the outboard section of the wings and added 1080 gallons of extra fuel. Similar to other tanks, they were self-sealing and were called "Tokyo tanks". The older B-17s, making the Schweinfurt raid, which included *El Rauncho*, were temporarily fitted with a 410-gallon tank. These were placed on one side of the bomb bay. These temporary tanks reduced the number of bombs that could be carried but not the weight. In the case of *El Rauncho*, she was bombed up with five one thousand pounders.

After lift-off, the eighteen B-17s of the 384th followed along behind their leader Major Thomas Beckett who was riding in the B-17 42-3429 *Flak House* with her pilot Johnny Butler. The 544th Squadron formed up in the low formation as their Group headed for the English Channel. Crossing the channel the low formation ran into lowering weather and began losing altitude to stay under the overcast and out of the way of the other formations.

Unknown to the B-17 crews, the Germans had an excellent radar system and they were watching and waiting for the Fortresses. The ground controllers were directing the fighters with their young aggressive pilots toward the unsuspecting B-17s.

After crossing into France, it happened: the dreaded yellow-nosed Focke Wulfs of the Abbeville boys following their ground controller's directions found the 544th Squadron of the 384th Bomb Group, flying beneath the overcast. This was the beginning of a Luftwaffe fighter attack that was to continue to Schweinfurt. The bombers that received the brunt of the attack were those leading the mission and in the low formations.

All along the route the Fortresses were under attack by various Luftwaffe Gruppes. The *El Rauncho* received her Abbeville welcome as her left wing was raked by a head-on attack by a Fw 190's 20 mm cannon fire. The top turret was partially disabled after a strike by a bullet from the Focke Wulf's cannon. With his damaged turret the engineer could only defend against attacks from 11 o'clock and 1 o'clock

The gunners on El Rauncho had figured rightly that this might be a tough raid as the armorers had stacked boxes of extra ammo in the radio room and had even notified the gunners prior to start-up, more was available if they wanted it. Fortunately, prior to reaching ten thousand feet, most of the boys had moved a couple of cases back to their stations.

On the trip to Schweinfurt the radio operator was directed to deliver ammo to the gunners in back.

The roughest part of the raid for the *El Rauncho* crew was the running fight to the target. There were fighters in sight all the way to Schweinfurt. Somewhere along the route, four 109s took on the tail gunner raking the tail several times, but missing Compton, the tail gunner. The attacking fighters damaged the rudder and elevator surfaces. *El Rauncho* and crew pushed on as another attack began from 1 o'clock low. This particular German fighter holed the bottom of the old Fortresses along with her main tires. The fighter also knocked the left landing gear out of commission. Before the target, the ball turret's oxygen system was damaged by flak.

As *El Rauncho* and the 384th approached the I.P. point, a wounded B-17 dropped down from a higher Group. The unfortunate Fortress *Peter Wabbit* 42-29830 hailed from the 379th Bomb Group. Approaching the flak fields she was swarmed by unrelenting German fighters. This Fortress was in serious trouble and was slightly ahead and approximately two hundred yards to the left of El Rauncho. Fire could be seen blazing from her open bomb bay doors and smoke pouring out from the radio room's roof-port. The crew of *El Rauncho*, were stunned as they watched the adjacent B-17 from the 379th Bomb Group fighting for all her worth against insane German fighters. The witnesses began describing the inferno on their intercom with the engineer shouting, "Why don't those guys get out"? Instead they watched as every gunner on the burning ship continued returning fire to the enemy fighters. There was not a single parachute seen to billow out from the fighting B-17 before she exploded with her full bomb load.

Only small fragments could be seen falling from the black cloud of smoke. The left waist gunner could feel a slight concussion from the explosion as *Peter Wabbit* (B-17F-70-BO 42-29830 FR*X 379th Bomb Group 525 Bomb Squad) and her crew disappeared into eternity. Later in a discussion with other 384th crews, there was a consensus that the crew on the burning Fortress was not only determined to run the Schweinfurt gauntlet but continuing her fight would allow other Forts to make it to the target.

Once the 384th Group dropped their bomb loads and turned-toward home, they could see the on-coming bomber streams fighting their way to the target. The enemy fighter pilot's attention was primarily on the B-17s driving toward Schweinfurt. This was some relief for the crew of *El Rauncho* until they felt their ship stumble from a flak strike. The pilot notified the engineer that the strike had damaged the aileron controls. The pilots must now coax their B-17 home. With both the rudder and the ailerons at less than one hundred percent, getting everyone home safely is left to the boys in the cockpit. The gunners will do their job as evidenced by their fight to the target.

El Rauncho made it back from the Schweinfurt raid but just barely with over 350 holes in her. The tower was aware that the battered Fortresses controls were shot-up. Just as the ships were entering the pattern, *El Rauncho* ran out of fuel. Jacobs called and notified the base of his ship's dire situation and was directed to make a one shot attempt at a straight-in landing. This put *El Rauncho* in front of the B-17s that had already notified the tower with their flares, that there were wounded on board. Fortunately the old "F" model came down with her right wing brushing a revetment protecting an older B-17E, and then crash-landing on the north-south runway. The Jacobs crew made a record exit, getting well away from the old Fortress when she came to rest. However, her Captain, Randolph "Moose" Jacobs, came strolling out of his Fortress nonchalantly with a cigar in hand asking for a light from a ground crewman as his lighter was out of fluid.
Another miracle: B-17F 42-29728 brought her entire crew back from Schweinfurt with no injuries. Her next stop was the salvage yard. .

Photo courtesy of Jack Goetz
42-29728 B-17F-65-BO SU*J *El Rauncho* 384th Bomb Group 544th Bomb Squad
Notice the cartoon character "Wimpy" below and in front of pilot's side-window

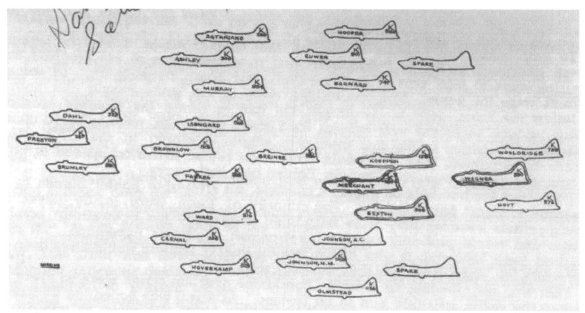

379th Box formation side view for Schweinfurt raid. With partial 379th pilot Sam Satariano signature
Notice the Wagner ship, *Peter Wabbit* 42-29830 is in the center of the 3 tail end Fortresses.
El Rauncho's and *Peter Wabbits* last crew list can be found on page xxii of the Appendices
Peter Wabbit was claimed by Heinrich Rudolph of JG 11/1

The *Tondelayo* 42-29896 was from the 527th Bomb Squadron of the 379th Bomb Group. She was assigned to participate in the Schweinfurt raid and like the other hundreds of shot up B-17s brought her crew safely home.

The armorers placed extra ammunition at each gun station. Prior to takeoff, a wagon loaded with cases of .50-caliber stopped at each B-17. One of the armorers inquired to the gunners if they wanted any extra ammo. The normal answer was "bring it on" and additional cases were then stacked in the radio room. The pilots were generally concerned with the extra weight especially when it was relocated to the tail and waist upsetting their weight and balance. The returning officers in the nose of the *Tondelayo* stated that the empty shell casings were above their ankles.

The 379th was in the high Group whereas the 384th was in the low Group. Upon reaching the coast, the Armada of B-17s encountered lowering weather. Following the Wing leader it was determined to stay under the heavy lowering overcast.

This move was beneficial to the Germans piloting Messerschmitt Bf 109s as these fighters found it difficult to operate at high altitude. Also the higher the Bf 109s were required to fly in their pursuits, the more gasoline their fuel injected engines required.

Once the 379th crossed the Dutch islands, the Group witnessed Spitfires escorting the Wing. Unfortunately, this service was short lived as the British fighters began wagging their wings. This salutation was either a good luck salute or perhaps a final goodbye to so many of the crews.

Reaching Antwerp the Schweinfurt raiders met their adversaries. Two Gruppes of Bf 109s, that had been battling the LeMay B-17s on their journey to Regensburg, had been refueled and rearmed. The greetings were not cordial as the young Germans attacked the bombers head-on. With their 20 mm cannons blazing, the fighters streaked through the formation with the intent of disabling a Fortress and scattering the big Boeings.

The German bandits stayed after the B-17s all the way to Schweinfurt. The route from Holland to the ball bearing plants was littered with the remains of burning B-17s. The only relief was entering the flak fields nearing and departing the target when the fighters turned away from the area of exploding shrapnel.

Unfortunately, once the surviving B-17s unloaded their bombs and turned for home, the fighters returned with vengeance. The German pilots had been gathering from their bases in France, Holland and Germany refueled and rearmed. The battles, with the returning big bombers was documented by the Allies listening to the aggressive German pilots radio chatter, along with the debriefing of the returning crews. Working together the Germans fought the retreating Fortresses all the way to the channel.

The returning bombers added more burning B-17s to the route along with unfortunate flyers. Including the Regensburg raiders, the remains of sixty B-17s littered the German countryside plus the remains of over one hundred flyers. There were forty-three wounded and five dead flyers removed from the returning Schweinfurt B-17s. In excess of one hundred Fortresses came home with moderate to heavy damage.

A 384th B-17F in 1943 with her ground crew making repairs for another raid.

Photo courtesy of Jack Goetz from his 1943 copy of "Plane News".

Crew list of the noted and pictured B-17s that participated in the Schweinfurt Regensburg raids can be found on pages xxii and xxiii of the appendices.

Chapter 13

Three Notable 379th Raiders

The Need for a Cigarette and a Nervous Navigator

After a 379th bomb Group crew attended their briefing concerning a raid on Berlin, the gunners assembled with the new navigator who explained that they could expect fighter escorts all the way to the target and back. The new navigator was a recently married man and to say he was nervous was an understatement. He gave a number of personal reasons the gunners should perform at 100 percent for him and his new bride. Although the men in back were somewhat surprised about the navigator's personal survivalist attitude, they kept it to themselves until some sixty years later at one of their Group reunions.

This was one of those one thousand plus plane raids, where the enemy is not only flak and fighters, but over nine thousand fellow B-17 gunners and their lethal 50 caliber machine guns. After the 379th had climbed to altitude and joined up with their Wing, the nervous navigator's pilot needed a smoke. So moving his oxygen mask aside, he lit up one of his Chesterfields. After taking one too many drags from his cigarette while being off of oxygen, he passes out. Falling across the wheel, the Fortress goes into a dive. While the engineer and copilot are struggling to get the unconscious pilot off the wheel, the rest of the crew, along with the nervous navigator are in a panic knowing that mother earth is heading their way. Fortunately, the pilot is up-righted and the copilot regains control of the ship.

The story continues as the B-17 has now lost the formation. The nervous navigator loads the flare gun and fires a flare through the opening in the roof of the Fortress. With this action, a P-51 comes down to investigate the problem only to be met by fire from the nervous navigator's 50 caliber cheek gun. The bombardier then makes the nervous navigator understand his mistake. The P-51 pilot cautiously brings his Mustang back up alongside the Fortress and gives the crew up front the middle finger salute. The fighter pilot then roars off climbing back up to rejoin the formation. Leaving the B-17 to fend for herself on her way back to Kimbolton.

A Scary Escape from a Determined 109

Sam Satariano's crew was returning to Kimbolton following a raid on an airdrome near Paris. With the propeller shaft broken on one engine, they began to fall out of their defensive formation. Once alone, the Satariano ship was attacked by an aggressive Messerschmitt. Sam piloted the B-17 with only one thing in mind: "getting away from that crazy German". Sam continued his story with an occasional comment from his top turret gunner, Louis Kline. "As we tried to shake the fighters loose, we went into a dive and darn near crashed in some woods. My engineer or the trees probably took out the 109, and the fear from the dive and the fighter caused our Navigator to bail out". Kline cut into the story and stated: that "he could not drive the fighter away and they were brushing the tree tops in some French woods. He yelled out; "that son of a bitch is trying to kill us." "Then suddenly the enemy fighter disappeared and I guarantee you he is still in those woods." Then Sam continued, "When we leveled out we were alone, so we asked the bombardier for a heading back towards base. His instructions were to take a course of 270 degrees. Pretty soon everyone realized that 270 degrees was gonna put us somewhere out in the Atlantic Ocean and we sure didn't have enough fuel to get to New York.

"When we finally got back to Kimbolton and got out of the plane, we walked to the front of our ship and were all shaking like leaves". Sam didn't smoke, yet he asked for a cigarette; half the crew stepped forward and offered brands from Lucky Strike to king-sized Pall Mall's. As Sam tried to steady his nerves to light up, he leaned against one of the propellers. Not realizing that the shaft had been broken, the prop spun dumping Sam on the tarmac. This was what the shaking crew needed as they all exploded in laughter."

The navigator evaded capture and was nearing freedom while crossing the Pyrenees Mountains. Unfortunately, he could not keep up with the guides, so they left him behind and he froze to death. With only two more days of hiking, he would have been in the warm sunshine, freedom and Spain.

The above story was described during an interview with Sam Satariano and Louis Kline at the 379th reunion in St. Louis.

On another raid while Satariano was acting as the Squadron leader, he noticed fighters to his right forming up so he moved his box to the left of another Squadron. This cost him the ire of the Group commander, in which Satariano received numerous expletives amid a colorful cussing. The proud and confident pilot reminded himself that he brought his entire Squadron home unscathed, which was more than the Group commander could say.

One can find records where a number of pilots appreciated the box formations until their ship was struck by anti-aircraft flak and could not keep up with the Group, then it was hang on for the crew. Gunners were sometimes thrown about so violently that they were injured, but these Mavericks were not about to be an easy target for any Luftwaffe fighter.

Satariano was one of the original 379th crews that completed twenty five missions. This was probably due in a large part in his desire to keep his crew alive at all cost.

Notable crewmen assigned to the *Tondelayo's*
The *Tondelayo* was in the same 379th Bomb Group and the 527th Bomb Squadron as the Brinkman ship. Her copilot, Bohn Fawkes, eventually was assigned as her captain after a number of issues with her original pilot, Johnny Simones.

Simones' problems began, per the navigator, when the *Tondelayo* was under head-on fighter attacks, while approaching the Wilhelmshaven target. One 20 mm live shell tore into the left hand seat cushion and lodged in the pilot's parachute. A second shell penetrated one of the pilot's rudder pedals and took the heel off his boot. It is understandable that trying to get your plane home, while sitting on a parachute with an unexploded shell, might prove just too stressful with all the thoughts of what damage an explosion might wreck on a man's personal anatomy. Thus, it would also seem reasonable that the next few missions were aborted for various simple reasons considering Lt. Simones' mental stress.

Whatever his supposed problems, Simones was KIA on the 25 June 43 Hamburg mission as pilot of 42-3023, *Boozeness*. The Simones Fortress was reported to have bombed her target and was shot down by fighters near Rhede, Germany. *Boozeness* apparently was on the same general route home as *Miss Deal* and the John Way crew. The Simones crew was lost at 0902 with the loss of five lives and the capture of five of her crew.

There was always grumbling by the crewmembers if their ship aborted and lost a mission credit, thus delaying their return home. It appears that the aborts may have been in the crew's best interest for aborting raids in June and July of 1943. Then after the Schweinfurt raid, there was much complaining about the losses of all the 8th Air Corps crewmen by the American public. This resulted in a number of so called "milk run" raids being set up. These raids resulted in fewer crew losses and improved the odds of completing the required 25 missions. However, from June 1943 until the end of the year, very few of the missions were "milk runs", as the chance of survival for flyers was still very slim. With the introduction of the P-51 and long-range fighter escorts, the survival rates for crews improved dramatically.

Elvin Doll was the *Tondelayo's* ball turret gunner. After completing four missions, he confided in Arooth that he could not take the combat in that damn ball anymore and he was going to hang it up. Mike was concerned for his friend since he had already heard stories that if one wanted out, it was a ticket to the infantry. Arooth went with Doll and stood with him in front of the C.O. The discussion was about the stress that Doll faced and he wanted out. The C.O. tried to talk Doll into staying with the *Tondelayo* crew, but Doll was adamant.

Finally, it was agreed that Doll would spend the rest of the war with the 379th ground crew as a PFC. Unfortunately, Doll had horrible memories for the rest of his life for witnessing the results of all the carnage when shot up Fortresses returned with wounded on board. He had the task of cleaning up damaged B-17s as soon as the wounded and dead were removed.

His stepdaughter relayed that he was in his sixties before he would fly again. Doll loved to go to Vegas and gamble and when the driving became too much for him, he finally began flying again. This old Missouri flyboy was a gambler from the start, and he quickly realized that riding in the ball of a B-17 was not something on which to gamble his life.

Michael Arooth, on the other hand, seemed to have been comfortable behind those twin fifties in the tail of *Tondelayo*. It was believed that he must have actually enjoyed taking on the enemy fighters.

Arooth once stated that the worst spot on a B-17 is in the ball and the other lonely position was in the tail. "It is a good spot for praying as you are on your knees all the time".

Arooth was credited for shooting down nine enemy fighters and is fifth on the list of B-17 gunner aces. He, like all tail gunners, probably saw more action than any other gun station. He seemed to enjoy his job, like his training friend Frank Murphy from the Brinkman ship. Murphy wrote in a letter to his mother after the St. Nazaire raid, "they shot at us and we shot back; what fun". The excitement of aerial combat enjoyed by these two gunners is a reminder of a quote from Winston Churchill in an earlier war. "Nothing in life is so exhilarating as to be shot at without result".

Arooth was overheard talking about the German fighter pilots once, when he stated: "the f---ing Germans must think all tail gunners are stupid as they just keep coming in for more, again and again"(this boast by the tail gunner was probably overheard after he had consumed a couple of pints).

Another saving grace for the *Tondelayo*, besides her gunner's, was her pilot Bohn Fawkes. If attacked by fighters, Fawkes had no problems with putting his plane through her aerobatic paces. He had not only brought his gunners back shot up, but also bruised and skint up from dodging the fighters.

Tondelayo's raid on Kassel

Bohn Fawkes piloting the *Tondelayo's* on her return from a mission to Kassel. After bombs away, the *Tondelayo* headed back west for home. Leaving the flak fields, the 379th crews witnessed a gathering storm of vengeful German fighters.

A half hour after leaving the target, two Focke Wulfs made a 6 o'clock pass on *Tondelayo's* tail. The exploding shells struck the Fortress sending shrapnel into the tail-gunners leg and hand. Further strikes severed the oxygen line and the intercom cable. With continuous strikes from the unrelenting Germans, Fawkes puts his Fortress through all kind of gyrations in his attempt to evade the attacking Germans. The *Tondelayo* pilot was not going to allow the enemy fighters an easy target. Unfortunately, the 20 mm strike that severed the oxygen line in the back of the ship left the flyers with cerebral hypoxia. Both waist gunners became disoriented and felt impending doom. Assuming *Tondelayo* was going down, the two gunners put on their chutes, released the waist hatch and jumped. The ball turret gunner, John Leary went to sleep, while the radio operator made it to the hatch but was unable to jump. Luckily, the wounded tail gunner was unable to get off the floor and make it to the tail hatch.

Fawkes took his plane and crew down near the deck over Holland, while the remaining boys in the back recovered from their lack of oxygen. Approaching Kimbolton, one of the boys up front would have placed the end of the flare gun in the roof opening and fired. This was the notice to the tower and to the returning B-17s that there was wounded on board. All the Fortresses would have given way to *Tondelayo* to go straight in. Also, emergency personnel, including the surgeon were waiting. And wouldn't you know it, after they got Mike on a stretcher and began attending to his wounds, up steps his old friend Elvin Doll handing him a lit cigarette. Even though Doll was elated to find his buddy had made it back from Kassel, he was directed by the *Tondelayo's* crew chief to clean up Mike's gun station so his men could get the repairs started.

There was always plenty of luck needed in completing twenty-five missions, but in the case of the *Tondelayo*, perhaps there was more. Fawkes, unlike most pilots and their crews, was not known to express his frustrations by swearing. He was more of the gentleman that we would all have aspired to be. So perhaps there was some divine guidance that was shielding *Tondelayo* and her crew from mortal doom.

Following the Kassel raid, the crew chief noticed a number of bullet holes in Tondelayo's wings with evidence of fuel leaks. After the smallest ground crewman got inside the wing, he had to wiggle the punctured rubber bladders out from all the truss material and then put in new tanks. This was one of the most difficult repair jobs on a B-17. After the tanks were removed, the crew chief was stunned to find eleven 20 mm shells were still in the old tanks. These unexploded shells were turned over to the intelligence officer. Sometime later the crew chief was notified that there was a note in one of the 11 explosive 20 mm shells taken from the *Tondelayo's* fuel tanks. Prior to the *Tondelayo's* next mission, the crew chief confided in the pilot that eleven explosive shells had been removed and none of the shells were loaded. It was further revealed to Fawkes, that in one of the shells was removed a piece of paper written on in Czech, the simple statement: "this is all we can do for you now."

Returning from one raid, the *Tondelayo's* number 2 and 3 engines were set afire by flak and fighters. The terrifying sight of an inferno within six feet or so on either side of the nose by the bombardier and the navigator peering from their windows would be enough for any sane man to abandon ship. Then they were suddenly thrown on the floor, as their plane was forced earthward into a dive. Neither of these two officers nor their crew had any idea whether they were about to join so many other flyers in being swallowed up by Mother Earth. Soon they realized that their pilot was intent on extinguishing the engine fires of *Tondelayo* and give her a chance to again bring her boys home to Kimbolton - and she did.

Tondelayo's final raid

On the Stuttgart raid, a combination of events put the *Tondelayo* on a course that might prove fatal for her and her crew. They followed an old leader who didn't understand the need to conserve fuel for so distant a target, to the loss of an engine, another fire, and then the loss of the formation, the Fortress was forced to zig-zag around looking for clouds to hide in on her return to England. Unfortunately, she ran completely out of fuel over the channel where she was gently put down on a large swell. Even Mike Arooth recounted he could not believe that she was going down to a watery grave. But again, even without gas, her last effort was in giving her crew time to exit into their life rafts. All the *Tondelayo's* crew was rescued and returned to duty.

Photo by Charles Crawford late1942 or early 1943.
Michael Arooth reclining on his bunk in a Wendover barracks with tarpaper exterior.

Buddies at Gowen field, Idaho: Mike Arooth and Charlie Crawford
Above photos from Charles Crawford's memorabilia

Following the 30 July 1943 Kassel raid Arooth was credited with shooting down three enemy airplanes and was awarded the Distinguished Service Cross.

The B-17F 42-29896 *Tondelayo*
Michael Arooth front row 3rd from left Elvin Doll 4th from left.
Photograph courtesy of the Doll family

Chapter 14

The Story of Bill Harvey

I first saw Bill Harvey at an air-show in Gilmer, Texas. The show was honoring the 384th and I was encouraged by my daughter to attend and take some printed flyers with pictures of Uncle Charlie and information about his fatal mission. The flyer was titled "Do You Remember Me?" After getting permission to use the table at the entry, in comes a big entourage of very confident and loud senior citizens. Confronting the Group, they asked when he was lost, and one of the ladies replied, "that was too early in the war". Unfortunately for me, none in the Group was wearing readable badges.

I kept noticing this one individual who seemed to be the head dog of all the honorees. If there were any questions or issues, he was the man who seemed to have more than his share of confidence. Probably one of those bold cocky, WWII pilots who thought he was God's gift to the free world.---Thought I.

After a few hours of flybys, stunts, old antique planes and skydivers, I left and decided perhaps I'd made a mistake.

Finally, after talking with other 384th members, my daughter got a letter out to Bill Harvey with a picture of part of the *Miss Deal* crew riding in a jeep. Harvey couldn't identify any of the crew, not even himself, sitting shotgun. A while after the letter, Harvey telephoned and he told me he was the original co-pilot on the John Way crew. I asked him if he knew my uncle and the phone went silent while the memories came back to him. He said that if I got a chance to get down to Jacksonville to come by and visit.

Sure enough, a few weeks later we met at Bill and his wife Betty's home. Spending a couple of days in Jacksonville, we learned that Bill was actually a super individual and not at all according to my first impression. A while later, we met up again at the 384th reunion in San Diego.

There was never a dull moment with Bill and after the reunion we made it a point to get together at each reunion and whenever we crossed into each other's backyard. After all the years, Bill stands with John Way, Uncle Charlie and Jack Goetz among my heroes.

The Story of Bill Harvey:
I have never forgotten the green, "farty shades of green," the Irish would say. After months of training in the western deserts, I couldn't believe how beautiful Ireland looked and then England equally as beautiful.

We flew our own plane, a B-17 "Flying Fortress", over from the States, landing in Gander, Newfoundland to refuel and spend the night. We ended up staying there for almost a month because of engine problems and because we needed a thirty-mile tailwind to make the big hop non-stop to the United Kingdom. We finally got the tailwind and headed east.

Problems started developing about halfway over. Firstly, we lost our tailwind, although we really didn't know it. Secondly, when we started to look for the Irish coast, it wasn't where it was supposed to be. Thirdly, when we thought we could see it, it turned out to be just some clouds on the horizon. Those low clouds really had us more confused and so, naturally, having no tailwind, we weren't even close to the coast.

Suddenly our bombardier, Tom Corrigan, who was riding up in the nose, shouted that there was a ship crossing our flight path. We all saw it and at first thought it might be a small aircraft carrier, but as we got closer, we realized that it was a submarine. "Is it ours or theirs?" someone asked. We hadn't a clue. We decided to radio our position and at least alert the English, if the sub was German.

Then at last, we really did see the Irish coast and what a beautiful sight. Didn't take us long to cross over Ireland and shortly thereafter, we landed at Prestwick, Scotland. Upon landing, a British staff car raced alongside and followed us into the parking area. They asked for two officers to come with them to explain the sub. Upon reaching their headquarters, they showed us a chart and laughingly pointed out the position we gave them for the sub. The coordinates were in a lake in the middle of Ireland. The navigator was forgiven by the English telling him, anybody can make a mistake. Of course, the submarine was German. As they explained, what would an English or American sub be doing out in the Atlantic. They would have nothing to shoot at but Allied ships. Then it occurred to us the sub could have shot us out of the sky if they had wanted. You've got to be lucky.

The next day we left Prestwick and flew to Grafton Underwood, which was to become my home away from home for the next year and a half.

We arrived at Grafton on a beautiful Saturday morning in early June, 1943, two or three weeks after the rest of the crews. By this time they were old hands with a mission or two under their belts. The next day, Sunday, was another beautiful day so my navigator, Dick Sherrer and I decided to go to Kettering, the closest town of any size, then take the train to Leicester, a nearby city, and be tourists for a day. At the Kettering station, I read the schedule and there was a train returning at six that night, which was perfect, getting us back to the base before dark. After a look see at downtown Leicester, we stopped in a hotel and they were having a tea dance. This turned out to be our first chance to see English girls. They were pretty and friendly and we had a great time. Five-thirty came all too soon, and we had to leave for the station. I checked at the ticket window to see if the six o'clock train was on time and was advised that this being Sunday, there was no six o'clock train and the next one was at midnight. I never could read a train schedule! Oh, well, back to the dance. Took two of the pretty girls to dinner and the movies, arriving back at the station in time for the midnight train. Our only thought was we will never get a taxi so late at night, so we'll have to walk out to the base -- which we did. As we got near, we could hear the roar of many engines. Deciding there must be a mission, we walked down to the flight line to watch the planes take off. We had only been there a couple of minutes when our Squadron Operation Officer, a fellow later known as

"Combat Brown," saw us and said, "Where the hell have you fellows been? We've been looking all over for you. Your plane and crew are on this mission and we've had to find a replacement co-pilot and navigator to go in your place." We couldn't believe it! We had only arrived yesterday. We hadn't even had an orientation flight. How could they send our crew? We weren't ready. Not even one practice mission. This is crazy.

Crazy or not, there was our plane just taking off and we were sick. "Combat" told us to go to our quarters until the Squadron Commander could see us. It wasn't long before we were standing at attention in his office. We felt terrible. We knew we hadn't done anything wrong, but he told us that the Group C.O. was really upset. After hearing our explanation, he said, "I'll do my best to save your asses". We were sent back to our quarters and told to stay there until the Colonel could see us.

Hours later, the mission was due to return and we said, "To hell with it, let's go down to the flight line and watch the planes land". One after another, the Forts came in and landed. Two didn't make it – one of them was ours. God, then we really felt terrible, thinking if we had been along, maybe we could have done something to bring the plane back. Just then, the Colonel spotted us and called us over. He said "I was all for court marshalling you two, but I can't because you really haven't broken any rules and I know how bad you feel. Anyhow your Squadron C.O. was the one who really saved your ass because I wanted to make an example out of you". What a way to start a tour of duty! As badly as we felt, we knew we were damned lucky to be alive, but I'll let someone else read the train schedules from now on.

One month from the day that our Squadron had flown its first mission, there were only three of us left out of the original ninety-three flying personnel; the Squadron Commander, the Squadron Operations Officer and myself. Of course, I was there because I had yet to fly a mission. Three out of ninety-three, my God! However, a few days later, Tom Estes's crew came back to the base. They had been all shot up over the Continent and on the way back, had to ditch in the English Channel. They were rescued by a Danish fishing vessel and then transferred to a British Air-Sea Rescue ship. So, now it wasn't so bad, our Squadron was back up to thirteen out of the original ninety-three; but it was a forbidding thought. At least replacement crews were starting to arrive and hopefully, I would get my first mission.

The next three months were the most frustrating of my life. Whenever a co-pilot was needed for a crew, I was picked. Seven times I started a mission and seven times we aborted and returned to base. One time, we got as far as the French coast, but when you turned around and came home, you didn't get credit for a mission. There were, of course, many reasons for these abortions …engine problems, control problems, weather, but the really bad one was the mental problems. Some pilots just lost their nerve when they got close to enemy territory and they would use any pretense to turn back. This was rare but it happened. That was my luck on my 5th, 6th, and 7th aborted missions. My pilot must have had a premonition that he was going to be shot down. So, he would drop out of the formation and turn back for the least little reason. After his second abort, I went to the Squadron Commander and asked to be taken off the crew. I didn't want to fly with this pilot again. After hearing my story, the C.O., Major Al Nuttall, said "Harvey, fly with him one more time. If he aborts again, I'll relieve him". I reluctantly agreed and a couple of days later, we were off on another mission. We hadn't even reached altitude when the pilot said, "look at the RPM indicator, it's jiggling all over the place". It looked okay to me, but he said, "We are going back to base". I pleaded with him to let me take the controls, but all he would do was shake his head. That was the last time I spoke to him. After landing and taxiing up to our hard stand, I got out of the plane and reported to Major Nuttall. The pilot was removed from command and a few days later was flying co-pilot for another crew. His premonition was right. He never came back. In the meantime, I made a vow that if I ever made a first pilot, I would never abort. More about that commitment later.

Finally, I made my first mission. It was to Stuttgart in southern Germany. I'll never forget it for two reasons. It was my first mission and we made two runs over the target. The lead bombardier didn't drop his bombs on the first run. Why, I never knew, but that day the Wing was being led by General Bob Travis and it was his first mission leading the Wing and he wasn't going to screw up and not bomb the target. So around we went in a 360 degree turn and made the bomb run for the second time. Needless to say, our Group was really shot up, but we bombed the target. Flew six more missions, as a co-pilot, then one day Nuttall called me in and said, "Harvey, you've had enough experience now, so I'm going to make you a first pilot, but I'm not giving you a crew. We need some experienced instructor pilots to fly with the new crews. Anywhere up to five missions. If you think the pilot and crew are ready before that – that's okay, too. Teach them well". Then he added, "As you know, most of our losses are on the first five missions. We should cut those losses with an experienced pilot aboard". I was so happy to be a first pilot that I didn't even think about having to fly with inexperienced crews all the time. I thought about it many times later, however.

We flew very little the next few months. The weather over the continent was miserable. We had to recover from some very serious losses. The two Schweinfurt missions, especially, were catastrophic. But to show you how lucky I was, on each of those two missions, I was on leave in London.

What a great city. About every ten days or so we got a 48-hour leave and usually it was to London we would go. And we had fun. I've mentioned the pretty and willing English girls. The saying then was "The British Eighth Army was in North Africa and the U.S. Eighth Air Force was in Britain," lucky for us.

The big problem in London was getting a hotel room. Once again I was fortunate. I had met a lovely English family who lived very near our base at Grafton. The family consisted of five people, Geoff and Mary Saunders and daughter, Lorna, along with Mary's father and his French wife who were living with the Saunders for the duration.

Mary's father, everybody called him Pop, had been a banker in Paris and he and his new French bride, Catherine had barely gotten out of France ahead of the Germans. These five people were just wonderful to the Americans who visited their home. We would go over and play tennis on their court. Then after an ice cold glass of milk and a hot bath, the cold martinis would be ready, followed by dinner. No matter how small the meat ration was, they would spread it out so that we all got a nice share. We could never pay them back for their warm hospitality, but we tried to reciprocate by bringing canned goods, cigarettes, liquor, or whatever else we could beg, borrow or steal.

One time over martinis, I was telling Geoff about how hard it was to get a hotel room in London. He said "Bill, my company keeps a suite of rooms for me at the Savoy Hotel. You can use it anytime you want". Believe me, you didn't see many lieutenants in the Savoy; but, one lieutenant certainly enjoyed the suite, the American Bar, and the Savoy Grill – with the world's best creamed spinach.

After my first or second London visit, I decided to have a pair of boots made. The boot-maker's shop, located in the Park Lane Hotel, was highly recommended, so I went in and ordered a pair of boots. While having my feet measured I asked the proprietor what kind of deposit he wanted. He said he didn't want a deposit but wanted to be paid in full. When I hesitated he said, "You come with me." He took me to a back room and pointed to 30 or 40 pairs of boots and said, "I only asked for a deposit on these boots and now they are mine forever. Those boys had been shot down and wouldn't be back to make the final payment". After paying him the full amount, I walked out a very sober fellow. London, even during war time, was exciting – good theatre and very inexpensive – plenty of private clubs which we all joined because they always had a good supply of liquor, and the wonderful tourist attractions that were a must see and, of course, the girls!

We couldn't get down there often enough, and a few weeks later I did get my boots. Now, fifty years later, I still have them. Was able to get on the right one the other day, but not the left one. I pulled so hard I actually tore the leather. After so long a time, the leather had finally rotted.

Of course, we only got to London on occasion, but we could always go into Kettering, only about five miles away. It had a couple of nice hotels, two theaters, and many pubs, and then again the girls! Dated one. Pretty as a picture with that lovely peaches and cream complexion so many of the English girls were blessed with. She later married a young lieutenant who eventually became the Commanding General of the Pennsylvania Air National Guard. Quite by chance, we met them a few years ago when we were up in Pennsylvania visiting our daughter and son-in-law, an Army Colonel who was stationed at the same base as the General. Small world! We see them now on occasion, both here and once in England, when we happened to be there for a Group reunion.

Slowly but surely I was getting my missions in, over France, Germany, Holland, even up to Norway. They were all tough, some tougher. Once, we came back with one hundred-forty holes in the plane. Once, made a dead stick landing. The fourth engine went out on final approach. Was later told that that was the first time in Eighth Air Force history that all four engines had to be changed while the plane itself was hardly damaged at all. You've got to be lucky.

In those days in England you had to fly 25 missions, which was your tour of duty, then you could go home. I had been looking at that magic number for months. I had been in the Group longer than any of the flying personnel, other than some Squadron and Group officers. The new replacement crews were coming and going so fast, I finally refused to eat in the combat crew mess and ate with the ground officers. I knew them; the new flying crews were strangers to me.

April 24th, was the day of my 25th mission. This was the sixth crew I had trained and my second time out with them. They were about ready to go on their own under their pilot, Bob Brown. The target for the day was an airfield and manufacturing plant in Oberpfaffenhofen, a suburb of Munich.

We were leading the low Squadron that day with Colonel Dale O. Smith leading the Group and the Wing, which consisted of three Groups. The high Squadron in our Group was to be led by Bud MacKichan. Bud was married to a girl from Saginaw, Michigan. Saginaw was the same town that my parents were living in. Bud's wife and my mother had, of course, become friends.

Take off was normal, but shortly after we began our climb to altitude, we lost a super-charger on one of the engines and as a result my low Squadron began to lag behind the Group. Colonel Smith radioed me to close it up, but I just couldn't do it while climbing. I thought to myself, once I'm at altitude we'll be alright and I can close up tight. During this period I began to think about aborting the mission. Something I had never done as a first pilot. I had had enough of those as copilot. Also, I had five planes flying formation on me and they were all inexperienced pilots with very few missions. I probably should have aborted, but I didn't. We finally got to bombing altitude, and little by little, we were closing in. I could see Paris far below and to the south of us. It was a perfect spring day, not an enemy fighter in sight, and our own escorts of Mustangs and Thunderbirds all around us.

Suddenly, the sky below was filled with little black puffs. Those innocent looking puffs were antiaircraft shells exploding just beneath our Group. A few seconds later, the Germans found our range and the puffs were all around us. Just then, our B-17 lurched and I knew we had been hit. I looked around and the back of the cockpit was on fire. This had happened to me on a previous mission and I had been able to get it out. So, I told Brown to take over and I would go back and try to put out the fire. No luck this time. So, I rang the alarm and told the crew to bail out, grabbed Brown by the arm and said, "Let's go". The bombardier and the navigator already had the forward escape hatch open and were waiting for my signal. A "thumbs down" sign did it and the four of us were out and away.

When we were lectured on how to parachute, three things were stressed. Number one, "free fall" as long as possible so the enemy fighters can't follow you down and shoot you. Number two, "free fall" so that the ground forces can't follow you down and be there to meet you as you land. Number three, save the ripcord ring as a souvenir. The first and second I did; the third I didn't. When the chute opened, and I thought it never would, it gave me a hell of a jerk. I realized I hadn't tightened my leg straps enough and they were really cutting into me. I would lift one leg at a time to release the pressure, which helped, but in the meantime, I was swinging back and forth and starting to get airsick. I couldn't see any other parachutes in the sky no matter where I looked. But I did think that Bud MacKichan must have seen what happened and would be able, through his wife, to tell my family that the plane didn't explode, that he had seen parachutes and that I would probably be okay. That report never got home however. Bud was killed a few minutes after I went down.

Then, on looking down, I could see a small village in a generally wooded countryside. On the edge of the village was a lone building with lots of people looking up at me. I thought, "Oh God, the Germans are just waiting for me". But as I got closer, I could see the building was a schoolhouse and the people were little kids waving and yelling and no Germans in sight. I landed about one hundred yards from the school in a freshly plowed field. Couldn't have picked a much better place to land. Tumbled over a couple of times and got to my feet hauling in the chute at the same time. Finally, got it altogether and started to run to some woods a couple of hundred yards away. Then I did one of the only really foolish things that I did in the four months I was in occupied France. I just wasn't thinking. After running about one hundred yards, I dropped the chute in the field and kept running. The chute was just too heavy and I kept getting tangled up in the shroud lines. If the Germans had found it, of course, they would have known right where to look for me.

Upon reaching the edge of the woods, I looked around and the schoolteacher had sent the kids out to get the chute and they were dragging it back to the schoolhouse. By the time the Germans got out there in their trucks and on their motorcycles, I was well-hidden in the woods and the parachute was well-hidden somewhere in the schoolhouse. Luck spelled with a capital L.

Over the years I've returned several times to visit the French people who helped me. When I would return to Faux Fresnay, which was the name of the little village where I landed, I would always ask about the schoolteacher. No one seemed to know what happened to her. Then one time on the thirtieth anniversary of my landing, I decided that this was probably my last visit, so my wife, Betty, and I decided to have a party at the hotel in Sezanne. We invited all the people in that area who had helped me. The local paper sent a photographer and a reporter and they did a nice story, including a picture. A few weeks later I received a letter from France. It was from the schoolteacher. She was still subscribing to the Sezanne paper after all these years. It was the first she had heard about my bombardier and me since the 24th of April 1944. Needless to say, I wrote a long letter back and although we never met, she at least had my sincere thanks.

About six that evening, after the Germans had given up the search, and after I had buried my flying clothes, and with great reluctance had included my roommate, Mike Mazer's leather flight jacket, which I had borrowed when I couldn't find my own. I crawled to the edge of the woods and soon saw a man who was obviously looking for me. Realizing that I had to have help and with the hope that he was not a collaborator, I stood up and waved my arm. He quickly saw me and walked over. I said, "American pilot", and he held out his hand and said, "Bon jour, American". After offering him a cigarette he signed language to me that I should wait for him at this spot and he pointed to my watch, letting me know he would return about eleven that night. After again shaking hands, he left. I soon learned that everybody was always shaking hands in France.

After a couple of hours, I decided that perhaps this man wasn't as he appeared, and I had better move away some distance so that I would at least have a chance to escape if he came back with the Germans.

It was just getting dark and now, for the first time, I began to feel fear. Every sound spooked me and every shadow looked like a German. "What the hell am I doing here?" I thought. Would I ever see home again? How sad it will be when my parents get the inevitable telegram. Well, at least, my brother is probably okay. Little did I know that he had already been wounded in Italy and was even now, a prisoner of war. My folks, I learned much later, had decided not to tell me that he had been reported missing in action.

After a few minutes of feeling sorry for myself, I thought about the matters at hand. We had been instructed, if we were shot down to head for Spain, and that the Spanish would see that we got back to England. The other alternative was to go to Switzerland, but the Swiss would not send you to England, being all but impossible from their land-locked country. There, you would be interred for the duration of the war. So, first things first. I would head for Spain. Of course, at that time, I didn't know that the English RAF were flying in at night and picking up evaders. I found out much more about that later.

After moving to a new spot, maybe a hundred or so yards away, for the first time I did some serious praying – for my mother, father, brother and myself. I wondered what Mike Mazer, my roommate, would think when he returned from the three-day armament school he was attending. I couldn't help but remember the day he had first shown me his new dog tags with his new name, Michael McMazer inscribed on them. With a name like Nathan Mazer, he wouldn't have a chance with the Germans if he were shot down. He said that he was damned if the Krauts were going to find out that he was a Heeb. After that, when we would be checking into a hotel in London, he would register in as Michael McMazer and then innocently ask the clerk for directions to the nearest Catholic church. What a guy! But he was still going to be pissed off about the flight jacket now buried about three feet under the ground. Many years later when back in the woods I tried to find the spot. I thought I could go right to it. I couldn't.

An hour later, I found myself studying the stars. My old Boy Scout training came in handy. Saw a few constellations I knew and then, of course, the North Star which I was to use many nights in the near future. First heading south toward Spain, later north back toward Paris, and lastly west toward the Allied lines after the June 6th landing.

Suddenly, and it was just about eleven, I heard a voice calling, "Big Dog," a name I had somehow acquired. It was Dick Rader, my bombardier, a tall lanky West Virginian from Huntington, along with the man I had met early in the day. His name Dick said, was

Charles Vallon and he had found Dick an hour or so earlier and told Dick that he had a comrade of his nearby. I'll say this, we were sure glad to see each other. Dick had seen some other chutes in the sky, but that was it. Charles took us to the small village of Faux Fresnay and on to his house. He had not sooner introduced us to his pregnant wife and pregnant daughter, when three or four men came in, and after shaking hands all around, we were soon communicating with a few words and much sign language. It's amazing how much information can be shared in that way. The men told us they would bring us clothes and that we must get rid of our own and especially our shoes, as they were dead giveaways. The problem was Dick, who is about 6'3" tall, while I am 5'9", more the average Frenchman's size. Anyhow, there was one tall guy in the village they soon brought him over and he said, "I'll give you my wedding clothes". Gaston and his wife, Bertie were wonderful people and we have seen them on all our visits back to Faux Frensay. The pants were a little short, but not bad. As soon as we changed and all our clothes were taken away, someone said, "how about an aperitif?" and out came the L'eau de Vie. The homemade white lighting, so common all over France.

We could barely get it down, but we had no choice. So, we drank it. Sometime later, we found another and much better use for it. Eventually, we both caught the crabs then, we discovered a real use for this "water of life". We rubbed it on ourselves and it put the crabs to sleep for two or three days, and when they awakened, we would put some more back on. What a relief.

For the next eight days, we lived in the woods. We had bales of straw to sleep on, some blankets and we built a lean-to, and even put up a sign saying "Savoy Hotel". We built the lean-to on the edge of a cool stream where we kept our supply of wine, including champagne, cold and ready to drink. We had both red and white wine, apple cider and beer. How good could it get? The whole village was feeding us. One couple, the Morant Gobins, couldn't have been kinder to us. We saw them many times after the war, but now they have both passed away. So, we lived the best we ever did while in occupied territory. Of course, it was too good to last. On the fifth day, Charles Vallon brought a man who could speak English. He told us it was time to leave. Too many people knew we were hiding, but the worst thing he told us was that Charles Vallon was a collaborator who was working for the Germans. Really a terrible man, who was the father of both his wife's and his daughter's unborn child. Dick and I were shocked because Charles had been so good to us. He really had no choice, the whole village had seen us come down and, if the Germans found out, they would know it was Vallon who had told them. So, we were temporarily safe. Our English speaking friend told us that there would be a man, a butcher from a nearby town, who would pick us up in his delivery truck and take us to the farm of two brothers who were the leaders of the local Marquis.

The details of the pick-up hadn't been worked out yet, but we had to be ready to leave the following night. He also asked us if we had any money and we said yes. Our escape kit included a silk map, a compass and saw, some high energy chocolate, water purifying pills and French Francs. We were advised to give at least some of our money to Vallon; because, if he had turned us in, the Germans would have paid him, so our cash might make up for his loss.

116

I must admit that when Charles Vallon came to get us the next night I had tears in my eyes. He had been good to us. When we reached the road, we saw the truck and standing by the truck was the butcher. We were introduced to Lucien Bonnet and it was time to say goodbye to Charles. After thanking him, I offered him the money and he took it. The butcher, Mr. Bonnet, immediately grabbed it back and said, "We are doing this for France, not for money". Unfortunately, this statement was his death sentence, because about a week later, Vallon turned in the butcher to the Germans and Lucien Bonnet was tortured and executed.

We drove for what seemed like an hour and pulled into a farm. Here, we met two young men, Hubert and Gabriel Jeanson, two out of four brothers. We said our farewells to the butcher, never to see him again.

The following week was exciting. The local Maquis members met at the Jeanson's farm almost every other night to discuss their plans, which was basically to hinder the Germans any way they could. They were all so young, basically kids; but I guess, so were we. On the second night, a real surprise, who should walk in our room but a British Flight Lieutenant. Damn, it was good to converse in English again and be brought up to date on what was happening. The Englishman was quite a fellow. He had been educated in France and so spoke perfect French, no accent at all. He had been shot down and decided to stay in France to help the Marquis and any Allied flyers who were evading. He had many opportunities to return to England, but felt he was more valuable here, and British Intelligence apparently thought so, too. His name was Leon. We never did know his last name.

The next night, another pleasant surprise awaited us. Leon told us an American who lived in Romilly sur Seine would be over to visit us. He had come to France during the First World War, met a French girl, married her and decided to stay in France. When he arrived, he had a stunning young French girl with him, decidedly not the one he married in 1918. He was quite a character and hadn't spoken English in so long he had a definite French accent. He invited Leon, Dick and me to come to Romilly the next night and have dinner with him. He came out to the farm and picked us up in his car. Dick and I were scared to death, but Joe, the American, as he was called, told us not to worry, and then Leon reassured us. It still seemed damn dangerous to me. We had a great meal preceded by champagne, then white and red wine.

After dinner, I noticed the pretty French girl took a small box out of her purse and from it took a gold toothpick, which she delicately proceeded to use, hiding the operation behind her napkin. I had never seen that before and almost laughed in her face. As we left, Joe told us we were in good hands and that there was nothing more he could do for us. As we got in the car, he handed me a book. "It's the only one in English that I could find, but I think you will enjoy it". It was titled; "The Portrait of Dorian Grey", by Oscar Wilde, and we did enjoy it. I must have read it at least three times.

Thirteen years later, Betty and I had dinner with Joe the American, in the same house, but this time with another good-looking French woman. We never did learn what happened to the first girl or his original wife.

A couple of nights later, we were awakened by people speaking English. One was Leon, the other a complete stranger, who turned out to be a British Intelligence officer sent out to the farm to check out our stories. The Germans, of course, had dropped English-speaking agents into the French countryside trying to ferret out the Maquis.

The Englishman asked me to come with him to the next room. After a minute or two of pleasant conversation, he asked me my favorite sport. "Football", I said. "How many on a team?" he asked. "Eleven", I said. "How many players are allowed to handle the ball"? I told him, "The four backs, the two Ends, and the Center". That was all he asked. Dick went through the same routine. We said our goodbyes and the fellow departed. Leon told us that he had already vouched for us, but that British Intelligence wanted to check us out anyhow.

The next afternoon, Leon told us the British were going to drop some supplies that night and would we like to come and help. We immediately said "yes", but later couldn't help asking ourselves, "What the hell were we getting into?" Leon later said, when he made radio contact with the plane, he would tell the pilot about us so that the British could send in a pick-up plane and rescue us. That was the first time we had heard that the British did that sort of thing. Boy, we might be back in Britain in a few days! Unfortunately for us, it didn't work out that way, but for a while our morale was really sky high.

About eleven that night, we heard a noise out in the farmyard and Leon and the brothers said, "Let's go". Outside was a broken down, beat-up old truck with a boiler in the truck bed – an honest to God wood burning steam operated engine. We were each given a flashlight and a Sten gun (submachine gun) and hopped on – seven of us, and the driver. Off we went. I couldn't believe the noise! The Germans would surely hear us, but on the other hand, they couldn't be everywhere and we weren't going to go through any towns or on any main roads. We stopped in a nearby village and picked up two more guys and headed for the country. After about thirty minutes, we arrived at an open field in the middle of a large forest, a perfect place for a drop. The plane was to fly over the field at 500 feet at exactly 12:30 on a south to north heading, Leon told us. After placing Dick and me in our positions, Leon told us to flash our light exactly the way the rest of the men did. He moved a few feet, and as he had the radio, I could plainly hear his conversation with the pilot. At exactly 12:30 we heard the plane. It was going to make two runs over the landing area which would give us plenty of time to talk with the pilot as he would be in range during the two passes.

The pilot split the field – what a navigation job, really on the money. Leon made radio contact. We were flashing our lights and down came the parachutes with the first of the canisters. Then after the plane made a three-sixty, down came the rest; but we lost radio contact and couldn't regain it. So much for our pick-up and ride back to England. We were sick.

118

But our immediate job was to pick up the canisters. We dragged them to the truck, covered them with parachutes and headed north. We had only gone a mile or so when one of the chutes caught fire. It had been too close to the wood-burning boiler. Flames shot sky high. We thought every German in the country would see the fire and we took off running, but Leon called us back and the fire was put out.

We kept expecting to see the Germans, but luck was with us again. Finally, we reached a desolate farm. This was where we were going to store the supplies and where we ran into two of our missing crewmembers. What a reunion. They had heard that four of our crew had been captured and were prisoners of war, and that two were somewhere nearby. What a relief for me. Everybody had bailed out safely and now everybody was accounted for. For the next hour, we unloaded radios, Sten guns, ammunition, k-rations, and various types of equipment that the Resistance would need. The next thing Dick and I did, a really sneaky thing to do, but we did it anyhow, was when the others left the barn and gone into the house, we opened all the k-rations and stole all the cigarettes. Each little Phillip Morris package contained four cigarettes. Needless to say, we smoked well for a while. As we left our newly found crewmembers, we were told the Marquis would bring us all together in just a few days.

We said our goodbyes and headed back to the farm. We had done a good night's work. The next day we celebrated the successful pickup by proceeding to get really drunk. Joe, the American, sent us a case of champagne and we managed to drink most of it in one sitting. We then spent the afternoon sleeping it off out in the yard. We would have been good pickings if any Germans had come by.

Shortly thereafter, the arrangements to move us south to join the Underground Army were completed, and we were told to get ready to leave. We were to be driven south by the local mailman in his mail truck. So early the next morning, a beautiful May day, the mailman picked us up and off we went. Leon sat in front with the driver and Dick and I in the back seat. As it turned out, we got away none too soon. We had been gone only a few hours when the Germans arrived at the farm. They had tortured the Butcher and found out where we had been taken. The Germans surprised the brothers, Hubert and Gabriel, along with some of the others. The Nazis made quick work of it. They made them dig their own graves and then fill it with lime. Then stood them in their graves and machined gunned them. I didn't hear about this until after the war when we heard from Yvonne, one of the boy's sisters, as to what had happened. After the Germans had left, she had taken some pictures of the bodies in their graves. I have these pictures today in my scrapbook. One traitor had caused the death of these brave men. Charles Vallon is now spending the rest of his life at hard labor in a French prison.

We met so many brave people. I'll always remember one family in Marcilly sur Seine. He was the local schoolteacher, Robert Menuier. His brave wife and beautiful sixteen year-old daughter Michelle, hid us in their home for about three days. On the second day, a neighbor ran into the house and told Madam Menuier that the Germans were in the village and were searching every house. She told us to go up in the attic and said, "Don't worry. I'll handle this". And she did. When the German soldiers came into the kitchen she had coffee and wine waiting for them. A typical wife, she wanted to be hospitable. The three German soldiers never went any further than the kitchen. How do you thank people like that? How can you ever repay them?

As we were riding through the countryside, the mailman had something to tell us that scared us to death. He told Leon in French and Leon told us that we're going to drive right through the German airbase at Romilly sur Seine. That we were going in the main gate and out the rear gate. He told us not to worry. He did this every day delivering mail. The Germans knew him – had known him for almost three years, so he was sure they wouldn't stop us. We were waved through the main gate, drove right by a line of Messerschmitt 109 fighters, watched the men take their exercises, stopped and dropped off the mail and out the rear gate we went. I could finally breathe again. Looked at Dick and he was as pale as I felt. A short time later, we were told that we were going to stop at a farm where a badly injured Brit was hiding. He had been badly burned when his parachute hit some high-tension wires. We could smell him the second we entered the house. We spent about half an hour with him, knowing full well that there was no way he could make it. We tried to cheer him up. Boy, was it hard; but damned if he wasn't cheerful all the while we were there. Tears came to my eyes as soon as I walked out of the room.

An hour later, the mailman dropped us off at the house of a wonderful old man. He had been a major in the First World War. He said he would guide us through the forest to where the Maquis had their camp. After an hour later, at a prearranged location, we met one of the perimeter guards. The old man waved his goodbyes and headed back down the path. The guard pointed to us down the path in the opposite direction.

The first person we met was one of our crew, Sgt. Atkins. You can imagine our excitement. First on finding out that he was okay, then being told that Bob Brown was in the camp. Six out of ten of the crew were safe. We had already heard that the other four had been captured. So all were at least alive and nobody had been hurt or wounded. Quite a joyful reunion at the camp. The crew's original pilot, Bob Brown, the navigator, Lt. Rule, and Sgts. McMahon and Atkins. We immediately brought each other up to date on what had happened since we were shot down. A good day.

Also in camp, along with our friend Leon, was a Scotchman from the R.A.F., Stewart Godfrey, a good guy that we naturally nicknamed Scotty. There were probably two hundred Frenchmen, all living in small tents and lean-tos. The leader apparently was a Lieutenant in the French Army. We were taken to him right away and he told us he was glad to see and help us, but there were problems as there was very little food for so many people. What food there was, had to be eaten cold, because building a fire was dangerous, especially in the daytime when the smoke could be seen from so far away. At night, the fires had to be carefully shielded because German planes were always overhead.

I will never forget listening to the French argue. Leon of course, would explain what was being argued about. The French didn't have just a couple of political parties as we do.

They had dozens and apparently they all were well represented in the camp. They sure could argue, and about everything. What targets to hit? What trains to derail? What bridges to blow up? What collaborator should be silenced? It was never ending. The Communist were well represented and naturally seemed to cause the most trouble, but they were all patriots and didn't hesitate to do what had to be done once agreements had been reached.

After we were there a couple of days, we found out that all of us must share in guard duty. There was an outer perimeter guard, maybe a mile or two out; and then an inner perimeter guard, out about a quarter of a mile from the main campsite. The Americans and English served only as inner perimeter guards. We all did guard duty and one day Sgt. Atkins, who had been there for a while, saw a man that didn't look familiar walking down a trail. When he came abreast, Atkins leveled his gun at him and marched him into camp. The Maquis leader asked what he was doing out in the woods and the fellow explained that he had been working and was taking a short cut home. The French didn't accept his story, and tied him up and threw him into a lean-to. A council was held and it was decided to really question this fellow. It turned out that he was working for the Germans and that each time he brought information to them he was paid the equivalent of ten cents in our money, plus a bottle of beer. What a price to betray your country!

That night they built a fire and placed an iron grill on it. When it was red hot, six of the French, three on each side, grabbed the collaborator and sat him on the grill. We were all watching. I shut my eyes, but you can't shut out the screams. Just before that, some of the Maquis had formed a circle with the traitor inside. They pushed him from one to the other beating him with their fists as they did. An Algerian was in the circle and suddenly he picked the traitor up, held him at arms-length. He then proceeded to take a big bite out of the man's arm, afterwards spitting it back out. We Americans later decided that he had done this to the collaborator to try to convince everyone that he, the Algerian, was a true patriot. More about this guy later. I was sick to my stomach, but traitors got what they deserved. After that, they dragged him away and hung him from a nearby tree.

A day or so before this big event, a Group of Frenchmen walked into camp with a big, and I mean a big, black from French North Africa. He had escaped, he said, from the Germans and was heading south to Spain. He, of course, spoke French and more than a little English. For the next day or two, he would come to our "lean-to" and talk. He flashed a heavy wad of money and had plenty of cigarettes. However, almost as soon as he arrived in camp, one of the Frenchmen came to Leon and told him to warn us to be very careful what we said to the North African. His story just doesn't jibe, so be careful. On the third afternoon, the Maquis leader came to our tent asking if we had seen the black man. I told him I had seen the Algerian that morning as he was heading out through the woods, but not since. The Lieutenant said, "We didn't trust him and it looks like we were right, because he has disappeared". The whole camp was aroused and sent looking for him, but he was gone. Someone was sent into town to see what they could find out. The word came back that the Algerian was a German agent.

It didn't take the argumentative Maquis long to decide this issue. All parties agreed, "Tout suite" to break camp and get out of this place. We walked all night, not easy in the woods. For two hundred or so of us. Rested the next day and then walked all night again. Finally finding what was thought to be a good place for a new camp. We had been without food for two days when finally some villagers came in with bread and cheese. Never tasted anything so good. Even had a little red wine from a bottle we Americans were given to share. A day or two later, another one hundred or so French joined us with six English R.A.F. Airmen with them. We now had a total of six Americans from our crew and eight R.A.F. Airmen, including Leon and Scotty. We doubled our inner and outer perimeter guards and didn't light a fire at all. We were really hungry, but maybe that was good. We didn't have to go to the toilet as often. This was a real problem for the Americans and, I'm sure, the English as well. There wasn't any
toilet paper and the substitutes we found out in the woods sure didn't work very well, but we did find a pretty good answer. In those times there just weren't many cigarettes available and what was, the infamous French "Gauloise", were so bad and so strong that the Americans would almost rather do without. There was a little loose tobacco available and for some reason, a plentiful supply of cigarette paper. We soon learned to roll our own, but what we really hoarded was the cigarette papers to use as toilet paper. You just had to be a little careful.

The whole camp was jumpy. The French had given us all guns when we arrived, but now they took them back. Seems as if the new Group of one hundred who had joined us were almost without weapons, so our guns were given to them. I was left with one hand grenade and I guarded it carefully. I wanted to at least defend myself.

One of the things we did have in camp was a radio, so we did listen to the B.B.C. and the Free French radio. By midmorning on June 6th, 1944, we knew that the Allies had landed on the French coast. We all thought we would be free in a few days, a couple of weeks at the most. But, it wasn't to be.

The next morning, early, we heard gunfire in the distance, out where the outer perimeter guard should be. Then more and more, definitely coming closer. By now the camp was in a complete uproar. The Germans had found us! What to do? The camp commander came running up and yelled at us, "You're on your own". I had already packed what little I had to carry and with hand-grenade in hand, I started to run in the opposite direction of the gunfire. Running with me was Dick Rader, Scotty, and another R.A.F. man who had recently joined us. We were about one hundred yards from camp when the Germans found the range, and mortar shells started dropping in the camp. Then we really took off.

Suddenly we heard machine gun fire and we hit the deck. The new R.A.F. man completely panicked and all of a sudden said, "I'm going back". We tried to stop him to no avail. He jumped up and ran back toward the camp. Dick, Scotty and I kept moving, actually on the ground most of the time because the machine gun fire was so bad. We eventually got to the edge of the woods where we stopped and hid in the high undergrowth. We could look down over a field of wheat onto a road and then more wheat fields on the far side, and then heavy woods beyond up to the hills. I still had my hand grenade, the only weapon among the three of us.

We waited, well hidden by now for the rest of the day watching the Germans go by in trucks and armored vehicles. Our plan was that as soon as possible, we would go down through the wheat field, cross the road and head for the woods on the far side. By late afternoon the guns were silent. We hadn't seen any Germans on the road for an hour or so and thought maybe it was time to make our move. Just about this time, we saw a Frenchman come out of the woods and casually start walking down through the wheat field. He had moved about fifty yards when we decided to follow him. Just then a shot rang out and the Frenchman pitched forward dead. There was a small barn and house near the road and the Germans had hidden a sniper or two in the barn. They had done their job.

We made an immediate decision to wait until it was dark – very dark. Unfortunately, that didn't happen. The moon came out. It was not a full moon, but it still gave out more light than we would have liked. Across the way, up near the woods on the far side, a rather large rock was glistening in the moonlight. The three of us decided to leave individually and meet at the rock. I would go first, followed by Dick and then Scotty. Down I started on hands and knees. About two-thirds of the way down, I heard a German patrol walking toward me up the road. I thought, "If they see me, I'll throw the grenade and run like hell". They didn't though, and finally they disappeared in the distance. After I quit shaking, I was across the road and up to the rock in no time. A minute or so later Dick arrived and said, "Damn, that patrol scared the hell out of me". All I could do was nod.

Where was Scotty? We waited and waited, fifteen minutes, thirty minutes. We couldn't hear a sound. What the hell had happened? The rock was still plainly visible. "We'll wait another fifteen minutes and get the hell out of here." That's what we did. Walked all night. Keeping the North Star over our right shoulder. Slept all the next day in the woods, a cold and miserable day. Then walked all the next night. Passed through a couple of very small villages. Damned barking dogs scared us to death. After two nights and two days, we had put some miles between us, and our old camp. We wondered if everybody, especially our crew, had gotten away and what had happened to Scotty.

That afternoon, we took yet another chance and walked into a farmyard and asked for help. The farmer signaled for us to follow him and he headed for the barn. As we went in, he said in French, "I have a compatriot of yours up above". Up we went to the loft and there sat our old friend Scotty. The question was how could the three of us, Scotty alone, Dick and I together, have walked all night for two nights and ended up in the same farmhouse? We never figured out how it could have happened, and Scotty still didn't know how he missed the moonlit rock.

Up and at'em early the next morning and after expressing our thanks to the good farmer, we took off, the three of us once again. Walked all day, saw no Germans, and slept in the woods that night. Nothing to eat all the next day and after another night in the woods, we came upon a lonely farmhouse. As Scotty spoke good French, he said he would go down and try to get us something to eat. When he left, I turned to Dick and said, "Dick, we're taking a hell of a chance with the three of us traveling together. Two is okay. Three is just too suspicious looking, but how in the hell are we going to broach the subject to Scotty?" Dick nodded in agreement. Well, we didn't have long to worry, Scotty brought back some stale bread, maggot filled cheese and a bottle of wine. He said, "I scared the poor farmer and his wife to death, but at least they gave us some food". Scraping the maggots off the cheese, we made short order of the food and then Scotty said, "Fellows, it's too damn dangerous for the three of us to travel together. I think it would be better if we broke up. I've been thinking that I'll go into Paris. My French is okay and I think I'll make out alright". We said we had also been thinking the same thing. So after memorizing each other's names and home addresses, of course, we wouldn't write anything down; we said our farewells and he headed north to Paris. We headed west to where we hoped to meet the Allied armies.

Never heard from Scotty again. I wrote to him after the war and had a reply from his wife. He had never been heard of since the three of us parted. Maybe he was caught in an air raid or maybe the Gestapo picked him up and shot him. We'll never know, and as I said before, a good guy.

It was now the end of June. We had been down in France for over two months. We were on our own. No help from the Maquis now. So, we did what we thought was best – just head west. More days of walking, passed many Germans. If it seemed necessary, we would say "Bon jour" or "Bon soir". Finally, south and east of Paris, we came to a river but no bridge could be found. Finally, decided to swim, but just then we saw a farmhouse down the road. So we agreed to go there and ask for help. As we approached the house, something did not seem right and we walked on. Found out later that the biggest collaborator in the area lived there. Luck, just plain luck.

We had many premonitions such as that and they usually proved right. All this time Dick was really worried about his new wife. They had only been married a very short time when he was sent overseas. He hadn't had time to arrange insurance. Didn't know how she was doing financially and as a result, we took chance after chance that we probably shouldn't have taken, only because he was so anxious to get home. What she was doing however, is another story.

We stopped at the next farm and, as soon as we got in the courtyard, I knew we had made a mistake. There were four big blond-haired men standing there talking. It was too late to turn and run, so I just asked in English if the patron was home. One of the men spoke a little English. "He's in town and should return anytime. Do you want to wait inside?" Nothing else to do, so we sat in the kitchen and told the English speaking one who had come in with us, that we were American pilots. He told us the patron spoke good English. "Here he comes now." In walked another tall blond, somewhat older than the rest. "Hello," I said, extending my hand, "We are American pilots." He gave us a great big smile, took my hand and said, "My name is Jacque Dykstra. I'm Dutch, but have lived here many years. Are you hungry?"

We stayed for a week. His housekeeper, Renee, soon to be his wife, kept us well fed. As Jacque was a dairy farmer, he had plenty of butter, milk and eggs. Boy did we eat. The only problem was that there were no screens on the windows and the kitchen was filled with flies. Oh, well, we could brush the flies off the food and pop it into our mouths. Thank God, flies go to sleep at night. I remember thinking, "After the war, I'll come back to France and sell window screens. I'll make a Fortune".

This was a dangerous place to hide. The Germans came every day for milk and butter. So we stayed hidden most of the time.

Jacque told us one night that it was too dangerous to stay at his place any longer and that he had arranged for us to stay in an abandoned hospital in Brienon, a nearby town. A friend would come tomorrow to take us there. He came the next day with a horse and wagon filled with hay (and me with hay fever). Something, by the way, I had never bothered to tell the Army Air Corp. The friend took us to his house and we found that he had a bathtub. This was something unusual in rural France in those days. When we told him we would like to take a bath, he said, "ah, oui, but come with me". We walked into the bathroom, sure enough a tub, but filled full of straw and the home of four baby ducks and their mother. Eventually we got our bath, the first in ten weeks. It sure felt good even though there was no hot water.

After feeding us, we were taken over to the hospital. It had been abandoned because it was directly across the street from the railroad station and the French thought surely, the Allies would bomb the station and the adjacent marshalling yards.

The following day we found out how right they were. That morning, we explored the hospital. We were on the third floor. In the next room there must have been fifteen or twenty stretchers for use after a bombing raid. Although, there had not been a bombing raid here, since the beginning of the war. The rest of the hospital was completely empty. After we finished checking the place out, a woman brought us some breakfast and said she'd be back around noon. We had just finished eating when we heard the bombers. We went over to the window to take a look and up there at about 20,000 feet, we could see the contrails of a stream of bombers. "Wonder where they are going?" Dick said. "I don't know," I said "Let's hope it's not here." Just then we saw a Wing of sixty planes break off and head toward us. "You know," Dick said very seriously, "they are going to bomb that damn marshalling yard." By now they were overhead and suddenly we heard the swish of the falling bombs. "My God, let's go." And we headed for the stairs taking them a flight at a time. Believe this or not, by the time the bombs exploded, we had gone from the third floor to the basement. I bet that record is still standing today.

As the sound of the engines faded away, we decided to go back upstairs. We couldn't see a thing. The smoke and dust completely blinded us, but we made our way up to our room. Looking out the window, it was much clearer by now. We could see people running around with red-cross armbands on. "They'll be coming up here to get those stretchers. If they look in here, we're dead." I think we both said it at the same time.

"Let's grab a couple of stretchers and bring them here to our room. If they come in here, we'll rush out as they come in." Looking out the window again, we saw men approaching the hospital. Again seeing the white armbands, Dick and I both reached for our handkerchiefs and tied them around our upper arm. We stood ready to rush the door if anyone came in. No one did. They went next door, picked up the stretchers and left. We were safe, at least for now.

A little while later, the stretcher-bearers returned, carrying bodies into the hospital. It was to be the morgue. Later that afternoon, our French friend came up and told us it was much too dangerous now to stay in the hospital and that he would come back after dark and take us back to Jacque's. He did and we rode back in the same wagon we had arrived in the day before. Well, it had been an adventurous couple of days. We had been in a bomb raid, had survived and were now back where we started. By the way, our Flying Fortresses missed the marshalling yard altogether, but destroyed part of the town and killed a lot of people. How could they be so bad? We thought. It had been a perfectly clear day and no anti-aircraft fire at all. We learned that day that bombing is not an exact science.

That night we returned to Jacque's farm. Believe it or not, Jacque really appeared happy to see us. He didn't seem to have any fear of the Germans at all.

The next day, July 4th, 1944, American fighter-bombers arrived in the late morning, attacking the marshalling yard again. This time, doing the job! Now they were circling over our heads. There was an ammunition train, which could not get into Brienon, parked on the tracks in back of Jacque's farm. What a target! I said, "Jacque they are going to attack this train in a minute or two. We've got to get out of here". I could hear Dick say, "Amen", behind me. There were six of us, Jacque; his housekeeper Renee, her daughter, Deena, another young girl, and the two of us. We left the house and ran down the driveway to the macadam road and jumped into the ditch on the far side. I was on the end, Dick next to me, then Jacque, Renee, her baby Deena, and the young girl. Thank God, it was a deep ditch because here came the fighters strafing the train, then flying right over us with empty shells falling all around. Then after making a 360 degree turn, back they came firing at the train as they crossed over us. Again, empty shells were falling all around us. What a sight! I noticed Jacque's cows were still out in the field. I said, "Jacque, they are going to kill all of your cows". He looked at me and said, "Don't worry, it is but nothing at all". I'll never forget that expression and have used it many times since.

By now the train was beginning to explode. Every third or fourth car was an oil tanker and they really blew. What a Fourth of July! About then a German truck careened down the road and stopped right beyond us. Two Germans piled out and jumped in the ditch right next to us. Jacque whispered, "Don't say anything". So we just watched. What a show we were watching! First, the dive bombing of the marshalling yards in Brienon and now the strafing of the ammunition train back of Jacque's farm. The Americans finally finished, reformed and were gone. The explosions went on for hours. The B-17s might have missed their target, but the P-47s didn't.

126

Jacque leaned over toward Dick and whispered, "You two casually get up and walk into the woods back of us. I'll handle the soldiers". We did and the Germans never ever looked at us. They were staring at their burned out truck.

Well, we couldn't stay any longer and we knew it was time to go. This time, we were heading toward Paris. The Allies were finally starting their breakout from the beachhead and we knew they would first head for Paris.

It was hard to say goodbye to Renee and her little Deena. Renee had been wonderful, along with those big blond Dutch boys who worked for Jacque. Jacque took us to Brienon and said his friend had purchased two railroad tickets for Melun. He instructed us to: "Get on the train, don't say anything, and then pretend to go right to sleep". We said goodbye to Jacque and told him we would see him after the war. Once more, I had tears in my eyes.

The train was crowded. There weren't many trains then. We had gone about two hours when the train stopped. Somehow we understood that the track had been destroyed and that we would have to walk about a mile and then there would be another train waiting for us. As we were leaving the coach, I noticed that the little old lady who sat across from us was having a hard time. She was trying to carry three or four packages and a suitcase. I pointed to one, signaling that I would carry it for her. I took one of the packages and immediately knew why she had been struggling. The damn thing must have contained lead bricks, maybe gold coins or both. It wasn't a mile we had to walk, but at least two or three. We stumbled, fell and crawled ahead and finally made it, with the little old lady not far behind. We crowded aboard and found a compartment. The lady thanked me for carrying her package and I nodded, "you are welcome." Then she reached into a small sack and handed me an egg. I said merci beaucoup and held it very gingerly. If I had liked raw eggs, I would have eaten it right then.

The next stop was Melun, where we were supposed to get off, but upon arriving at the station, the platform was overrun by German soldiers. To hell with getting off, we would jump at the first opportunity between Melun and Paris. We could now talk because the people in the compartment had tried to talk to us when we got on the second train. First French, then German. So we finally told them that we were American pilots trying to escape. There were a lot of ooo, la, las and smiles. We shook hands all around. Then we quieted down as the train was boarding a lot of German soldiers. Dick and I decided to jump at the first opportunity. As the train slowed down, for a curve, we decided, this was the time. We said goodbye to our friends, opened the compartment door and jumped. Believe this, too, I didn't break the egg even after rolling over many times going down a steep embankment. Well, no one had seen us jump and we weren't any worse for wear, but what to do now? We sat on the bank of the river resting and thinking. We were just north of the city center of Melun. There had to be lots of bridges across the Seine in this area. Some probably not even guarded. We soon saw one. I crossed it first and Dick followed a minute or two later. Meeting again on the other side, we walked down what looked like a soon-to-be busy street. I still had my egg in my hand and we were hungry.

We looked into two or three restaurants but passed them by. Then I said, "Dick, let's take a chance on that one". We did and a little lady was standing behind a zinc metal bar top. I said in English, "We are American pilots and we're hungry. Will you feed us?" She got so excited I thought she would do it in her pants, but she put her fingers to her lips and signaled us to go in the back room. Then she said in French, "My son speaks English. I'll get him".

A couple of minutes later he came in and said, "You don't know how lucky you are. I'm the only restaurateur in town that speaks English. I am Marcel Govin". We explained our situation and asked him if he could feed us, handing him my egg. A second later Marcel popped out of the kitchen saying, "Didn't you know your egg is hard-boiled?" It would have been eaten long ago if I had known that.

After a few hours' sleep, Marcel took us to the interurban station saying that the streetcar would take us another ten kilometers west. Slept that night in another haystack after making another pinpoint hole in my roadmap. That afternoon we had seen a well camouflaged factory and I was keeping track of those things on my road map. Awakened very early to start the day on which, we were picked up by the Germans.

We headed west and as we approached a small village, we noticed a new building on the left side of the road. As we passed it, a German came out with his rifle on his shoulder. We probably should have said "Bon jour" as we had done so many times when passing Germans. But, we didn't and the soldier yelled "Halten". I whispered to Dick, "Well, I guess we've had it". We heard, "Halten", again. This time we also heard the rifle coming off his shoulder. We turned and stopped. The German approached us with his rifle pointing right at us. "Papers", he demanded. In my terrible French I said, "We have no papers. We are going to the fields to work. Our papers are at the farm". If the soldier had spoken any French at all, we would have been finished. Apparently he had just arrived, because most German soldiers that had been in France for years spoke the language quite well. The soldier then noticed my road map. It was in the inside pocket of my old suit coat and the very corner of it was showing. "No papers", I said. With that he reached over and pulled out the map. "Oh boy!" I thought, "This is it". A real farmer wouldn't have a road map in his pocket. The German pointed toward the village and said, "March", and fell in behind us. Dick and I, of course, didn't say a word. Upon reaching a building that the Germans had taken over as their headquarters, we stopped and met another German. Our man explained to him what had happened and the second soldier said, "They are just going to work, let them go". No such luck. We were taken inside of what turned out to be a small mess hall and a few soldiers were having breakfast. Not having eaten for about 24 hours, it sure smelled good, but we were ushered into the next room and told to wait at the door. Our captor walked across the room and knocked on the door. After being told to enter, we could see it was a bedroom, as the foot of the bed was plainly in sight. Our man gave, to whomever was in the bed, a Nazis salute and handed over the map. As I saw what was happening, I said to Dick, "Take my sweater," which I was carrying in my hand, "and let me move over so, if he looks out, he will see me." "I'm more the average Frenchman's height". Dick took the sweater and I moved, but it wasn't necessary. I saw the man in bed hand my map back to the captor. He again gave the Nazis salute, came out of the room, closed the door and marched over to us.

He handed me the map and said, "Allez!" which, means get out. I took the map, we turned, went back through the mess hall and out the door, smiled at the Germans who were still standing there and casually walked down the street. As soon as we turned the corner, we started running, and we ran until we fell exhausted at the edge of a small woods.

As soon as we got our breath, I said, "Dick, you have any cigarettes"? He reached in his pocket. "One", he said. He lit it and we passed it back and forth. "By the way, Dick do you have my sweater?" "Oh God!" was the reply. "I left it on the table that I was standing next to."

Let me describe the sweater. One of my roommates had been shot down in the North Sea and rescued by the British Navy. He was given dry clothes, including a blue pullover sweater, British Navy issue. It was too small for my roommate, "Moose" Jacobs, and upon his return, he gave it to me. Ever after, I wore it on missions because it looked like a civilian sweater and I figured if I was ever shot down, it would come in handy. However, I failed to do one thing. On its label was the statement "Property of His Majesty's Navy".

Dick and I looked at each other and words weren't necessary. We got the hell out of there. We ran off and on all day long, keeping off the roads and in the woods. About dusk, we saw a likely looking farm and went in to ask for help. When the farmer appeared, we said we are hungry and tired. When he started to question us, I said we only speak a few words of French because we are Dutch. Jacque Dykstra had told us to say that if we ever needed to. I said, "We are Dutch", exactly as a Hollander would say it. (I had practiced.) The farmer said, "I am also Dutch". Then he started talking a mile a minute. We then confessed we were American pilots trying to escape. He told us a doctor would be there in a few minutes to treat his sick wife and he speaks English. We were hidden in the barn and in a very few minutes, the doctor rode in on a motorcycle.

Introductions and explanations were made and the doctor's first words in English were, "I have been stopped at least five times today and they never stop me because they know who I am. But, today they stopped me and asked if I had seen two men who didn't look familiar. Of course, I hadn't, but I must tell you, the Germans know you are in the area and they are looking for you." So much for not cutting the label out of my sweater. The doctor left to go in to treat the sick wife, saying he would talk to us when he was through.

Dick said, "You know, Harvey, we should ask the doctor if he has anything for the crabs." We had run out of eau du vie. "I hope he has got something," I replied. "All the running we've done today has really got them moving."

The doctor came back saying, "You men have really got to get out of here. Walk at night until you get out of this area". He did have some medicine for us and he also gave us some aspirin and some extra francs. With a "Merci", a quick handshake and a "Bon chance" from him and the farmer, we took off.

It was now about the first of August. We had been down nearly fourteen weeks. We had nothing but good luck, albeit, a few scares and were held in brief custody once. The invasion was starting to gain momentum and we knew with a little more luck, we would soon be meeting the advancing armies. Dick and I decided to be extra careful from now on. We didn't want to be taken prisoner at this late date.

A couple of nights were spent traveling through the woods. We weren't covering many miles, but we weren't taking many chances either. Along the way, we had been supplied with identity cards. We had carried pictures with us. All flying personnel had their pictures taken in civilian clothes. The French Gendarmes in one small town had the cards made for us. They were darn good forgeries. There's quite a story about the pictures however. It seems that every Bomb Group photographed all their airmen in the same civilian coat and tie. It wasn't long before the German Intelligence knew what Group you were in just by what civvies you wore. However, we were never called upon to show our identity cards. Just as well, our terrible French would have done us in anyhow.

Once more, lady luck was with us. We stopped at another farm. The man answering the door looked like a saint, with gray hair flying in the breeze, long apron, and wooden shoes. (I thought the Dutch were the only people who wore them.) Not only that, but as he invited us in the house, he spoke perfect English. He told us his name was George Perache. He introduced us to his "brother", Henri. It seems they were both from Paris. George sang in operettas and musicals and his "brother", was an architect. George had refused to entertain the Germans so he and his "brother" had bought a place in the country and were farming. It didn't take us long to learn that they weren't really brothers, but gay lovers; but they were patriots and couldn't have been better friends and saviors to us.

It was wonderful to be able to carry on a conversation with George in English. It wasn't long before others in the village knew we were hiding at George's farm. So, we had plenty of visitors. One day a cute young girl called Raymonde, whose mother was the village postmistress, came to visit. They lived in an apartment over the post office. We tried to figure a way to go visit her, but it was just too dangerous. Furthermore, she had a boyfriend, Charles, who was in the Maquis. Oh well, our adventure was a little different than all the movies we had seen. You know, the ones about the shot down pilot who is found and hidden by a beautiful girl.

One afternoon, George came rushing in. "Go out in the back garden", he said, "and get yourself well hidden. There is a company of Germans outside. I'm going to try to get rid of them". Out we went! Our hearts were in our mouth. None of the shrubbery seemed big enough to hide in, but we did by burrowing down and barely breathing. It seemed the German officer wanted a place to billet his men. George told him there was just no room in his small barn, but he suggested a place about a kilometer away, and the Germans left. George came out to the back and gave us the all clear. Our shirts were sopping wet.

It was time to go again. Too many people now knew we were hiding in George's house. So, once more with tears in my eyes, we headed west, waving our goodbyes to two good Frenchmen.

The activity in the air had really picked up. American fighters and light bombers were overhead all the time, and high above the heavies, the B-17s and the B-24s. We knew it wasn't going to be long, but again we had to be more careful than ever.

A couple of more days of walking again, while avoiding the roads. The Germans were all over the place. Convoy after convoy heading east back toward Germany. Lots of the trucks were painted with a red cross, as if they were ambulances. Now, in the distance, we could hear artillery fire still far away.

We stopped at one more farm. The farmer was another Dutchman and he spoke a little English. He took us in and told us that three Russians were also hiding there. They had escaped from a prisoner of war camp. The Dutch farmer told us that he was going to tell them that we were students from Paris. So don't speak when you are around them. One night, the Dutchman asked one of the Russians, who before the war had been a schoolteacher, what he thought of the Americans. This was his reply in a combination of Russian, German and a little French. "Right now America and Russia good friends, but after the war, America and Russia boom, boom, boom, boom." So that was their thinking even at that time.

Again we headed west and stopped for help at yet another farmhouse. The patron, this time a Frenchman, spoke just a little English. When we walked into his living room – kitchen, we could hear over the radio, the sound of Glenn Miller's band. Did that sound good! After his opening number, Miller introduced his guest star, Dinah Shore. We just sopped up that music and singing. Miller and his band were entertaining in England for morale purposes. He sure helped ours! We were able to thank him personally about a month later. Dick and I saw him in the lobby of the Savoy Hotel in London. I decided I would go over, introduce myself, and tell him our story. He really enjoyed it and asked us to come and see him broadcast his show. After the show, he invited us up to his suite for drinks. A really first class guy and, as we all know, he had only a short time to live.

We stayed with the farmer for four days. On the second day, three Germans came into the courtyard. They told the farmer they were deserters who wanted food and some place to hide. I couldn't blame them. They were old men – no business being soldiers.

French farms are different from ours. Firstly, they are hundreds of years old. They consisted of a series of connected, usually one story buildings, built around a courtyard. Almost like a Fort with one main entrance or gate. All rooms opened onto the courtyards. The farmer took them into the kitchen to eat and the soldiers stacked their rifles against the outer wall. Dick and I looked at each other, looked at the guns and then one of us said, "Let's capture the bastards". As one we arose, we each took a gun, walked in the kitchen and said, "Get up. Hands up". A little dramatic but that's what happened.

131

The farmer, more than a little surprised said, "What are you doing?" I said, "These people are prisoners of war. The Americans will be here in a day or two and we'll turn them over to them. Where can we put them?" There was a place: the milk and butter room. It had a barred door and big lock. After relieving them of their belts and bayonets, we told them to move out. They were scared to death. They naturally thought we were French Maquis. They well knew what would happen to them. We told them we were American, but they wouldn't believe it. One of them made a sudden move and Dick fired a shot over his head and out the open window. They then meekly left the kitchen and we locked them up. I still have the belt and bayonet to this day. The buckle is inscribed, "Got mit uns", meaning God with us.

All the next day, August 18, 1944, the road in front of the farm was crowded with retreating troops, convoys and tanks. The Americans had to be nearby. About four p.m., a Frenchman came riding into the courtyard shouting, "The Americans are in the village". The farmer said, "You better get going and take the Germans with you". We intended to do that anyhow, and off we went. The three Germans in front with Dick and me, with our belts and bayonets strapped on and rifles at the ready, bringing up the rear. It was about one kilometer into town. The longest walk I have ever taken. I could just see German soldiers behind every tree, but we made it. Sitting there, the most beautiful sight I have ever seen, were three, light 2-man tanks, a scouting force way ahead of the main body. The tankers were sitting on their tanks. They were dirty, unshaven, but they looked like Greek Gods to me.

I yelled to them, "I'm Lieutenant Harvey and this is Lieutenant Rader". "We were shot down". "What's taken you guys so long to get here?" And in the next breath, "How about a cigarette?"

One of the tankers threw me a whole pack. After lighting up, we did a lot of explaining about who we were, why we were there and what we were doing with three Germans. They explained to us that they were a scouting party out ahead of the main force of tanks and that they were just ready to turn around and go back, when we arrived. Our luck was still holding.

They could take us back, they said, but there was no room in the light tank, so we would have to ride on the outside. They gave Dick and me a helmet, and also gave us each a machine gun. They put the three Germans on the first two tanks, and Dick and I rode on each side, of the third. "Hang on," they said. "We are not going to waste any time and it's a rough road."

Hang on we did for what was the longest ride we've ever had. Again, I could see a German behind every hedgerow and around every curve. After what seemed like hours, we came up over a ridge and there before us, were more tanks than I had ever seen in my life. What a sight! We were taken directly to the commander's tank, jumped off and saluted a tough looking Lt. Colonel. Our friend, the tank driver, told the Colonel who we were. By this time, we had drawn a crowd and there were hundreds of questions and hundreds of answers. The Colonel told us refueling trucks were on the way up and afterward we could ride back with them to Army Headquarters. "Now," he said, "go get yourselves something to eat".

As we were eating, our old friend, the tank driver, came over to us and said, "We've got a new intelligence officer, fresh from the States, and he seems to think you guys might be German spies so be careful what you say to him". A little while later this Major came over and said he wanted to ask us a few questions. Apparently, we answered them satisfactorily for he finally said, "Okay, I guess you guys are who you say you are". I'll never forget saying to him, "Yes sir, Major, we knew who we were all the time".

Well, we thought we had it made and were home free, but it didn't turn out quite that way. Finally, late that night, a convoy was formed of twelve trucks. The first six gasoline tankers were to lead the way. The second six trucks were empty, except for some odds and ends, and we were told to hop on. Again given a helmet and gun. After about two hours of rough riding, way too rough to sleep, the convoy stopped. Dick and I jumped out to see what was wrong and the lead driver said, "I donno. Lieutenant, I've lost the tankers that were ahead of us. They must have turned and I didn't see them. They had all the maps." What to do? Firstly, it was starting to get light and Dick and I knew we had to find some woods and get the trucks hidden. We had watched the German "Dawn Patrol" many times. They were out every morning, making their runs before the Allied patrols appeared in the skies. We barely had gotten the half-tracks hidden in the woods, when here they came. Two flights of two 109s each, low and fast. "We'll stay here until they come back and then we'll try to find out where the hell we are."

Twenty minutes later the 109s reappeared. After they disappeared Dick and I, along with a sergeant who spoke a little French, started down the road looking for a farm house. Again with machine guns and tin hats, we stopped in the first place we saw and created quite a stir with the appearance of disreputable guys in civilian clothes with machine guns and helmets, and an American soldier. With many "Viva la France" and "Viva Americ", the farmer got out a map. We were out in the middle of nowhere, certainly in German occupied territory. We were shown how to get back, but not before a bottle of champagne was consumed. A little early in the morning, but not bad! After alerting all the drivers that we were in enemy territory, we started down the road, a little tense, to say the least. Up ahead we spotted a village and stopped to decide what to do. "What the hell, we've got to go this way, so let's go."

It was amazing, as the farmer must have telephoned someone in the village. The whole population was out in the street laughing, crying and shouting – "Viva la France", "Viva la Americ". We must have been there at least thirty minutes. Never was kissed by so many girls in my life and my right hand was almost broken by the hearty handshakes. It seemed everybody had one or two bottles of champagne in their hands. "Where did it all come from after four years of occupation? And the French flags and even one small American flag". Our six trucks, eight soldiers, two Airmen armed with two machine guns and two pistols had liberated a town. We hated to leave, but the Germans had been there yesterday and they might return.

No further incidents, and after about an hour, we were back on the right road and soon came to General Patton's headquarters. Unfortunately, we didn't get to see or meet him, but were given a jeep and driver who would take us to Cherbourg.

The next few hours were full of excitement. Couldn't believe the number of German prisoners of war we passed. I'm sure they couldn't believe what they were seeing. Giant heavy equipment, stuff that Dick or I had never seen: there were earthmovers, cranes, and bulldozers by the hundreds. Convoys of tankers, trucks, replacement tanks. We couldn't believe it. The German prisoners knew why they had been defeated. We passed through many French towns, including Caen and Caretan. We couldn't believe the destruction. How could they ever be rebuilt or would they? A road had been bulldozed through the towns, but that was all. The side streets were impassable. At last after a day of wonderment, we reached Cherbourg. We were dropped off at headquarters and were taken to an old German airbase to spend the night. But first, a shower, it had been four months and there was plenty of hot water. I could feel every pore in my body breathe. A sensation I've never had before or since. That shower had to be better than sex. After the hot bath, a bed with clean sheets. We were gone.

Next day, we were picked up by two officers in a jeep and were told that we would spend the day with them, as they made their inspection route around Cherbourg. After a couple of hours of gentle questioning, they admitted that they were intelligence officers just checking to be sure we actually were Americans and our stories rang true. During that day, I spotted a long line of soldiers – GI's, officers even saw a Major. "Why are they standing in line?" I asked. "Waiting to get in the whorehouse" was the reply. And – this was two in the afternoon! "Hey, that's not such a bad idea", I said to Dick, but by then we were four or five blocks down the road.

We were all set to fly to London, standing on an emergency strip on Omaha Beach, when a C54 taxied up and discharged its passengers from London. A few minutes later, they told us to get aboard. We had been watching a Group of German prisoners, all Generals, it appeared. After we got in our seats, the five generals came aboard with an American escort officer. A conversation started and we found the generals all spoke English quite well. The conversation got around to the fact that Berlin was almost completely destroyed. One of the generals said, "Well that's true, but then again so is London." "No." I said, "You have to really look to find damage in London." They looked at me as though I was crazy. I got up and went into the pilot's compartment. "Captain," I said to the pilot, these generals in back are a pretty haughty Group. They think London is in ruins. Why don't you give them a little "look see" and fly them over the Mayfair area. There's hardly any damage there." He said okay and I returned to my seat. Shortly thereafter the pilot announced that we were over the center of London. I watched the generals as they lost their haughty demeanor. Their faces fell. They now realized for the first time that they had really lost the war. I then looked away from them and down on London. The pilot had picked a perfect place. I couldn't see any damage at all. The generals didn't say another word. We turned into our final approach and touched down. Dick and I looked at each other, smiled and reached out to shake hands. We had made it!

Arriving at Station 106, our old base a few days later, I found that my ex-roommate, Mike Mazer, was again off attending another armament school, but was due back that night. So I went to his room and sacked out in his bunk. A little while later I thought the building had collapsed on me. Mazer had heard I was back and in his bed. He made a flying leap at me and didn't even say "Hello" – "How are you" – "Glad your back" -- just "Okay, Big Dog, where in the hell is my God-damn flight jacket?"

Miss Deal crew overloading the jeep at Wendover.

Photo Courtesy of Ellen Corrigan.

The Jeep Photo of 384th BG, 544th BS members consist primarily of the John Way crew, their B-17F was 42-30049 *Miss Deal*. Bill Harvey riding shotgun, John Way sitting on back of jeep with his right arm across his knee and wrist bent. Behind Way and to his left (with his tie out) is William R(Red) Feagin, (the gunner that got the Bf 109),
To Feagin's left is the Bombardier Bill Corrigan, Standing next to Corrigan is Raymond Dodge (Young Dodge or Trigger Dodge), sitting behind the driver and in front of Feagin is Bill McGeehan.
McGeehan, the Navigator that was assigned to the Halseth crew. Their original Fortress was 42-30039 *Liberty Belle*.

Photo courtesy of Betty Harvey

Bill Harvey (Big Dog). Of interest, a Fortress from the 384th the B-17G 42-102662 "Big Dog" carried Harvey's nickname. Harvey's good friend, Nathan Mazer, had the B-17G 42-9800 *Fighting Hebe* carry his nickname.

B-14G-15-BO   SU*Q   42-31346   *Shack Rabbit*   384BG, 344BS
Crew list of 24 April 1944 when *Shack Rabbit* was hit by flak and lost; all crew survived

P	Lt	W.L. Harvey	CP	2/Lt	Bob Brown
N	2/Lt	Johnson Rule	B	2/Lt	Dick Rader
TTG	T/Sgt	Dewey Smith	RO	S/Sgt	Stan Sturak
BTG	S/Sgt	Charles Roberson	RWG	Sgt	C. McManus
LWG	S/Sgt	Jim Atkins	TG	S/Sgt	George Vann

Photo and information courtesy of the 384th Bomb Group, James Traylor and Tony Plowright

Bill Harvey, standing in front row wearing leather jacket and parachute
after aborted mission to Hamburg. Harvey was observer/tailgunner
on the Hausenfluck crew. All 10 crewmen are at the side of their Fortress 42-30039
Liberty Belle. Notice the fifty caliber hanging in the right waist port.
This picture must have been taken right after their B-17 reached her hardstand,
as the guns have not been removed for cleaning and storage.
Gilmore, the Air Commander elected to return his Group to base as he could not
identify his Wing during assembly.

B-17F-85-BO 42-30039 SU*H Liberty Belle 384th Bomb Group, 544th Bomb Squad

P. Commander	Capt	William Gilmore	Radio Man	S/Sgt	John Kelly
Copilot	1/Lt	Jesse Hausenfluck	Ball Turret	Sgt	James Traylor
Navigator	2/Lt	Charles Everson	Right Waist	S/Sgt	Sebastian Bucheri
Bombardier	1/Lt	Robert Kennedy	Left Waist	S/Sgt	John Blauer
Engineer	T/Sgt	John Kilcourse	T. G. Observer	1/Lt	Walter Harvey

Jacque.Dykstra was the Dutch dairy farmer that helped Bill Harvey evade capture while journeying through
the area near Brienon, France. After the war with Harvey's assistance, Dykstra immigrated to Michigan.
Finding a farm in the Mt. Pleasant area he returned to farming. Unfortunately Dykstra was killed by a drunk
driver and he left his wife Renee, two daughters and a son. The one daughter Dina Desormes operates a
successful bakery in Mt. Pleasant, Michigan

137

Chapter 15

Eight Memorable Experiences from 384ᵗʰ Crews

Patches, One Rugged Old Fortress

The first raid of the 384ᵗʰ was to be an attack on the General Motors truck plant in Antwerp, Belgium. Scheduled to participate was the Donald Ogilvie crew with B-17F Number 42-5848. The 384th referred to this original Fortress as *848*. On this first mission the Group leader was the 384ᵗʰ commanding officer Budd Peaslee. This raid on Antwerp was thought to be a quick and easy "milk run" with the target only 50 miles from the English Channel.

With the Bomb Group departing England without their scheduled fighter escort, three Staffeln of Focke Wulf, Fw 190s attacked the Boeings head-on. The B-17s were now experiencing the light cannon fire from the enemy fighters that were closing at over 500 miles per hour. The *848*, the Fredrick Disney ship, and the Oblinski B-17 were heavily damaged and struggled after bombs away to return to base. Oblinski's Fortress 42-30076 again was attacked by several fighters and exploded in mid-air, crashing at Wilhelminadorp, Holland.

The Disney Fortress was the 547ᵗʰ Squadron leader and began losing altitude on her way back toward the English Channel. Ogilvie and one other B-17 followed their leader as he was going down to give protective fire support. Fortunately, the Focke Wulfs did not pursue the falling Fortress and the two escorting bombers realized that their action was useless and attempted to regain their Group on their return to base. The Ogilvie and the other B-17 that broke formation were severely reprimanded, for their chivalry had not only endangered their crew, but the entire Group.

On the way back to base, a number of English farmers were harvesting barley and noticed a B-17 approaching Grafton Underwood that was in bad shape and firing a flare from the nose. The farmers commented that they could see right through one of her Wings and parts of her tail-plane were missing.

Finally, it touched down and the ambulance took the injured away. The crew chief and his cadre of mechanics for *848* could hardly believe how badly their ship had been shot up from nose to tail; and yet she was able to make it back home. It took the ground crew a week to get *848* ready for duty. When the other crews saw all size aluminum patches scattered over this olive drab B-17, she got her name change. *Patches*.

Patches made six more missions and finally on her raid to Kassel, Germany, she again was shot up bad. Taking a flak hit near the waist, both gunners were wounded. On the way back toward Holland, the Focke Wulfs came out of the blinding sun, raking *Patches* with their cannon fire. This first pass left the engineer, the pilot, the co-pilot and the navigator severely wounded. The engineer was hit in the leg and knocked out of his station. With a broken leg he climbed back into his gun turret and continued to defend the

ship. The injured navigator stayed at his station giving directions for the lone B-17.
Soon enough the fighters returned and the pilot told all the gunners to give him the
approaching directions of the attackers. When an approaching fighter started an attack,
the position was relayed to the pilot and he made evasive moves, confounding the fighter
pilots, who couldn't get a good sight on the dodging bomber. Although taking numerous
additional hits, *Patches* finally got her crew back to England where she was landed at a
B-26 base near Colchester. The pilots were challenged to get their *Patches* down with
throttles and controls stuck, they could not hit the main runway. When they did get
down, one of her tires was flat from a 20mm hit causing the big bird to wander to her port
side, crossing taxiways and finally coming to rest in the grassy infield.

When the 384th came calling for their beloved *Patches*, it was decided that she just had
too much damage and would be marked for salvage.   *Patches* brought the William R.
Harry crew back home to England following her final raid on the Fieseler aircraft
assembly plant at Kassel, Germany. All her flyers returned to duty. Lt. Harry was
awarded a Silver Star for his actions in piloting *Patches* back to England.

Photo Courtesy of Quentin Bland
The Ogilvie Crew posing in front of Patches prior to the Antwerp raid
Also shown in photo is Delbert McNasty the 384th Mascot
Patches Ogilvie crew list, and William R. Harry crew lists can be seen on page xxv of the Appendices

The Only Raid of "April's Fool"
Ralph J. Hall crew's B-17 was lost on the second Hamburg raid on 25 July 1943.
The target was a diesel engine plant in Hamburg. Because of cloud cover and heavy
smoke, *April's Fool* attacked an unknown secondary target in the area. She was severely
damaged due to the heavy concentration of flak stations around Hamburg. After falling
back, she was quickly attacked by an enemy fighter, although the pilot had already set the
Fortress on auto-pilot and given the bailout order. *April's Fool*, while on fire, continued

her trek after the pilot had bailed out and crashed a few miles north of the German seaport near Glashutte. All 10 flyers safely bailed out to become prisoners of war.

Photo courtesy of Olaf Timmermann
The crew list for April's fool can be found on page xxv of the Appendices

Weary Willie's Last Raid

The second Hamburg raid also saw the loss of one of the last original crews from the 544th bomb Squadron. The Tom Estes crew seemed to be about the happiest 384th gang at Grafton Underwood. The proud crew left early on 25 July for their seventh mission and their second Hamburg raid. Their ship was hit by flak near the target and then viciously attacked by fighters on her departure route. Heading north out over the North Sea, her sister ships are outdistancing *Weary Willie*. As usual the flak damaged B-17s are falling back trying to stay in touch with the retreating raiders.

Approaching the island of Heligoland, the swarm of fighters began a ruthless attack on the battered 42-5883 *Weary Willie*. Her crew put up a valiant fight as Estes and his copilot Jim Merritt try their best to get away from the swarming fighters. With the gunners doing their utmost, Estes can feel the hammering 50 calibers and hear the crews calling out the warnings of the attacking fighters.

With only the rudder and the elevator controls left that still function Estes realized that soon the battle will be lost. Putting the B-17 into a near vertical dive in an attempt to shake one persistent Focke Wulf is the pilot's only choice. With no restraint system the gunners are thrown about as *Weary Willie* surpasses 250 miles per hour air speed. With all the shaking and banging it was worse than a high-speed ride in the back of a 1940 Ford pickup truck over a washboard road full of potholes. Or as Cochran, the top turret gunner and engineer from Texas, commented over the ten station intercom while in the dive, "this is as rough as breaking in a bronc".

Pulling 4 to 5 Gs coming out of the dive near the drink, the wings stayed on the old bird. Unfortunately, her end was approaching, as the Fortress did not have the power with only one engine to keep up her retreat. Hearing the ditching order from the pilot, every crewman began tossing everything they could lay their hands on out of the old battered Fortress. The boys even dumped their machine guns and any ammo that was left. *Weary Willie* did her best, but had simply suffered too much damage to make it home. Next to the last of the original 544th crews, she lost her battle with German fighters and became another MIA. She was ditched northwest of the island of Heligoland, Germany.

It was estimated that the Estes ship settled in the North Sea approximately 65 miles from the German mainland. Although *Weary Willie* failed to make it back to Grafton Underwood, she was gently put down on the top of a large swell. As a result all members of the crew easily and safely made it to their life rafts. A talented and confident Tom Estes and his crew watched as *Weary Willie* slowly sank into the North Sea.

After drifting for a while, one of the crewmen complimented the pilot on what a great landing he had made. Estes replied "I didn't do it, when we got down to about 20 feet above the water, I told the Lord he had control and the good Lord sure made a wonderful landing". After drifting a while longer one of the waist gunners commented to his formerly cocky crewmates; "My, my, isn't this an embarrassing situation for the *Weary Willie* crew to be in".

Drifting to the Northeast for two days, the luck of the Estes crew continued to stay with them as a Danish fisherman came to their rescue. The fisherman pulled the crew on board and headed for Denmark. Estes and his navigator, realizing they would be POWs if the boat returned to her Danish port, begged the captain to head back toward England. The fisherman agreed to help the crew but he was also concerned for his own skin. He knew the Germans would have no mercy on a Dane transporting ten 384th flyers toward England. The fisherman also had his concerns for all the dangerous mines near the English coast.

The crew decided to rig up an SOS sign on the fishing boat using their "Mae Wests". Sure enough they were spotted by a British ASR (air sea rescue) launch that came along side to bring the flyers on board and back to England. In an act of courtesy the fisherman was offered a full load of fuel. However, he explained that the Germans monitored the amount of fuel used and recorded it at each fueling. Too much fuel on board might lead to a Nazis investigation and possibly a charge for treason.

Less than three weeks after their return to Grafton Underwood, the Estes crew was back in combat participating in the Le Bourget raid on 16 August 1943.

The 379th also participated in the 25 July 1943 Hamburg raid with the loss of only two B-17s with sixteen flyers became POWs, and four of the unfortunate flyers KIA. While the 384th lost seven Fortresses with twenty-one flyers KIA, thirty-nine crewmen became POWs, yet all ten from the Estes crew returned to duty.

Sissy **Loses Her Radio Operator**

The Estes crew was credited for their 25th mission on 4 February 1944. Prior to take off, the pilot had a meeting with his crew to remind them that Captain Alfred "Coach" Nutall would be on board and that completion of this mission was their ticket home; so, "no mistakes period".

This was on the Kiel raid with their new B-17G 42-37848 *Sissy*. While approaching the target, her bomb bay doors swung open and the bombardier took control of the bomber. Inputting the necessary information into the bombsight to bring *Sissy* in line with the target, the bombardier actuated the bomb release at the correct time. Losing five thousand pounds, there was a sudden upward movement when the bomb load was released in a timed string.

The bomb bay doors did not close after bombs away and were blocking some of the ball turret gunner's sight lines. The bombardier, Joe Baggs, radioed to Fred Wagner, the radio operator, to get in the bomb bay and to manually crank the doors closed. Wagner did not need a lot of encouragement to crank the sixty plus rounds to get the doors closed as he'd had his fill of the Air Corp. With *Sissy* moving steadily along, he opened his radio room door to the bomb bay and strapped on a low-pressure oxygen bottle. Wagner plugged the hose from the bottle to his mask and began his trek across the catwalk with the wind whipping through the open doors. Wagner got a good view of the German farmland miles below. With all the wind from the open bomb bay and nothing between Wagner and German soil but a narrow piece of metal, his nerves were tested. Wagner, either didn't notice when his oxygen bottle slipped from its strapped on location, or with only three minutes of oxygen, he used up what little was in the bottle before he finished his task. Obviously, he was very involved in getting the bomb bay doors closed and once Wagner lost his oxygen bottle or lost pressure, it was just a matter of time.

Per his crewmates, Sergeant Wagner did not tumble right out of the bomb bay; instead he was seen holding on to the racks as he slowly lost consciousness while trying to hang on. Finally, he lost his grip passing on through the open bomb bay doors. While, *Sissy* roared on toward home. Wagner was now on the same route as *Sissy's* bombs albeit a few miles behind.

Wagner's crewmates watched him fall, never seeing a parachute open up. Thankfully, he was wearing his parachute and upon reaching a lower altitude, he came around. Realizing that he was rapidly approaching "Mother Earth" at over 100 miles per hour, the radio operator was able to open his parachute and land safely in the "Fatherland". Upon reaching the ground, Sergeant Fred Wagner was greeted by German soldiers, taken to an interrogator who was acutely interested in why the radio operator was the only crewmember that had parachuted out of B-17 number 42-37848. Wagner, like most of the early flyers that survived the raids, spent his remaining war years in a prisoner of war camp.

142

The bombardier got the bomb bay doors closed and the crew got credit for their 25 missions. The other members of the Estes crew were welcomed home without their radio operator. They were able to relay to Wagner's family how lucky they were to have known the radio operator and what a hero he was.

The Estes crew was first of the 384th crews to make 25 missions.

Standing L to R, McDuffie, Estes, Ursta, Merritt, Davis, Gilmore.
Kneeling L to R, Self, Wagner, Dubois, Cochran
"Sissy's" crew list when "unlucky Wagner" fell from the B-17 can be found on page xxv of the Appendices

An Unfortunate Escape from *Sugar Puss*

A replacement crew that was lost on the Hamburg raid from the 384th Bomb Group and the 544th Bomb Squadron was the Christman crew flying *Sugar Puss*. Although the crews from the 544th reached the target area, which was a diesel engine works facility in Hamburg. There was so much cloud cover and/or smoke obscuring the target that only eleven Fortresses from the 384th successfully attacked the secondary target. *Sugar Puss*, may have been struck by flak setting off an inferno in the hydraulic oil and oxygen tanks. Also a Focke Wulf 190 attacked from 11:00 o'clock knocking out the number one and number two engines.

The bombardier at his station in the nose and adjacent to the number two engine was severely wounded and never fully recovered his memory from his head injury. As a result of the loss of power from the two left engines, the Fortress went into a flat spin that the pilot could not recover from. There was such tremendous centrifugal force caused by the spin, a number of the crew were fatally trapped inside.

The crew members that did manage to escape were falling with the Fortress as she had practically lost her forward motion and there was no slip-stream to carry the men safely away from the falling craft.

Unfortunately, the navigator, Vern Dennett, after bailing out realized that his parachute became tangled in the spinning craft and he would soon join his trapped crewmates in eternity as "Sugar Puss" crashed in a German wheat field.

It was reported that the pilot, Clarence Christman, departed his B-17 42-3088 through one of the side window of the spinning craft. As a result, he lost both legs from hitting the propeller of one of the engines. Considering the raging fire in the area just behind the pilot's station, engulfing the ships ladder and bomb bay, Christman had no choice but to exit one of the pilot's side windows. An armchair Fortress pilot might have suggested that the captain should have feathered the propellers prior to his departure.

The Christman crew.

Photo courtesy of Quentin Bland
For MIA Christman crew list see page xxv of the Appendices

Sea Hag: The Engineer's Story

Jacobs, the pilot, was a big man and found that boarding through the bomb bay was just too difficult for him to squeeze between the bombs to get to the ships ladder and up to the cockpit. Thus he would always board by taking hold of the bombardiers hatch frame and curling himself up into the bombardier/navigators station. The engineer would always enter through the waist hatch. Before entering he would place his chewing gum on the exterior of the fuselage and bump it with his fist. Just like Clark Gable would do in the 1938 film "Test Pilot". The tail gunner had always signed one of the bombs "To Hell with Hitler". For some unknown reason the three flyers failed to perform their ritual before departing for the Ludwigshafen raid.

After going through the check lists, all seemed to be in order except the number four engine would not hold her rpm and would fall off 375 rpm during run up (per the rules 175 rpm fall off was all that was allowed during the pre-take off checks). The pilot assumed that a couple of cylinders had some excess oil that fouled the plugs. Normally setting the number four to full rich and after start up leaning her out would bring the engine temperature up enough to burn the oil out of the cylinders, plus it would clean up the plugs, it was thought.

The engineer requested that the pilot abort the take off with a reply that the C.O. had been all over him because of the number of aborts the crew had made. Finally, it was agreed that they would fly with the Group as far as the coast and if the problem persisted, at that point they would abort the mission. (Goetz knew the pilot well since training days and Jacobs respected his engineer's opinions, unless it meant aborting a mission.)

Reaching the coast the engineer relayed to the pilot that number four had a bad vibration and was smoking; "so turn around, Moose". The pilot who was more concerned with facing Dale O. Smith (the men of the 384th had another name for Colonel Smith as they had dropped the Dale and inserted an A.O., thus abbreviating his new nickname at the 384th) protesting the decision to turn around, Jacobs convinced the engineer to put the plan to abort to a vote.

The radio operator called all the stations on voting whether to continue the mission or to abort and the results were 6 to 4 to stay with the Group. Crossing the enemy coast the formations set their course for Ludwigshafen and her chemical plants. *Sea Hag's* number four engine was beginning to have serious problems as the right waist gunner was notifying the engineer that an enormous amount of oil was building up on the wing from the stricken engine.

The engineer kept reminding the pilot of the issues with their far right engine. He also notified the Captain that the cowling flaps were coming off of number four along with what looked like pieces of the top cylinder head had broken off. Deciding to visit the back of the ship, Goetz entered the radio room and saw a hole in the right side of the fuselage two feet in diameter ("big enough to crawl through"). After visiting the back of the plane, he returned to his station directing the pilot to turn around before it was too late.

While turning back toward England, it was estimated that the North Sea was about 75 to 100 miles distant. With the engine still running, oil had built up on the wing, Goetz said to the pilot, "you had better feather number four". The pilot turned, shook his head, as *Sea Hag's* number 4 engine's oil reservoir was empty. The same waist gunner (Gregori) called Goetz and said, "You've got a problem with the oil build up from number 4". With the oil reservoir empty, the number 4 propeller could not be feathered.

About 70 miles or so from the coast, the propeller from the right outboard engine suddenly came off sending *Sea Hag* into a spin. The pilot nosed the B-17 down telling his rookie copilot to, "Get your feet on top of the rudder bar and brace yourself". His next statement was, "You follow through with me when I say pull, PULL". With their feet braced on the bar they pulled back hard bringing *Sea Hag* out of her spin and dive near 6,000 feet. Goetz stated that, "coming out of the dive the shaking and rattling stopped, the G forces threw the waist gunners to the floor and she shuddered like hell: Hard." Goetz grabbed his chute asking Jacobs, "Should we hit the silk?" Jacobs shouted back "No"!

After pulling out of the spin, the number one engine caught fire. Goetz relates, "Heading back we were on the deck" and again with the argumentative pilot saying, "We're gonna make it". Seeing the water getting closer and closer, I told him, "We are not going to make it". With my statement and with the intercom out, Moose Jacobs told me to notify the crew to get ready to ditch. "Going through the radio room, I saw that Gregori had released the waist hatch and was getting ready to jump". Grabbing the right waist gunner and signaling the other boys in back to follow me, we headed for the radio room. When we got in the radio room, the bombardier, the navigator and the radio operator were already sitting on the floor. We all piled in, bracing ourselves the best we could against the bomb bay/radio room bulkhead. Some of the guys had their backs against the bulkhead, while others were lying on the floor with their feet up against it.

Goetz could see through the big hole in the right side of the radio room as *Sea Hag* was nearing the point of hitting the water. Just before hitting the water, he yelled out, "Here we go". The ship hit hard and the bomb bay door popped open, sending Goetz onto the catwalk of the flooded bomb bay with the navigator on top. Then *Sea Hag* went right into a ten-foot swell, stopping the Fortress hard.

Sea Hag went down in less than thirty seconds. Miraculously, all of the crew escaped the sinking B-17, except Gregori. The right waist gunner was the hero of the ditching, helping the crew out before going down with the old Fortress. Within the hour, the Royal Navy came to the rescue, delivering the flyers back to England and terra firma. The nine flyers were soon on their way to a short hospital stay and back to Grafton Underwood.

Photo courtesy of Jack Goetz.
Sea Hag Gunners wearing British Naval uniforms after their rescue and return to Grafton Underwood. Standing (L to R) Donald Gorham and Robert Compton, Kneeling Jack Goetz and Doy Cloud
*Randolph (Moose) Jacobs was one of Bill Harvey's roommates. Upon returning to base he gave the undersized sweater he received from his rescuers (His Majesty's Royal Navy) to Harvey. This sweater is part of The Bill Harvey Story.

The *Dallas Rebel* and the Runaway 50

With clear weather on the morning of 16 August 1943, the one hundred and seventy-one heavy bombers had a "demolition derby" of a day spreading over twenty-seven hundred bombs, each weighing 300 pounds across the French airfield. After bombs away and leaving the flak fields, the Groups of B-17s were flying away from their target, La Borget airport, which had been the termination point for Lindbergh's historic transatlantic flight in 1927.

Fortunately, the bombers were escorted by P-47 Thunderbolts with their new long range drop tanks. These fighters got an introduction to the dreaded yellow nose Focke Wulfs of the "Abbeville Boys", thus relieving some of the pressure from the B-17 gunners.

Robert Compton, the tail gunner on 42-5051 *Barrel House Bessie*, had already claimed two Messerschmitt Bf 109s. Compton was elated at his two victories and was receiving congratulatory calls from his crewmates via the 10-station intercom. Suddenly he was shocked back to reality to discover he was completely out of ammunition, and fighters were approaching between 7 and 7:30 o'clock. To his right a B-17 nicknamed *Dallas Rebel* was quickly moving into a tight left wing position of *Barrel House Bessie.* Bringing the two ships close together would bring more guns to bear on the enemy fighters and improve their chances of surviving the approaching attack of the 109s.

The tail gunner began calling for help to the left waist who had already engaged the enemy fighter at 7:30. Without releasing the trigger, the waist gunner moved his gun to the left picking up the Messerschmitt that was slipping toward a 6 o'clock position and was firing at his bomber's tail section. The B-17 in the left wing, *Dallas Rebel* continued to move closer in while her ball and tail gunners successfully drove off the one fighter. With the other Bf 109 moving directly behind his Fortress, the left waist gunner shot off his own left horizontal stabilizer. The continuous fire sent the enemy fighter into a spin. With shouts of victory from the crew, the gunner released his hold on his machine gun. Since the gun was hot, she kept firing. The runaway 50 caliber swung to the right firing a dozen or so bullets. The left waist suddenly had a sick feeling come over him as he realized that his gun had sent bullets into the *Dallas Rebel*.

Approaching the base, two of the Fortresses fired flares, signaling all returning B-17s to give way for wounded crewmembers. With both pilots in 42-5849 wounded in the hands and legs from a flak burst, it was a struggle to land their ship nicknamed *Helles Belles II*. Safely down and out of the way, the two pilots were quickly rushed to the base hospital.

Next the *Dallas Rebel* came in and was quickly shutdown near the waiting emergency crews, well out of the way of the other Fortresses. The 384th' remaining sixteen B-17s began touching down and taxiing to their hard stands. During approach and landing the left waist gunner on *Barrel House Bessie* had seen the emergency crews swarming around the left waist hatch of the *Dallas Rebel*. With the sick feeling returning, he along with one of his crewmates walked over to the *Dallas Rebel* and found a hole, about the size a 50 caliber bullet would make, in the right side of the fuselage in the radio room area.

Many years after the war, the waist gunner returned to the abandoned airfield at Grafton Underwood, England. Meeting with Quentin Bland, the 384th historian, he was given the location of the *Dallas Rebel's* radio operators' grave. Driving up to the American Cemetery in Cambridge, he located Melvin Feigenbaum's final resting place. Placing flowers on the grave and praying silently with his wife at his side, the old gunner finally made peace with himself after bearing this cross for over sixty years.

Flight Leader Lt. Robert E. Fortier, while flying escort duty for the La Borget raiders in his P-47D, encountered friendly fire by a B-17 gunner. The Thunderbolt was struck by three 50 caliber bullets, one about three feet aft of the cockpit, one striking the inner cooler doors, and one striking a supercharger line.

The *Dallas Rebel*, was last seen under attack by six German fighters while returning from a raid on Aklam, Germany. It was reported that she ditched in the North Sea with no survivors.

Four crewmembers from the *Dallas Rebel*

Top row unknowns
Bottom row L-R Morrison (e/ttg) Brescia (tg)

Randolph Jacobs posing with 3 of his gunners after his 25th raid

Photos courtesy of Jack Goetz.
(Left to Right) Larry Wager (left waist), Jack K. Goetz (engineer top turret) , Randolph Jacobs (pilot), Donald Gorham (radio operator gunner).after 20 March 1944 raid on Frankfurt, Germany.

After completing 25 missions Jacobs re-upped and was killed on the April 29, 1944 raid on Berlin when the cockpit was struck by a flak burst.

Chapter 16

Mourning Relatives of Charlie and his friends

Growing up about a mile from where Uncle Charlie was born was memorable. What was exciting was to visit and spend a night at Grandmother's house.

There was an upstairs room, which still had Charlie's things. On one end of the room was a short little door, which offered access to this area, the attic. Peering through the little doorway, although quite dark, you could see unfinished and unused millwork and lumber. This mysterious part of the house was forbidden. Even in Charlie's room rarely was anyone allowed to play, but I do recall finding some of the largest bullets there that I had ever seen. There were maybe five or six with the tips painted red, they were all hooked one to the other with metal clips.

Near one corner of the room was an ornate metal double bed, which you might imagine as a brass bed painted white. On this bed was an old quilt, which was covered with tiny blue flowers scattered in a recurring pattern. Opposite the bed was a dresser in which the finish was almost black. A big mirror stood on top and in the center, while a narrow drawer was on each side of the wide middle drawer.

There was a rocking chair near the stairs and another contraption shaped somewhat like a sawhorse near the rear window. The layout of Charlie's room was never changed, so Grandmother could somehow hold onto the memories by always keeping his room as he left it.

Late one afternoon I fell asleep on the bed and I remember awakening to hear Grandmother praying and asking for Jesus to please bring Charlie home. This still haunts me and was my only recollection of hearing my Grandmother in prayer other than her blessings at mealtimes. Maybe she led the congregation in prayer at our old church at Center Grove but I don't recall it. For we were always in attendance and so was Grandmother unless she was visiting or ill

Grandmother always projected a pleasant persona especially around her Grandchildren. However, her children were always concerned for her, as she never accepted Charlie's death. There was no closure for the mothers of the "missing in action".

Frank Murphy Jr. became friends with Charlie after they were both selected for the Brinkman Crew from the 379th bomb Group.

Frank perished when on 11 June 1943 their B-17 went down in a meadow just after 6:00pm, near Marx, Germany. His mother searched diligently for months, writing numerous letters to crewmate families of the Air Corp and others that Frank had mentioned in letters.

Betty Banks, editor of the Greene County Independent, rode the school bus with Frank Murphy when he lived in Benevola, Pickens County, Alabama. Betty recalled Frank's mother as withdrawn after word of his death.

After the war, Mrs. Murphy traveled by train to the St. Louis area. There, at Jefferson Barracks, she attended a memorial for Frank and three of his crewmates as they were interred in a mass grave. It was of small consolation that she met parents and relatives of three of Frank Jr.'s friends at the military cemetery, although she did try and glean information about her young son's last days while he was stationed at Kimbolton, England. After returning from Missouri, Mrs. Murphy spent the rest of her years mourning for her son Frank.

The pilot's mother was overwhelmed by the loss of her only child, Billy Brinkman, as a result of the head-on collision with the attacking German fighter. William Brinkman was brought back to Pocahontas, Iowa and interred in Clinton Garfield Cemetery. When his Mother and Father passed on, they were buried next to Billy.

Similar stories can be told about the mothers of the bombardier and the engineer/top turret gunner. Lt. Donald Andrews is resting in the American cemetery near Ardennes, Belgium. Sgt. Clarence Watkins was laid to rest in the Fort Snelling National Cemetery in South Minneapolis. Another 176,000 plus WWII dead are buried in American cemeteries around the world.

Families of Charlie's crewmates lost on the Fortress *Miss Deal* corresponded with Grandmother in their futile effort to locate their lost boys, after they received formal notices of missing in action. One of these was the mother of eighteen years old, Raymond Dodge.

All of Mrs. Dodge's letters inquired for any positive information which might give her hope for the return of Raymond. This sad story ends following the return of young Dodge's remains to Clear Lake, Wisconsin. All of his family and friends attended the moving funeral service and burial at Moe Lutheran church and cemetery. Raymond Dodge's father dropped dead the very next day. The family buried Father next to his first-born and favorite son.

The left waist gunner on *Miss Deal*, William (Red) Feagin, had married when the 384th moved to Sioux City, Iowa. So Grandmother not only faithfully wrote to Red's Mother, Lena Feagin but also stayed in touch with his wife Margaret, all the while praying that one day, she would receive some good news about her youngest, Charlie.

The pilot of *Miss Deal*, Lt. John R. Way's mother seemed to be unable to even consider that anything unfortunate could happen to her son or Charles. After the war, Tom Corrigan, the bombardier on *Miss Deal*, wrote to Bill Harvey that after visiting with the Way family he found that all but John Way's mother had accepted his death. Mary Way did her utmost to locate her son and in a letter to Grandmother she indicated that she had even written the Vatican asking for their help. She also offered the Vatican address to

Grandmother, although I never came across any evidence that there was any correspondence to Rome.

Word was never received concerning the recovery of John Way or Uncle Charlie's remains. Neither their mothers nor any mothers of the missing rarely accepted the fact of their boys' death. Rather, always believing that one day he would come home walking up that old road.

After the war's end, Charlie's good friend Robert Wilson (Dub) Wright would quite often drive down to the peaceful valley and visit his buddy's old home. He spent time with Grandmother, talking about all the old friends and neighbors. Visiting with Charlie's old pal out on that old front porch swing brought a flood of good memories and eased the loss.

Charlie's fiancée also searched numerous hospitals for Charlie and visited Grandmother often, which certainly was comforting. Eventually though, she had to get on with her life and she married and bore a daughter.

The loss of a mate was expressed to me by another aunt, while updating her on some new information during a visit. She told me that after receiving a telegram in 1943 that her husband was missing in action, she always believed that one day he would walk through that front door. "And oh my, how good life would be again"! "If only" with tears in her eyes "he could come back to me."

Grandmother like all Mothers who lost their boys in the war, mourned her son until the last day of her life.

The never-ending mourning of the parents brings to memory King David's loss in II Samuel 33. "O my son Absalom, my son, my son Absalom! Would God I had died for thee, O Absalom, my son, my son"!

Shirley Smith Haskell lost her brother, Lt. Paul Smith, when his B-17 caught fire over the Ardennes Forest on the 22nd of February 1944. While returning from a raid on the Junkers fuselage plant at Aschersleben, Germany, Smith's Fortress was suddenly attacked by 10 to 15 Me 109s. His ship 42-39809 received heavy damage with an ensuing fire, which forced the entire crew to bail out.

While escaping the burning ship Lt. Smith realized that his parachute was on fire. Unfortunately Smith had little time to ponder the fortunes of war or his rapidly approaching eternal home.

Although her mourning softened over the years she continued her annual trip to visit her brother's grave at the American Cemetery in Ardennes, Belgium. Upon learning of the loss of Charles Crawford and John Way, Shirley also annually visited the American Cemetery at Margraten, Holland, placing flowers on the Memorial Wall for both Crawford and Way.

Below is part of a letter that Shirley sent before she passed on a few years back:

I am Shirley Smith-Haskell, kid sister of Lt. Paul Matthew Smith Jr. a B-17 pilot – posted station 106 – UK –384th BG (H) 547th BS – 1943-44. Tragically my "Knight" (for such he was, and such he remains) was lost 2/22/44 – his chute failed because of flame, in the Forest of Ardennes. My "Nu-Nu" rests among his comrades. As I kneel before his cross my eyes scan the countless crosses and Stars of David --- to each I am "Sister" and each "Big Brother" to me. My pilgrimage is not made in sorrow – long passed – sorrow became triumph! Pride! Surely these valued beautiful young boys dwell in the "Splendor of Eternity"!! Small sister will seek each in the Nurseries of Heaven.

On August 15, 1945, I was at our family home in New Orleans. My school was in mid-term and I – before I returned shopped the familiar stores. I stood in a queue waiting to charge my selection when the strange words fell upon my ear – "Hiroshima" – "Atomic Bomb" – "Mushroom Cloud" - I had no need of "definition" – instinctively I knew – The war was over – I knew that never again would "Nu-Nu" toss me-squealing! – High in the air – that my "big brother world" was forever shattered. Still, my predominate thought was – our boys would come home now – our boys would not die upon the earth of the Empire of Japan!

I silently replaced the sweaters, the skirts, the "bobby sox" – I walked down Canal Street to Bourbon – to the incredible beauty of "refuge"- the Cathedral of St. Louis where I burned 2 tapers – one for those who would soon come home – one for my "Nu-Nu" and his comrades who would never – save for memory. I walked to the pew where each Eve of Christmas we sat with Nanny – Celina Cazanave – and were witness to the beauty of the mass – Celina upright and proud – Paul holding me upon his knees so I could drink deeply of the splendor of the Eucharist (we were no Roman! – Our beloved Celina was – it was enough – 2 Episcopals! One Catholic! A wondrous Mix!!)

When I emerged the "coloration of Victory". Touched all I saw – as I walked up the many steps of our Prieur Place home, I saw our mother, our father, Celina – waiting to gather me. I still recall those embraces – the tears now co-mingled with smiles – "Safe Harbor" now assured for our boys!

When I dwell upon those days – especially the "dark" – "lost" patches, I am proud of the little sister – although inexperienced in tragedy – and so very young – she was the one to lead her mother – her father back to life. I am humble before this gift of God.

After reading the story about the loss of Charles Crawford and John Way, by Doug Gross, in **B-17 Combat Crewmen & Wingmen**, Shirley Smith Haskell had flowers placed in their memory on the wall of the missing at the American Cemetery at Margraten, Holland. This occurred during her annual pilgrimage visiting her brother's grave at the American Cemetery in Ardennes, Belgium.

After completing 25 missions 384th airmen were allowed to return home. However, at the completion of the 25th 384th raid at the Nantes submarine repair facility on 23 September 1943, the B-17F 42-3459 *Jolly Roger* was lost. This was the 43rd 384th B-17 that crashed since the Group arrived with 36 new bombers and their crews. Obviously, the odds of surviving 25 missions before long-range fighter escorts was dismal.

Chapter 17

Events in Charlie's War

Training

On the 27th of April 1939, Charles Earl Crawford graduated from Cotaco High School in north Alabama at the age of nineteen. His father had passed on a year earlier, leaving him pretty much alone with his mother. The youngest of ten children, Charlie had to listen to all the wisdom of his older brothers and sisters. This was probably enough to encourage anyone to strike out on their own

By the time Charlie was twenty years old he and his buddy, Arvil McKee, were working for AT&T building phone lines in the South. They were hired at Decatur, Alabama where they boarded with Charlie's sister Elsie and her husband R. Leldon Penn for about three months. They belonged to a ten-man crew that was transferred to the Mobile area.

In October 1941, after being drafted, Charlie learned the Army's art of cooking at Ft. McClellan, Alabama. Here he was induced to resign and re-enlist in the Army Air Corp. It should be noted that there is a document with a date of July 8, 1941, that indicates that Charles E. Crawford had applied for appointment as an aviation cadet.

By the middle of December 1941, Charlie was in the 417th School Squadron of the Air Cadet Training School at Sheppard Field near Wichita Falls, Texas. At Sheppard Field he sent a letter back home noting that there were 15,000 Air Corp trainees and six airplanes. Next, we find that in April 1942 he was in the 417th Technical school Squadron in Fort Sill, Oklahoma, training as a radio operator. Here he applied to purchase savings bonds through the pay reservation system.

In August, he was back at Sheppard Field sitting in a dentist chair. In the month of September, he completed a course in arithmetic from Scott Field in Illinois. So much for pilot training.

Finally, in September 1942 after an additional four months training at Sheppard Field, Charlie apparently completed all his courses as a Radio Operator. His training records are skimpy at best and it is assumed that his training as a radio operator was at Fort Sill and Sheppard Field. Fort Scott also had a radio operator school as evidenced by an acquaintance of Charlie's from Hulaco, Alabama --- Willie Price, who was attending there while Charlie was at Sheppard.

Radio Operator: The Army Air Corp
Training for radio operator was as demanding as any position in the military as trainees would spend six months, twelve hours a day, seven days a week in training.

By graduation the radio operators had been physically and mentally prepared to take their position in combat. Following graduation, the minimum proficiency in Morse code was sixteen words per minute. Plus, he had to be able to operate communication equipment carried on a B-17. This included an FM transmitter for communication between B-17s, a continuous wave transmitter, an AM transmitter for long distance phone operation, a radio compass, an advanced short wave radio, plus a ten-station Intercom. The radio operator would utilize the radio for direction finding and pass the information along to the navigator or pilot.

The ten-station intercom was very important as there was near continuous checking of each position for each crewman's well-being. Also during fighter attacks, the crews could work as a combat team sharing information to defend their Fortress.

(With Charlie's experience working for AT&T, he would have probably been an excellent candidate for base maintenance of telephone equipment, radio equipment maintenance, and continuous development of base communication equipment.)

On the 17th of September, he was promoted to Private, which probably indicates that he was nearing completion of this phase of training. Ten days later, he was in the 927th Guard Squadron at Sheppard. This was prior to shipping out to Las Vegas, Nevada. On October 12, 1942, Charlie was a member of the class 42-45 in the Air Corp Gunnery School in Las Vegas. We have very little information on Charlie's Gunnery training other than from an interview with Jack Goetz during a 384th reunion at Wright Patterson near Dayton, Ohio, which would have been similar.

Operating the ball turret was a bit different from the other stations, as the operator would be lying on his back with very little protection from flak or the fighters. The tight quarters prevented the wearing of a parachute except for the smallest of gunners. The ball was actually suspended on a shaft that appeared to be similar to an automobiles drive shaft. The aiming of the twin fifty calibers was accomplished by a computing gun-sight. All the WWII so called computing gun-sights were gyroscopic. The bullet proof circular sight/aiming glass was between the gunners legs, with a foot rest on each side. One foot rest pedal operated the 10 station intercom while the other foot operated the gun sight. Also the gunner had to input the type of fighter. The aiming glass had one horizontal reticle lines with a vertical reticle line on each end. The gunner would bring the fighter's fuselage on the horizontal reticle while closing the two verticals on each wing tip. With the correct fighter inputted, then the gun sight knew the target's wingspan. The distance between the vertical lines told the gun sight the range of the target. As the fighter closed on the bomber, the gunner operated the left pedal to keep the lines on the wingtips. This told the gun sight the rate of closure. The rate at which the turret turned, computed the targets speed relative to the bomber. Once the gunner had the fighter in the reticles and within range, he would be the victor. All this was to reduce the problem for the gunner on how much to lead the target so that the bullets would meet the target aircraft at a point in space to score hits on the target.

In October 1942, Charlie sent a letter home indicating that he liked to listen to the Blues network and liked the sounds from Bob Chester and his band.*

On the 9th of November, he was promoted to the rank of Sergeant, another indication that he was ready to take a position on a B-17.

Next, Charlie and most of the gunnery students in his class were sent to the Army Air Base in Salt Lake City, Utah. Here, he and five other gunners were selected for the Brinkman crew.

The Brinkman Crew was assigned to the provisional Squadron "C" at the Army Air Base, Salt Lake City, Utah. Two days later the crew was re-assigned to the 411th Squadron of the 29th bomb Group in Gowen Field, Idaho. Here the 379th bomb Group was formed with the 524th, the 525th, the 526th and the 527th Squadrons making up the Group.

Of interest, it was learned by the Group's personnel that most all the homes in Gowen were heated by water piped in from the local hot springs.

Charlie and the Brinkman crew in ship number 42-29892, along with the crew assigned to the *Tondelayo* were part of the 527th Squadron. Most of Charlie's closest training friends were in these two crews during their final training and when heading overseas.

A few weeks later the 379th was moved down to Wendover, Nevada. Here training continued for the gunners as they became acquainted with the different stations. Many of the captains allowed each of the crewmembers to take turns at the Fortresses controls. This would certainly help offset the boring flights and add to the crew's team spirit. During bombing practice and close formation work, the pilot kept everyone at his station, as this required his full attention.

While stationed at Wendover, Charlie acknowledged that his Uncle Lewis Prince had died from injuries he received after being struck by an automobile in Oklahoma City.

In February 1943 the 379th while moving by train toward Sioux City, a coal and water stop was made at North Platte, Nebraska. This ten-minute stop allowed the troops some time to enjoy the free beverages and food furnished and prepared by the area farm families.

After the customary two blasts from the train whistle, the troops cleared out, as their train continued its eastward journey. It took another full day of riding the rails before Charlie and the 379th reached Sioux City, Iowa.

Sioux City is where most of the 379th crews would receive their new Boeing B-17 for their final phase training and then on to the European theatre.

*Unknown to Charlie, in seven months his pilot would be John Way who before his entry into the Air Corp had been employed by Glenn Miller.

With the terrible winter weather in Sioux City, the 379th moved down to El Paso. Here the crews were introduced to a number of returning Air Corp veterans from the ETO. These combat veterans gave a number of motivational lectures, which seemed to have a positive effect on Charlie's outlook on his participation in the coming air war. In a letter to home he indicated that he didn't think Germany would be much of a problem.

In late March 1943, the 379th Air Echelon completed their training. Brinkman and the other crews received their final furloughs for a visit home. Charlie and his crewmate Frank Murphy rode the trains together on their way to Alabama. Murphy was a farm boy from Benevola, which is in Pickens County near Gordo.

On Charlie's return to Sioux City, he boarded the train at Decatur, Alabama. In a letter to his Mother, he stated that once he boarded, the train was so crowded he could not move to get a final glimpse of her.

Charlie wrote little about his train travels, but we know the 384th's Ground Echelon traveled by train to the various bases during each phase of training.

The last Train Ride
Charlie's crewmates and friends that made a final ride by train were: Sergeant Raymond Dodge whose remains were shipped to Clear Lake, Wisconsin and interred next to his Father at Moe Lutheran cemetery. 1st Lieutenant William F. Brinkman whose final interment was adjacent to his Mother and Father at Clinton – Garfield Cemetery Rolfe, Pocahontas County, Iowa.
William A. Carver, Robert B. Todd, Ralph J. Smith, and Frank Murphy Jr. are all resting in a mass grave at Jefferson Barracks, MO., arriving by train after their crossing of the Atlantic by freighter.

Photo of troops in the North Platte Canteen

On 25 June 1943 *Miss Deal* leaving her target was struck in the ball turret by flak. Charlie was moved to the radio room, where a Messerschmitt Bf 109 raked the Fortress 42-30049 with her 20 mm cannons. For Charlie the war is over.

157

Chapter 18

The Search for Clues

After nearly two years and hundreds of phone calls, plus letter writing to members of the crews of the 379th and 384th Bomb Groups, we found Albert Westlake. He was the tail-gunner who was put on Uncle Charlie's plane at the last minute. We also located Stephen Fabian in Ohio, the copilot for the fatal mission.

Albert Westlake lived in Brighton, Colorado with his wife, Marie. Al invited us for a visit and agreed to answer any questions we might have. As it turned out, my brother Joe had a business meeting in Denver prior to my appointment with Mr. Westlake and he agreed to stay over and go to Brighton with me. We had a bit of a time locating Al and Marie's bungalow near downtown Brighton. After a little backtracking, we navigated to the correct address. Al got right down to business, while Marie kept the coffee flowing.

Al quickly revealed how vicious was the battle between the B-17 gunners and the fighter pilots defending their Fatherland. He recalled that he was wounded defending the tail of the B-17 and a guy was lying in the radio room, also apparently wounded.

Al also observed that the right waist gunner lost his duel with a German fighter after a strike by an exploding 20 millimeter shell. During all this carnage, the left waist gunner, although wounded, continued his mortal engagement with another German fighter.

All this left us with lots of questions that we needed to get answered. Mr. Westlake told us that when *Miss Deal* exploded, he had been blown from the plane and came down next to one of the gunners that he thought was Raymond Dodge. However, he was probably confused as Dodge had no hands and could not have opened his chute. This left three individuals that could have come down next to the tail gunner, John Way, Charles Crawford or Red Feagin.

Westlake also related that he was hospitalized in Emden and that later in his life he corresponded with another airman named Stew Cooper who also had been hospitalized in Emden. Mr. Cooper revealed to Westlake that while in the hospital, an orderly had indicated that an American flyer had been brought in with a severe neck wound. Unfortunately, the doctor could not save this American soldier. Who was this American airman? Westlake gave me copies of Cooper's relevant correspondence, which is another part of this story.

In early November 2002, my wife Betsy and I visited with Quentin Bland the historian for the 384th Bomb Group. Quentin lived in the village of Grafton Underwood, England with his wife, Barbara. This village was adjacent to the 384th Bomb Group's old airbase, also known as Station 106.

What remains of this old airfield consists of a few old buildings and an area for armament storage. All the hardstands, taxiways, and runways, had been reclaimed as farmland.

Airmen from the 384th rode their bicycles to the nearby village of Brigstock frequenting its several pubs. This quaint little village was only 3 miles to the northeast. One notable flyer from the 351st, Clark Gable kept an upstairs room at the pub known as "Old Three Cocks" for his private retreat. Gable was very fond of this little town and it was rumored that he enjoyed competing at cards. Considering that Gable survived 24 missions, then perhaps lady luck stayed with him at his card games.

Soon we were meeting with air war historians in Holland and Germany. We enjoyed meeting Ab Jansen. Ab is a researcher, writer and author, who has spent most of his life compiling and documenting information on the air war, with excellent historical books on the Allied raids and the Axis fighters defending their country. Mr. Jansen and his fellow researchers supplied much information and provided meetings that were priceless in our research.

Lenny Schrik, one of Ab Jansen fellow researchers, proved most helpful in providing information and introducing us to additional researchers that specialized in different air war areas. Lenny was very knowledgeable on Luftwaffe fighter history. His research on the missing Messerschmitt Bf 109 G and her pilot Albert Oexle provided the information that led to their recovery. Both were lost on 25 June 1943. See recovery photos below courtesy of Lenny Schrik.

Photo 1

Recovery operation has begun by the Royal Dutch Air Force

Photo 2

Control building for the recovery operation in september1999

Photo 3

The recovered armament is in good condition

Photo 4

Cleaning of one of the Bf 109's propeller blades

Lenny had arranged a meeting with the Mayor's office at Finsterwolde in an attempt to enlist his help in locating and raising the wreck of *Miss Deal*. This was such a surprise and reflected Lenny's intensity in his research work. We also visited one of the village cemeteries where Lenny pointed out graves of the three Dutchmen that he believed were killed when *Miss Deal* salvoed her bomb load so that the crew could bail out. The three men were working on a farm adjacent to the inner dike of the Dollard and about nine or ten kilometers from where *Miss Deal* is lying. This farmland is known as Carel Coenraad polder and lies within a line from the wreck of *Miss Deal* to the recovery location of Albert Oexle and his Messerschmitt Bf 109.

Above photograph: Lenny Schrik, the Dutch airwar historian who chose the date 25 June 1943 as his primary research date. Picture taken near buoy 17, the general crash location of 'Miss Deal's" tail section. Background diver departing in his zodiac, in the distance is Germany.

Olaf Timmermann pictured on one of the big gun turrets at Fiemel pointing toward Emden. Olaf is the dedicated Ostfriesland airwar historian who supplied many original images and documents necessary for completing this work.

Numerous meetings with Olaf Timmermann, a German air war historian, resulted in his sharing of documents that he had accumulated over the years concerning the area air crashes of June 25, 1943. He loaned us a good number of these documents, which led to a few more questions. Late one day, Olaf went with us to small German villages on the east side of the Dollard, putting up posters requesting any information concerning the crash of *Miss Deal*.

While on the east side of the Dollard, we walked the area on the dike where Raymond Dodge, *Miss Deal's* right waist gunner, and another unknown washed up. This area of rich farmland is known as Kanal Polder and is adjacent to the frontier between Germany and Holland. The recovery location is three to five kilometers west of the German village of Ditzumer-Verlaat.

A preplanned meeting was held with the Minister of The Northern Water District and his staff in Delfzijl; this was attended by another air war researcher, Sicco De Vries, and lasted for over two hours. The members of the Water District were concerned with any wrecks lying in their waters and any search plans, as there were areas relegated to wildlife management and entry was prohibited.

There was some confusion as to the exact location of *Miss Deal*, as it was the general consensus that she had broken into two parts, and the tail section was near Buoy 7 and the fuselage was on the Maanplaat**. The Minister indicated the location of additional wrecks lying in the Dollard.

*Dollard an inland sea, is spelled Dollart in German.
**Documents acquired later reflect that *Miss Deal* broke into three large sections. Maanplaat means moon plateau.

A meeting at the Emden hospital proved somewhat fruitful considering that the archives were searched for a Charles Crawford. Like the Minister's staff at the Northern Water District, the doctors and the hospital management were very understanding and congenial. The same can be said for the Emden librarian who provided assistance in searching and reviewing of old documents.

Another most interesting meeting was with the old retired fisherman, Pieter Kolthof, who lived by a canal near Nieuw-Beerta. Kolthof had visited *Miss Deal's* tail section following the crash. He described her condition as having numerous tears and holes in her seven-meter length. Also of interest, was the fact that the twin machine guns were still protruding from the tail and appeared to be in good shape, "like a stinger".

Franz Lenselink and his friends at the Emden Bunker Museum, supplied information they had for 25 June 1943. Franz was able to supply information on the naval flak stations in the Emden and the Dollard area. The Bunker Museum sent the content of a report for 25 June 43, which stated: "one observed which fell an airplane burning from the clouds or in 220 degrees". Per Franz, this was from a Naval observing station in Emden and the 220 degrees would have approximated the direction of the crash site from the center of Emden.

One of the most interesting meetings was held in the home of Mr. and Mrs. Roel Nap. They resided in the little village named Oude Pekela, which like most of the Dutch towns in this area, had her canal. This meeting, like many that we had in Dutch homes, was very hospitable with the matron serving everyone coffee along with sweets.

Roel spent several minutes telling about his experience as a young boy while at school on the morning of June 25, 1943. I began questioning him about the air battle that he witnessed and he indicated that the American bomber was visible and perhaps at 6,000 meters in altitude. He stated that the fighter was approaching the bomber very rapidly and he could see tracers emanating from both planes. I showed Mr. Nap a picture of a B-17 and asked if he could identify from where the tracers were coming. He pointed out the left waist, and indicated that the fighter came down near their school. I was surprised that he correctly identified the left waist and thus realized that this engagement must have occurred where Lenny believed that *Miss Deal* released her bombs. This would have put the air battle witnessed by Roel Nap within about three miles of his school. Also, Mr. Nap stated that while the fighter was coming down in the direction of Finsterwolde, the bomber was moving off over the Dollard in the opposite and general direction of Emden. Also of interest, he said that he did not see nor hear the bomber explode. He stated that he counted four parachutes leave the airplane, while his father told him at dinner that evening that there had actually been five fliers that came out of the bomber by parachute.

Of all the documents that we were privileged to study, the most intriguing, were produced by the American Graves Registration Command (AGRC). These documents were the results of two investigations following the war.

One report was dated 17 December 1948 while the other had a date of 14 June 1944. The latter date is questionable as this area of Holland was one of the last areas liberated by the Allies.

The report of 1948 actually refers to two plane crashes. An interview with the chief of the Water Police revealed that three planes had crashed in the Dollard during the war. Besides *Miss Deal*, a British Lancaster had also gone down. The Chief may have been also referring to a de Havilland Mosquito, which per Dutch researchers, crashed in the southwest part of the Dollard, as the third plane. Other researchers have indicated that a fourth plane, a German fighter, crashed north of where *Miss Deal* is lying. Although the investigator in his conclusion, thought the third plane crashed near Rysum, Germany. The police chief's Master Policeman, Bayon, assisted the Army in the investigation and indicated that one crash site was about 10 kilometers west of Ditzum (*Miss Deal*?), and per his recollection, four flyers were taken prisoner, while an additional crewman was taken to a navy hospital in Emden.

A Mr. Pastoor, one of the witnesses, refers to a crash in the early morning, "about 0300 hours", when he saw a burning four motored plane coming from Emden, crash about six kilometers west of Ditzumer Verlaat. This was, apparently, a British bomber lost on a night raid, as the liftoff for the Hamburg raid was between 0400 and 0500.

Mr. Pastoor further described how he and another fisherman going out on the Dollard with their sleds in the darkness, led three flyers ashore. The tide was rising and they were in impending danger of drowning. After the crewmen were led ashore, they were taken prisoner by The Coast Battery Polder. The following day, Mr. Pastoor* went out to the wreck with several other fishermen and one (1) deceased was found next to the plane in the direction of Heintz Polder. He brought this body to shore and delivered it to the coast battery. The present whereabouts is unknown to him. He only remembered that this body had a left fractured leg and that one of the crew was a tall Lieutenant who spoke "perfect German." On the date of the interview with the Captain, Mr. Pastoor indicated that he thought that some of the wreck might still be visible, and that two months earlier, he thought he had spotted some remains of the wreck.

The investigator Captain Herbert L Swanson reported that the Water Police Chief, Mr. Knut, supplied the searchers with boats and they navigated out on the Dollard. Coming alongside a Dutch fishing boat, they were informed by her Captain, that he had personal knowledge about two plane crashes. One plane crashed in the Maanplaaten, and a second one crashed right next to the buoy number 7. The fisherman stated that he was certain that the plane that crashed near the buoy was still where it originally went down.

The dedication of Captain Swanson and the AGRC to locate one of the planes is noted by the following statement, which is assuming that the bottom of the Dollard at the Maanplaaten was similar to the bottom near Buoy 7.

The statement by Captain Swanson: "On the next day, we returned to Ditzumer Verlaat and in the company of Mr. Pastoor. At 0500 hours, started a walk of about six kilometers through the mud in an effort to locate the wreckage of the plane, which crashed in the Maanplaaten. During the walk, we were unable to locate a single piece of a plane and even at sunrise, nothing could be sighted."

The rest of Captain Swanson's narrative: "After returning, we questioned several more people but could not obtain any further information except the statement given by Mr. Wenninger**, former member of the Battery Polder. He stated that four (4) instead of three (3) prisoners were taken and that some of his friends will still be in possession of pictures taken one day after the plane crashed". The four prisoners brings *Miss Deal's* crew back into the picture concerning the Maanplaaten as, Hill, Gadomski, Fabian and Corrigan were POWs brought together by the Germans after the crash, as Westlake was taken to the hospital in Emden and Janson had jumped earlier and was taken to a hospital in Papenburg. Swanson continued his narrative about the pictures: "He (Wenninger) is now trying to get the pictures and he will forward them to this headquarters as soon as possible. Later, Mr. Pastoor and the other witnesses remembered that one (1) additional body was found in the seaweeds not far from the Polder Battery. At that time, Mr. Pastoor*** marked the place and later the body was picked up by members of this Battery. This body did not have a head and none of the witnesses knew whether or not papers or identification tags were found on the body. Also, the whereabouts of this body is unknown to these people."

CONCLUSION:
According to all circumstances and statements obtained, it seems to be that subject plane may be the one which crashed at Maanplaaten about 6 km west of Ditzum Verlaat (see attached sketch). It is certain that this plane wreckage will be under mud and probably unrecoverable. When Mr. Karl mentioned five (5) airmen he saw, it is possible that he saw the three (3) crewmembers mentioned by Mr. Pastoor and Mr. Pastoor and the other fisherman who accompanied the airmen to safety. The fourth prisoner mentioned by Mr. Wenninger presumably tried to reach the coast by himself, and was not sighted by Mr. Pastoor. If this is the plane in question, Sgt. Westlake was found somewhere else near Emden by the Navy Observing Station and brought to the hospital. The other three (3) still missing crewmembers presumably drowned while trying to reach the coast or after jumping from the plane prior to the crash.
Search of records of this headquarters shows that the last mentioned body and marked as No. 3 on sketch, are the remains of Dodge, Raymond E. Information about body No. 2 (see sketch) – the one found next to the crash plane, could not be obtained yet. The third plane crash we learned about occurred near Rysum but date and circumstances do not correspond with subject case.

Evert Pastoor

Photo courtesy of Harm Pastoor III
Picture is stamped with Hankenkreuse

*Evert Pastoor, the fisherman who led three flyers to safety.

**Mr. Wenninger, the spelling is incorrect, Lubbert Wenninga was the individual whose friends had pictures of the wreck of *Miss Deal*.

***Harm Pastoor, the brother of Evert Pastoor, found Raymond Dodge's body washed up on the dike.

<u>*RECOMMENDATION:*</u>

It is recommended that an additional investigation be conducted in the same area in an effort to obtain the correct dates of the plane crashes in Maanplaaten and near Buoy* No. 7 and to locate the three (3) still missing crew members which might have been washed ashore on the Dutch side. It is, also, recommended that an office investigation be conducted in an effort to establish the name of body No. 2 (see sketch) which might have been temporarily buried in Wittmund, Germany. The establishment of his name will show what plane crashed at Maanplaaten. Statements obtained concerning the second plane crash do not correspond. Some people stated that the plane crashed in 1943 while others said it crashed in 1944, therefore, as long as the name of body No. 2 or the correct date of these plane crashes are not known, it is impossible to say which of these two (2) is the subject plane. If the one at Maanplaaten is not the subject plane, the possibility exists that the second plane which crashed into the water next to the buoy No. 7 is the plane in question. The second plane is about ten (10) feet under water (at low tide) and it would not be too difficult to salvage the wreckage of this plane by divers.

ADDITIONAL NOTES:

a) *A phone call with the Burgenmeister of Nieuw Beerta that the body found by Mr. Karl and mentioned as washed ashore at Nieuw Beerta** in basic documents are the remains of Feagin, William R. ****

b) *Examination of records pertaining to unknowns recovered from the North Sea indicate a possible association with No. X-1448 (Neuville-en Condroz) with Sgt. Charles E. Crawford, one of those missing in this case.*

Peer O. Witthaus
Interpeter

s/t/ Herbert L. Swanson
Capt. Inf. O-33645
Investigator

Raymond Dodge, Right Waist Gunner on the B-17F
42-30049 *Miss Deal*

Photo courtesy of the Dodge family

*Buoy 7 location is now marked by Buoy 17
**The village of Nieuwe Beerta does not physically adjoin the Dollard
***Feagin, William R. was recovered by two fishermen that worked the Dollard.

This is the second narrative of the follow-up investigation by Hendrick L. Veigh.

NARRATIVE

As ordered in paragraph 2 of Basic Communication, an investigation was made of the Dutch side of the Dollart-Emden bay. Washed ashore Americans who may possibly be associated with Lt. John R. Way and for S/Sgt. Charles E. Crawford. Every town, village, and hamlet from Nieuwe Schans, on the German border till Uitwierda (North of Delfzijl), were thoroughly investigated. Investigations and subsequent statements show that all American personnel that met with death in this coastal region, either through plane crash or drowning, were identified by the Germans and after the liberation recovered by AGRC.

All other military personnel buried in this region have been definitely identified by name, rank and serial number as non-American.

Conclusion: Attention is invited to the attached sketch. According to this sketch William R. Feagin was recovered in Nieuwe Beerta. Remains 2 and 3 washed ashore at the German side of the border. Remains 2 were identified as S/Sgt Raymond E. Dodge. Sketch also states that Dodge was recovered from Wittmund. On checking map of Germany, it was found that Wittmund is situated about 31 miles N.E. of Emden, roughly between Emden and Wilhelmshaven, and only a few miles from the German coast, opposite the German Frisian Islands. It is nigh impossible to believe that even the Germans would go through the trouble of transporting the remains found at the spot indicated on the sketch, to a town situated between Emden and Wilhelmshaven. *

The sketch does not say what happened to remains 3. If Dodge washed ashore close to the town from which he was recovered, it is evident that remains 2 and 3 are the remains of Way and Crawford. If the area in which 2 and 3 washed ashore has not yet been searched for the remains of Way and Crawford, it is requested that this area be investigated.

If this investigation proves negative, it is recommended that an effort be made to lift the cockpit of the A/C in question.

/s/t/ HENDRICK L. VEIGH D-150596
INVESTIGATOR

*It is apparent that this investigator was ignorant of German protocol concerning the recovery and disposition of Allied flyers. The German Air Force was responsible for the recovery of crashed airplanes and flyers, and at Wittmund was a fighter base and the headquarters of the responsible commander for this area of Northwest Germany.

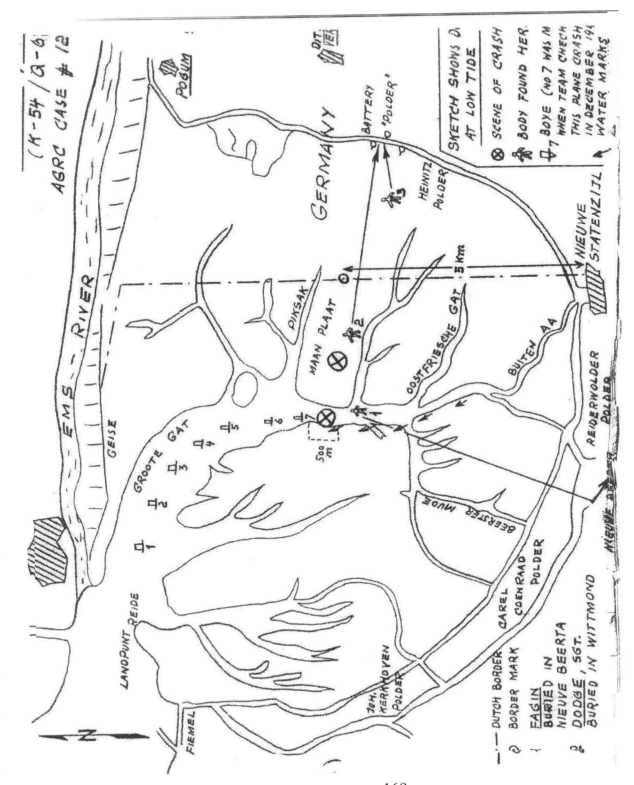

The Searchers with the Dutch witness.

Back row: Lenny Schrik, Roel Nap (The Witness), Betsy and Tony Crawford
Front Row: Sicco de Vries, Lottie and Ab Jansen

The Dollard Trip

We met our friends Ab and Lottie Jansen when we arrived at the Delfzijl docks to board the dive boat Zeester. Betsy and I had another good friend Lenny Schrik, in tow (Lenny a studious air war researcher who located and recovered the Bf 109 near Finstewolde, Holland with the pilot Albert Oexle still entombed in his fighter). As usual some were late for the departure time for our Dollard expedition. Also, already on board were some old fishermen who were aware of the crash site of *Miss Deal*. One old fisherman named de Boer, later stated that he and a friend recovered one flyer's remains that had been removed from the wreck by a Group of "Hitler Youths" that had placed him face down in the mud of the Dollard. De Boer stated that after the youths left, the deceased flyer was taken to the German military station at Pogum, Germany.

The Expedition in search of the B-17F *Miss Deal*, by Ab Jansen
This story was on the weekend of 4 October 2003 aboard the Zeester, a tour-boat captained by Klaas Koch of Groningen. Tony Crawford hired the boat and crew for the search-trip on the Dollard. Lenny had arranged the presence of a diving-team with rubber-boat and technical equipment to search for the wreckage of *Miss Deal*. It was a mixed company: besides the ship's crew and Tony Crawford, his wife Betsy and cousin Richard Penn, a number of eyewitnesses, including a few fishermen in their eighties, a journalist, tour organizer Lenny Schrik, the Ostfrisian air war historian Olaf Timmermann, and this author.

That whole week the weather forecast had been particularly unfavorable and indeed it was as it usually is in October in these parts: heavy overcast, windy and rainy. But the "Zeester" had a spacious cozy cabin, there was coffee and "grub and bub", so that the occasional showers could not do much harm.

Though the search party, equipped with modern metal-detecting devices, searched the presumable crash-location for hours, at first solely by boat, later when the tide was low, by foot, not the tiniest bit of the aircraft was found. Disappointing? Yes, of course, but not unexpected. After all, the Dollard is a large sheet of water and also sea-bottoms do change, certainly in the course of some 60 years! Notwithstanding this, it was a perfect day.

A dreadful find
The same weekend of 4 October 2003 ex-fisherman Simon de Boer (82) told us that some five or six days after the crash, a colleague had come to him saying: "Good heavens, hear what happened to me: I found a dead guy in my nets." Simon went with him and saw a heavily clothed man hanging over his nets with his head and arms down. He was clad in a coverall, had a flying helmet on his head, and an oxygen-mask covering his mouth and – as would turn out later – heavy fliers' boots at his feet. When they could not possibly get the water-logged airman into their boat, they decided to tug him to Nieuw-Statenzijl.

The conclusion of his account is just dreadful: by order of the Germans (practically each village had some 'garrison') the fishermen were not allowed to take the body ashore. "And so it was lying there in the waste water for about a week, before it was finally pulled out," Simon told us, still with indignation in his voice. In the boots that had to be cut from the swollen legs, the Germans found some paper money, no doubt belonging to the man's escape-kit. The corpse was then buried in Nieuw-Beerta. This information identifies this crewman as S/Sgt. William R. Feagin, the right waist-gunner. He is now resting in the U.S. National Cemetery at Arlington, Washington D.C.

Additional Search Clues:
I received e-mails and letters from Jan Stegmeijier, a Dutch air war enthusiast and writer that we had visited a number of times. Jan lived with his wife Riek in Woldendorp, Holland. On one visit he showed us a 24-volt generator, which he implied came from

one of *Miss Deal's* engines. Also it was recovered from the nets of a fishing boat. Another gift from the Stegmeijiers was a brass hook-on device that was removed from *Miss Deal*. This device came from Pieter Kolthof and he apparently had another connecting part that was used to mount the carbine scabbard to the radio room/waist bulkhead.   In one of the e-mails Jan stated that the fisherman Kuiper had removed two engines from the B-17 that crashed near the sandbank. One engine was removed 10 to 15 years after the crash and sold to the son of a vicar that was living in the area of Emden.

The Wellington lost in the Dollard   from Ab A. Jansen. Wespennest Leeuwarden. DI. I. Pg 196

Crash of Vickers Wellington DV423 of 304 Squadron from Polish Air Force the night of 10 or 11 January 1942. The Polish Squadron was based in Lindholme, England and lifted off at 1741 hours. There were 7 Wellingtons in the 304 that attacked the Wilhelmshaven railway station. Two of the Wellingtons were lost in the 10 January Wilhelmshaven raid. A German night fighter, that was based in Wittmund, Germany, claimed one of the bombers from the Polish Squadron. The German pilot was Oblt. Schoenert.

Wellington DV423 304 Polish Squadron
Pilot Officer	+J. Zajac
Second Pilot, Sergeant	+Stanislaw Garstka
Pilot Officer, Observer	+Josef Mazynski
Radio Operator Gunner, Sergeant	+Jacek Stryzewski
Air Gunner, Flying Officer	+Tadensz Klewicz
Air Gunner, Sergeant	+R. Pokrzywa
All were assumed as KIA	

Perhaps this was the early morning bomber that Pastoor went out on the Dollart and rescued four flyers. Although this was a two engine bomber that came down in the Dollart, 18 months before the crash of *Miss Deal*.

Olaf Timmermann, the Ostfrisian airwar historian indicated that a B-17 made a belly landing in the Dollart on 17 April 1943. The target on 17 April 1943 was Bremen, Germany. Sixteen B-17s from the 91st and 306th Bomb Groups were lost that day.
The bomber that may have crashed in the Dollart on that date has not been identified or verified.

Chapter 19

Riddles and The Good Germans

The following two letters seem to imply that perhaps John Way or Charles Crawford's remains may have been recovered.

Translated letter from the mayor of Finsterwolde, Netherlands. Presumably sent to Charles Crawford's sister, Miss Gay Nell Crawford, from the Mayor in 1955. *In reference to your letter of May 31, 1955 the fisherman lived in my community. Fisherman Tammo Kuiper had confirmed that during the war years an American airplane, a Boeing, had crashed in the region of the Netherlands. During that time the place where the airplane crashed was evident. Now everything has sunk to the bottom. However, Kuiper can point out the place where the remains of the airplane existed. The airplane has not been raised and would have to be removed.*

The fisherman, Imko Bakker lived here. His nets set down where the airplane had crashed. On July 7, 1943 he found the bodies of some flyers. The parachutes of the flyers sat on one of his net's poles. Bakker asked his colleague from Nieuwe-Statenzijl, where at that time the German military station was. Where did they give up the bodies? Presumably, these are the bodies of the flyers. They were hidden in the deep water and were buried in Wittmund.

The wreck of the airplane was not raised and surely can accept that the eight crewmen were wounded and in the deep ground they disappeared.
It is from me that all the Mothers share their sacrifice with you. One way or the other, I wanted you to know. In advance, I will gladly give you any further information.
With my deepest respect,
The Mayor of Finsterwolde
Translation by Lenny Schrik

Translated letter from German Red Cross, Emden office 8 June 1955.
In my letter of June 2, 1955, that I sent you, the Holland (Dutch) fisherman had attempted to lift the wreck and I wrote to the mayor in Rheiderwildersiel and requested some information.

Only today did I receive an answer from the mayor (which was in the Dutch language). I have the letter that the Holland consulate left with the transcripts for your information. From the letter of the mayors, it is apparent that the wreck still lays there today in the Dollart and is not going to be raised.

I will later inquire into this business. The mayor writes that on July 7, 1943, fisherman Imko Bakker found the bodies (corpses) of the flyers. The letter from IRRK, Geneva on

*January 13, 1955, he said the body of Raymond E. Dodge was found on August 26 1943.
It supports the opinion that two bodies were found. It now needs to be clarified where
they found the two bodies on July 7, 1943. Also that he died with his parachute. Perhaps
your brother could ask for it.* (Tony, I am not sure if that previous sentence is translated
correctly. Or perhaps it says that the parachute opened but that your brother was unable
to survive.)

*As I already mentioned, I will continue to attempt to clarify this matter. I will gladly tell
you any results that I have to report.
With friendly greetings,
Adolf Siefkes, Eggenastr. 24*
Translated by Lenny Schrik

The following statement leads us to believe that the remains of Charles Crawford and
certainly John Way are still in the wreck that is lying in the Dollart:

Mr. Meinto Oosterhuis, address A-253 Drieborg, Community of Beerta, declared that 25
June 1943 at about 1100 hours, he was fishing on the Dollart when he saw a four engined
American bomber, flying above the Dollart, was attacked by several German fighter
planes. The American plane exploded in the air and came down in three large pieces.
The cockpit crashed into the water about 200 meters south of the southern tip of the
sandbank "Maanplaat". The tail section fell close to buoy 7 and the wings came down on
the "Maanplaat". Three men fell out of the plane and landed in the water. They were
picked up immediately by Germans in a speed-boat. The German speedboat commander
told Mr. Oosterhuis later, that these three men were only wounded and had been taken to
Emden. A few days after the crash, a Dutch fisherman found a corpse in his nets and
took it to Nieuw Statenzyl, from where it was transported to and buried in Nieuwe
Beerta. Mr. Oosterhuis declared further that it is quite possible that there are still remains
in the cockpit of the aircraft.

s/s/ Meinto Oosterhuis

Certified True Copy   Certified True Copy

Raymond G. Johnson   Hendrick Veigh D-150596
1/Lt   Inf   Investigator

The chart indicates that *Miss Deal* crashed near buoy 7. Some of the researchers had
assumed that a second bomber on 17 April 1943 crashed-landed after a Bremen Raid near
the Dollard frontier between Germany and Holland. However, the chart indicates that
Dodge and another unknown washed up on the dike west of Ditzumerverlaat.

The fisherman named Pastoor had stated that a four motor bomber came down at 0300.
This would have been a British bomber returning from a night raid. There is
documentation that a British Wellington IC crashed in the Dollard on January 10, 1942

from the 304 Squadron piloted by J. Zajac. Now, we have 3 bombers lying in the same inland sea along with a British Mosquito. Also, the researcher Lenny Schrik indicated that there is a German fighter lying one and one half-km north of Miss Deal.

A Dutch researcher indicated that high tide on 25 June 1943 at Emden was around 0600. Today's tides, swing 12 feet from high to low. If *Miss Deal* crashed around 0900, then the minimum depth of the Dollard should have been around six feet. It is likely anyone, coming down in the Dollard, either by parachute or falling, would likely have drowned, unless they were wearing an inflated Mae West (life preserver). It would have seemed likely that the tide would not have had any effect on the movement of any remains to the east in the direction of the Battery Polder. The Dollard drains to the northwest, an incoming tide, from zero to 12 feet, would likely move any floating object to the east. The recovery area for Raymond Dodge was approximately 5 kilometers to the east of *Miss Deal*. The second B-17 is approximately 2 kilometers east of where *Miss Deal* is lying. So, without more information, we cannot be certain which crashed plane is our *Miss Deal*. In 2006, I requested the help of my Congressman Jeb Hensarling in locating the remains of my Uncle Charles Crawford and his pilot John Way.

In July I received a copy of the following letter, from Acting Deputy Assistant Secretary of Defense, Robert J. Newberry, which is retyped below:

Date stamped Jun 29 2006
The Honorable Jeb Hensarling
United States Representative
Attn: Margaret Smith
6510 Abrams Road, Suite 243
Dallas, Texas 75231-7217

Dear Representative Hensarling:

Thank you for your recent letter to the Joint Personnel Recovery Agency on behalf of Tony Crawford. Mr. Crawford is seeking information about his uncle, Army Sergeant Charles Crawford, who is missing from the Second World War. Since my office, the Defense Prisoner of War/Missing Personnel Office (DPMO) is the Department of Defense Agency responsible for the Prisoner of War/Missing in Action Issue, your letter was forwarded to me for response.

As you know, Sergeant Crawford was lost when his B-17 aircraft was shot down on the Dutch-German border in 1943. JPAC believes the best course of action to resolve this case is to locate and investigate the wreckage. JPAC hopes to conduct a preliminary survey in the vicinity of the crash site this fall to see if they can find any additional information about this case. Additionally, I have directed my staff to conduct an in-depth analysis of the Ardennes "X-files." I will contact you within 90 days to update you on our progress. Information we discover on this case will be relayed to Mr. Crawford via the Army Casualty Office.

DPMO, JPAC, and all Department of Defense organizations involved in accounting for our missing servicemen conduct operations worldwide to locate, identify and repatriate the remains of our servicemen missing from all our Nation's wars. Discussions to investigate a particular loss are based on operational criteria such as location and accessibility of the site and availability of investigative and recovery teams. Since 1976, JPAC and its predecessors have recovered, and returned to their families the remains of more than 300 servicemen missing from World War II. We will continue to investigate these cases.

I hope this answers your concerns. If you still have questions, you are welcome to contact me and I will do whatever I can to resolve your concerns.

Sincerely,

Robert J. Newberry
Acting Deputy Assistant Secretary of Defense
POW/Missing Personnel Affairs

Cc: Army Casualty Office
JPAC

Sometime after this letter I was contacted by two Dutch researchers that there was a meeting with JPAC concerning the proper course of action to recover the remains of John R. Way and Charles E. Crawford. Near the end of the meeting there was a consensus that the best course of action was to locate and investigate and/or raise the wreck. It was reported back that during this trip to the Netherlands and Germany that JPAC had searched out the availability of necessary equipment to conduct their search.

We traveled with the German researcher, Olaf Timmermann, putting out flyers requesting information concerning the crash of *Miss Deal*. Olaf also submitted a story with an appeal for information about *Miss Deal* to the newspapers on the German side of the Dollart. He received three responses. One was from Pastoor's daughter. Her name is Mrs. Schulte. She had reported that one of "Miss Deal's" crewmembers wrote letters after the war to the village. She did not recall his name but perhaps other old people might, and also know the whereabouts of the letters. Mrs. Schulte also stated that three American soldiers visited the crashed plane and tried to get one crewman out, but could not.

Olaf had another meeting with a local German citizen that told him about a Dutch fisherman that visited the plane and took some parts i.e. compass etc. and kept them. The man said that the Dutch fisherman stated that the wreck has sunk down in the Dollart. A third man reported that his father was a member of the flak battery and he had taken a picture of *Miss Deal* following her crash.

The president of the Bunker Museum in Emden, Germany, Franz Lenselink, indicated that as many as 10 aircraft wrecks are lying in the Dollart. Thus, the unknown that washed up adjacent to Dodge, may have been mistaken as an unknown British flyer. If so, he may have been interred in the Sage Cemetery in Oldenburg, Germany or one of the other British cemeteries in the area. The Sage cemetery has 178 unknown flyers and could be the resting place for Charles E. Crawford or John R. Way. There is another theory about the disposition of the unknown that washed up adjacent to Dodge. Since the Luftwaffe reported that they had lost a fighter in the Dollard on 25 June 1943 then perhaps he is buried in a German military cemetery.

For obvious reasons all the above leads need to be tracked down.

Below are portions of a transcript from an interview with the retired Dutch fisherman Simon de Boer, concerning the crash of the B17F 42-30049 *Miss Deal*. This interview was conducted at Simon de Boer's home at Nieuwschans, Holland, shortly after the expedition on the Dollard. Each individual's initials are used DB (de Boer), LS (Lenny Schrik), SdV (Sicco de Vries) and TC, (Tony Crawford):

DB: There was a big plane that came down near the fishing nets. Some of the crew flew out of the plane. Some of them drift toward Pogum, Germany.* We went on the Dollard with me and Tammo Kuiper and found one body and fixed him unto the ground with a pin (so that he could not float away). There came some boys from the Hitler Youth and later we took the body in and brought it to Pogum. (There was a German military station at Pogum during the war).**

LS: Ditzumer.......?

LS: That side more or less at the German side?

DB: Verlaat. Yes.

LS: Ditzumerverlaat okay, this was Dodge, more or less to the side of the German border, he was?

(The above four lines look as if Lenny is leading de Boer, that it was Dodge that he, and Kuiper recovered and took to Ditzumerverlaat. However, Dodge was not recovered until nearly two months after the crash of *Miss Deal*, and his documented recovery was west of Ditzumerverlaat on the inner dyke).

LS: How many came out of the plane?

DB: We could see that there were about five men jumping out of the plane.

DB: The tail of the plane stuck, about one week out of the water. And a body found in the fishing nets: (Imko Bakker told de Boer that he had something in his nets) we took him on a rope behind our boat to Nieuwe Statenzijl, where the body laid several days in the water. Then they took it on the quayside. (To bury it in Nieuw Beerta.) The man had on a (oxygen) mask but did not wear a parachute.

LS: How long was this man in the water before he was found?

DB: About one week after the crash (de Boer thought he had drifted out of the plane.)

(Now de Boer gets to other stories about several crashes)

LS: Now back to our plane. For how much was the tail of the plane stuck out of the water?

DB: Oh, a pretty end. About, three meters long.

TC: Three meters from the front of the tail, or front till the middle?

LS: What was the color of the tail?

DB: I don't know.

SdV: You did not see the plane come down?

DB: No I did not.

LS: Was it, perhaps a silver colored wing?

DB: Could be, it is possible.

LS: It is almost impossible. At this time, they were green colored.

TC: That is correct.

SdV: There is an indication that, where the tail was lying in the water, for many years there was a large piece of the plane visible at that place.

DB: I did not see this.

LS: Did you see any survivors?

DB: I did not see them only the dead man.

(Now de Boer talks about two men in a rubber boat, shot down by flak at Fiemel, taken in by German soldiers from the battery, but this is another story and de Boer does not remember the day.)

Sdv: Let's see on the map, here is the plane, the wreck and hardened sand.

TC: Did the plane hit the buoy? There is a reference that the buoy was missing.

DB: We did not see it, because we were not on this place, so we could not find out, if the buoy was missing.

DB: Imko Bakker was fishing there, and there was never a thought of the presence of a buoy.

SdV: Do you remember this tail? (Showing de Boer a picture of a B 17F tail.)

DB: Yes I do recognize it. Such a tail it was.

SdV: A man in the ball turret was hit, his comrades took him out and put him in the radio room

DB: Yes, there was a man who lay in the mud, I think the Hitler Youth had put him out of the plane.

SdV: They the Hitler Youth, did they bury him at the spot?

DB: No they did not.

TC: Did you see the fighters at the moment of the crash?

DB: No, I did not see them. At the moment that the bombers did fly, for example to Wilhelmshaven, we stayed at home, because of the danger.

LS: The tail, at which side did it pointed to?

DB: In the direction of Delfzijl, or better Termunten, yes.

LS, TC: Later on, there were people who had tried to lift up a part of the plane. Do you know something about it?

LS: Not in wartime, but after. I heard something about from Tammo Kuiper, in 1991.

DB: No, I don't. But Tammo Kuiper had a boat with a concrete shelter. And when there was shooting, he hid in that shelter.

LS: Tammo Kuiper, Tommy Cooper was his nickname. Ha-ha, he tried to lift up parts of the plane, he told me, several years ago. I did show him a map on which he marked some positions from crashed planes, including a B 17. And that was what he stated to me.

The translation was by Lenny Schrik.

* Winds at the target were reported at the briefing for the Hamburg mission were estimated to be from the west at 45 MPH at 25,000 feet.

**There was a German military station at Pogum during the war. (It should also be noted that it was stated by others that the Hitler Youth took the flyer from the plane and placed him face down in the mud as this was the proper way for fanatics to place the fallen enemy of the Reich).

The Battery Polder

Kriegsmarine Flak Battery Turret Emplacement with soldiers taking a break. This is a permanent turret built below grade with concrete retaining walls. Also, there appears to be fishnet poles in the background. Photo from Tony Crawford's collection

After locating Harm Pastoor from Ditzumerverlaat, Germany, I received an e-mail of great interest. Some of Harm's family owned the property known as Kanal Polder and sometime during the war, the Nazis military seized a portion of their farm, paying nothing and built a flak station. The battery contained the normal structures needed for the operation of the flak guns, including barracks, officers housing, operations office, guns and turrets, remote ammo bunker with railway to gun emplacements. See the chart on page v of the appendices. Notice the house and other farm structures adjacent to the outer dike. The gun emplacements are inside the inner dike next to the Dollart.

Members of this flak station recovered Raymond Dodge's remains after they were found washed up by Harm Pastoor. Today, this area is a German National Park where the wildlife is protected along with some of the remaining structures of the old battery.

The Good People of Northwest Germany

Harm Pastoor stated that in 1946 there was quite a stir in Ditzumerverlaat and other surrounding villages. It seemed that most all the people were alarmed as suddenly the wreck of *Miss Deal* was visible again. It was as if she had returned or perhaps her ghost had come back. Whatever occurred, it was believed that two American flyers were trapped in the wreck. There was so much excitement and local talk about the wreck being suddenly visible, that one of the young local boys just had to go out and have a look for himself. He walked the three miles to the wreck and then back home*. That young boy is now much older and is Harm Pastoor's father-in-law. The American authorities were notified and two years later the American Graves Registry Commission finally came calling on Mr. and Mrs. Pastoor.

*It was likely that the young boy took one of the fishermen's sleds for ease of travel. See picture on pg 184.

179

The ever gentleman, Evert Pastoor, shared all the information that he knew about the wreck and then later went with the soldiers to search for the wreck, but by now she had been reclaimed by the Watt/Schlick or Dollart mud. Upon their return, the soldiers were covered with mud and without any complaining, Mrs. Pastoor laundered the two American's uniforms, and then, served them currant bread and coffee. This was in 1948 and there is no record of any additional searches being performed by the AGRC.

I have found nothing in any of the military records about any airplanes rising up out of the Dollart in all my searching. Lenny Schrik, from The Dutch Air War Study Group, had indicated to me once that wrecks would suddenly appear in the Dollart. I always assumed they were old fishing vessels, etc., disturbed by a storm, and that Lenny was simply trying to humor or keep me motivated.

This leads us back to the conversation that Olaf Timmermann had with a Mrs. Pastoor Schulte in 2004. Mrs. Schulte had stated to Olaf that three soldiers had accompanied her father to a wreck out on the Dollart, and they tried to get a flyer out but could not. It would seem logical to conclude that the soldiers had no equipment and that the wreck was loaded with mud. Perhaps, the Army had become aware of the wreck rising out of the Dollart in 1946 and sent out another search team of which we are not aware.
So now, the Dollart has *Miss Deal* and waiting to give her and her two flyers up when DPMO honors their commitment, a WWII historian, or archeologist comes searching. The people of Ditzum, Ditzumerverlaat and the Ems/Dollart area of Germany learned firsthand after the war, their good Fortune of living in an area of rich farmland and good fishing grounds.

Evert Pastoor went out on the Dollart and rescued the three flyers from the rising tide and drowning by directing them away from their trek towards the 400 meter wide Ems River and toward Ditzum. Pastoor was told by the flyers that there was a crewman trapped in the plane with a broken leg. He immediately went to the ship removing the flyer and placing him upon his sled. He was able to beat the rapidly rising tide bringing the seriously injured soldier to the dyke and safety. He was well aware that the Nazis might take vengeance for his saving the lives of the Allied flyers. He was reminded many times that his actions were not in the best interest of his family by his wife. Whenever he was asked about his heroic rescues, his answer was; "If there is someone in danger and in need of help, I will help him."

Statements from local German citizens living in the Dollart region in 2012: From Ms. Frauke Buhs, who was about 12 years old at the time of the crash, said that three men were captured and driven over the dyke. Then, they were advised by the soldiers to clean off the mud and take a bath in the channel. Mrs. Anni Wenninga said that her husband, Mr. Lubbert Wenninga, who served at the battery, had stated that the captured flyers were given clean clothes and they were served some food. The prisoners would not eat the food as they feared it had been poisoned (this does not sound like American flyers). The flyers waited until the Germans began eating before they would eat.

Photo courtesy of Harm Pastoor
Evert Pastoor and his wife

After the war the barracks at Kanalpolder were used to house displaced German citizens. Fortunately, these people found some of Germany's most fertile land and were rewarded with plenty of vegetables from their gardens.

Photo courtesy of Harm Pastoor

This picture reflects some of the Fortunate Germans that fled from the eastern territories escaping the terrors of the brutal Russian onslaught by any means possible. One East

German woman attempted to escape to West Germany with her children by boarding a ship for refugees bound for Northwest Germany on the night of 30 January 1945. A submarine fired three torpedoes into the ship. Our East German woman lost four of her children that night, which has been recorded as the greatest maritime disaster in history, with the loss of an estimated nine thousand four hundred lives. The "Gustloff" quickly sank in the frigid waters of the Baltic. During the summer and spring, thousands of bodies of women and children washed up on the Swedish beaches and shorelines of the islands of Oland and Gotland, as well as Sweden's mainland. Once any displaced Germans got to the Dollart area of Germany, they were immediately well taken care of and placed in housing such as the Barracks at Kanalpolder.

Dr. Ernst Oppermann
Photo Courtesy of Albert Westlake Tailgunner on *Miss Deal.*

Doctor Ernst Oppermann practiced at the Marine Hospital in Emden, Germany. He treated numerous Allied flyers, saving many lives of the Nazis' enemy. One of the flyers that Dr. Oppermann saved was Albert Westlake, "Miss Deals'" tail gunner. All the allied flyers agreed that Dr. Oppermann treated everyone of his patients the same. At the surrender of Germany, he was forced to search for mines by the occupying British. During a research visit, I met with three doctors at the Emden hospital, and they were well aware of Dr. Oppermann's service to his fellow man.

Dr. Oppermann sent the following reprinted letter to another former patient and flyer, Stewart Cooper. He expresses his gratitude for gifts sent to his family. Plus, he describes his life after the war, during the occupation of Northwest Germany by the British.

Bielefeld, 28th April 1956

Dear Mr. Cooper,

When you rang me up, I was extremely pleased. It was a happy feeling to hear from a good pal again after a long, long time. I hope that, even at the time when our countries were at war, you had the feeling of being treated as soldiers and pals.

Please excuse me for not thanking you sooner for your wonderful parcel. The reason being I haven't had any practice in speaking English these past two years. My two boys they are 10 and 12 years old now; were delighted about the clothes, especially the warm jackets during this cold winter.

The end of the war wasn't very pleasant for me. During the last days of the war, we were in the front line without the field hospital being seriously damaged. After the occupation by Canadian Troops, I stayed as senior doctor of the hospital occupied by many wounded soldiers until the beginning of 1946. I was then imprisoned as I had been a member of the "party" and spent 3 very hard months in an internation camp. I was then ordered to the German mine sweeping service until the end of 1947.

After that, I could not regain my position as surgeon and I had to be thankful for the chance of obtaining a small practice as a general practictioner.

After having been in a leading position, this start was not at all easy for me.

I'm including a few photos of the children. You can see that the jackets fit perfectly and that they play with the balls.

I should be very pleased to hear from you again.

With sincere greetings from my family, also for Mrs. Cooper

I remain yours,

Dr. Ernst Oppermann

Photo from Tony Crawford's collection

Luftwaffe Flak Crew with their cannon. This Luftwaffe cannon could be quickly relocated when compared to the Kriegsmarine cannon, many of which were affixed in a concrete emplacement usable as a shore battery. A number of Luftwaffe flak crews took credit for the downing of *Miss Deal*.

Photo courtesy of Harm Pastoor*

Evert Pastoor, the fisherman, with his sled** that he used to bring the flyer with the broken leg to shore and safety from the rising tides. Mr. Pastoor forsook the Nazis rule of helping the enemy by assisting three other flyers from the Dollart and to safety.

*In November 2012, Harm Pastoor while searching for documents in Leer interviewed an old German who witnessed on 25 June 1943 an American bomber streaming smoke and under fighter attack. Suddenly a parachute appeared as the planes continued on to the west.
**Dollart fishermen used sleds for ease of travel with their daily catch between their fixed nets and home.

A tantalizing statement from the interview with the old fisherman, Simon de Boer: "There was a big plane that came down near the fishing nets. Some of the crew flew out of the plane. Some of them drifted toward Pogum, Germany. We went on the Dollard with me and Tammo Kupier and found one body and fixed him unto the ground with a pin (so that he could not float away). There came some boys from the Hitler Youth and later we took the body in and brought it to Pogum." (There was a German military garrison stationed at Pogum during the war.)

1. **The German records for this military garrison must be searched. Families of soldiers stationed at Pogum may have letters attesting to the disposition of these remains.**

The chart indicates that *Miss Deal* crashed near buoy 7. Some of the researchers had assumed that a second bomber on 17 April 1943 crashed-landed after a Bremen Raid near the Dollart frontier between Germany and Holland. However, the chart indicates that Dodge and another unknown washed up on the dike west of Ditzumer Veerlaat.

2. **Harm Pastoor is interviewing old Germans living in the area of Battery Polder, Ditzumerhammrich, Ditzumerverlaat, and the villages east of the Dollart for information concerning the disappearance of the unknown remains that washed up adjacent to Raymond Dodge. Was the unidentifiable flyer assumed to be British and taken to a German cemetery for British war dead? Perhaps he was assumed to be a German fighter pilot lost in the Dollart on 25 June 1943.**

Mr. Meinto Oosterhuis, Community of Beerta, declared that 25 June 1943 at about 1100 hours, he was fishing on the Dollart when he saw that a four engined American bomber, flying above the Dollart, was attacked by several German fighter planes. The American plane exploded in the air and came down in three large pieces. The cockpit crashed into the water about 200 meters south of the southern tip of the sandbank "Maanplaat". The tailsection fell close to buoy 7 and the wings came down on the "Maanplaat". Mr. Oosterhuis declared further that it is quite possible that there are still remains in the cockpit of the aircraft.

3. **The above statement leads us to believe that the remains of Charles Crawford and certainly John Way, may still be in the wreck of the cockpit that is lying some 200 meters south of the southern tip of the "Maanplaat" Dollart.**

Below is a section of AGRC chart reflecting the location where "Young Dodge" and the unknown flyer washed-up. Notice battery polder location relevant to the recovery of the two flyers. Also, note that located in Pogum, was a German military Garrison. This is where de Boer and Tammo Kuiper took a flyer from near the wreck.

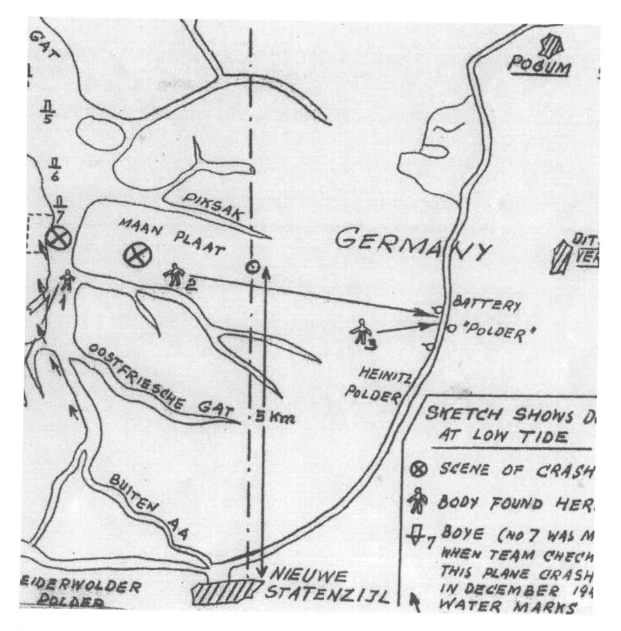

Per Meinto Oosterhuis, the cockpit is lying 200 meters south of the southern tip of the Maanplaat. This would locate this part of the wreck on the Oost Friesche Plaat. Thus, there are three major sections of *Miss Deal* lying in the Dollart.

With these three trails not searched and 2013 coming to a close, I am hopeful that an interested reader will take on the challenge of finding John Way, Charles Crawford and *Miss Deal*. Returning of these two warriors to their families and the recovery of their B-17 would be the final chapter of the 25 June 1943 Hamburg Raid.

Tentatively
The End

Charles Earl Crawford
MIA 25 June 1943

Appendices

Copy of Luftwaffes report of condition of four crashed AAF planes and crews on 11 June 1943. Number 3 is the Brinkman ship.

384th Formation Chart for 25 June 1943 Hamburg Mission

i

Luftwaffe Claims 25 June 43

25.06.43	Oblt. Heinz Knoke	5./JG 11	B-17	□ 05 Ost S/AO-3/3, 5.500 m.	08.34	11	-	yes
25.06.43	Fw. Wolf	4./JG 11	B-17	□ 05 Ost S/AQ-4/7, 8.500 m.	08.45	1	-	yes
25.06.43	Uffz. Gaedicke	3./JG 11	B-17	□ 05 Ost S/CR-8/3, 7.500 m.	08.45	1	-	yes
25.06.43	Fw. Höltken	Stab/JG 11	B-17	□ 05 Ost S/AP-8/6, 7.000 m.	08.46	1	-	yes
25.06.43	Uffz. Römling	4./JG 11	B-17	□ 05 Ost S/AQ-5/7, 8.000 m.	08.47	1	-	yes
25.06.43	Uffz. Kurz	II./JG 11	B-17	□ 05 Ost S/AQ-5/5, 7.900 m.	08.50	1	-	yes
25.06.43	Hptm. Helmut Specht	II./JG 11	B-17	□ 05 Ost S/AQ-5/6, 7.900 m.	08.52	12	-	yes
25.06.43	Hptm. Anton Hackl	Stab/JG 11	B-17	□ 6 km. S.W. Freisoythe, 7.500 m.	08.59	125	-	yes
25.06.43	Uffz. Güthenke	3./JG 11	B-17	□ S.W. Papenburg	09.02	2	-	yes
25.06.43	Lt. Heinert	3./JG 11	B-17	□ 12 km. S.W. Emden	09.02	1	-	yes
25.06.43	Uffz. Robert Spreckels	2./JG 11	B-17	□ 05 Ost S/AP-2, 7.500 m.	09.02	3	-	yes
25.06.43	Uffz. Robert Spreckels	2./JG 11	B-17 HSS	□ 05 Ost S/BC-1, 7.500 m.	09.26	4	-	yes
25.06.43	Oblt. Pancritius	2./JG 11	B-17 HSS	□ -	-	10	-	yes
25.06.43	Ofw. Gaumert	4./JG 11	B-17	□ -	-	1	-	yes
25.06.43	Oblt. Frey	7./JG 11	B-17	□ -	-	8	-	yes
25.06.43	Fw. Siegfried Zick	7./JG 11	B-17	□ -	-	2	-	yes
25.06.43	Hptm. Schnoor	I./JG 1	B-17	□ S.E. Groningen	09.10	8	-	yes
25.06.43	Ofw. Laun	I./JG 1	B-17	□ -	-	10	-	yes
25.06.43	Oblt. Hardt	III./JG 1	B-17 HSS	□ Munderloh, 15 km. S.E. Oldenburg	08.50	1	-	yes
25.06.43	Fw. Fordemann	7./JG 1	B-17	□ -	-	1	-	yes
25.06.43	Fw. Lindenschmid	9./JG 1	B-17	□ -	-	3	-	yes
25.06.43	Ofw. Husser	III./JG 1	B-17 c.V.	□ -	08.58	-	-	yes
25.06.43	Lt. Ullmann	III./JG 1	B-17	□ -	-	1	-	yes
25.06.43	Hptm. Luckenbach	III./JG 1	B-17	□ -	-	1	-	yes
25.06.43	Maj. Karl-Heinz Leesmann	III./JG 1	B-17	□ -	-	34	-	yes
25.06.43	Uffz. Koch	6./JG 1	Beaufighter	□ AN-4, 20 nm. NNW Frisians, 20 m.	16.15	2	-	yes

Luftwaffe Damages and Losses 25 June 43

25.06.43	1./JG 1	N.N.	-	Rollschaden, Schiphol, 15%	Fw 190 A-4	140 601	ws. 4 +
	3./JG 1	Uffz. Kurt Lessnitz	verl.	Bedienungsfehler, Bruchlandung Schiphol, 10%	Fw 190 A-5	840 191	ge. 8 +
	I./JG 1	N.N.	-	Rollschaden, Schiphol, 15%	Fw 190 A-4	0608	
	III./JG 1	Olt.Friedrich Hardt Gruppen-Adjutant	+	Luftkampf, Absturz Friesoythe, 100%	Bf 109 G-6	15 394	ws.<1 +
	7./JG 1	Olt.Heinrich Klöpper Staffelkapitän	-	Luftkampf, Notlandung Oltmanns- fehn, 15%	Bf 109 G-6	15 442	
	7./JG 1	Uffz.Hans Lehmann	verw.	Luftkampf, Cloppenburg, 100%	Bf 109 G-6	15 397	ws. 4 +
	8./JG 1	Uffz.Albert Oexle	+	Luftkampf, Leer, 100%	Bf 109 G-6	20 103	sw.10 +
	9./JG 1	Lt.Helmut Müller	verw.	Luftkampf, Absturz Neuschanz, 85%	Bf 109 G-6	19 613	ge.29 +
	9./JG 1	Ofw.Fritz Timm	verw.	Luftkampf, Raum Wilhelmshaven/ Emden, b	Bf 109 G-6	19 432	ge.28 +
	III./JG 1	N.N.	-	Luftkampf, Absturz Terborg, 100%	Bf 109 G-6	20 032	
	9./JG 1	N.N.	-	Luftkampf, Leeuwarden, 15%	Bf 109 G-6	15 481	ge. 3 +
	2./JG 11	Uffz.Johann Kohler	+	eigene Flak, Absturz Dörpen/Ems,	Fw 190 A-5	410 263	sw. 8 +
	5./JG 11	Olt.Heinz Knoke Staffelkapitän	verw.	Luftkampf 4-mot, über See, 5%	Bf 109 G-		sw. 1 +
	5./JG 11	N.N.	-	Spritmangel, Notlandung Peize, 10%	Bf 109 G-1	14 038	
	II./JG 11	N.N.	-	Spritmangel, Notlandung Dedems- vaart, 20%	Bf 109 G-6	18 229	
	9./JG 11	Lt.Dieter Paetz	+	Luftkampf, Absturz Wilhelmshaven, FSA, Schirm zu früh gezogen, 100%	Bf 109 G-6	20 056	

B (handwritten)

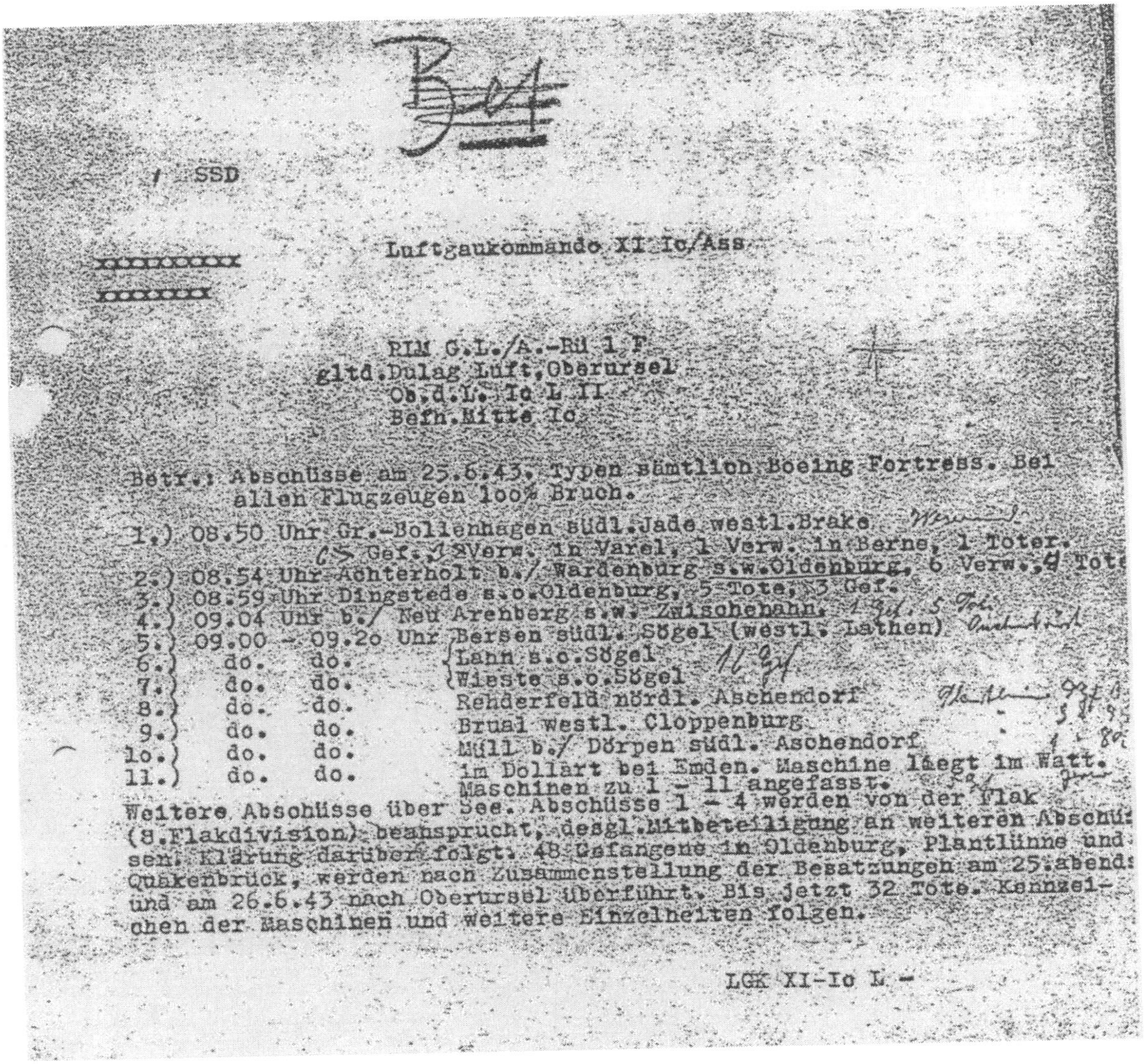

/ SSD

XXXXXXXX
XXXXXXX

Luftgaukommando XI Ic/Ass.

RLM G.L./A.-Rü 1 F
gltd.Dulag Luft,Oberursel
Ob.d.L. Ic L II
Befh.Mitte Ic

Betr.: Abschüsse am 25.6.43, Typen sämtlich Boeing Fortress. Bei
allen Flugzeugen 100% Bruch.

1.) 08.50 Uhr Gr.-Bollenhagen südl.Jade westl.Brake.
       3 Gef. 1 Verw. in Varel, 1 Verw. in Berne, 1 Toter.
2.) 08.54 Uhr Achterholt b./ Wardenburg s.w.Oldenburg, 6 Verw., 4 Tote
3.) 08.59 Uhr Dingstede s.o.Oldenburg, 5 Tote, 3 Gef.
4.) 09.04 Uhr b./ Neu Arenberg s.w. Zwischenbahn, 1 Bd. 5 Tote
5.) 09.00 - 09.2o Uhr Bersen südl. Sögel (westl. Lathen)
6.) do.   do.   (Lahn s.o.Sögel
7.) do.   do.   (Wieste s.o.Sögel
8.) do.   do.   Rehderfeld nördl. Aschendorf
9.) do.   do.   Brual westl. Cloppenburg.
1o.) do.   do.   Müll b./ Dörpen südl. Aschendorf
11.) do.   do.   im Dollart bei Emden. Maschine liegt im Watt.
                    Maschinen zu 1 - 11 angefasst.
Weitere Abschüsse über See. Abschüsse 1 - 4 werden von der Flak
(8.Flakdivision) beansprucht, desgl.Mitbeteiligung an weiteren Abschü-
sen. Klärung darüber folgt. 48 Gefangene in Oldenburg, Plantlünne und
Quakenbrück, werden nach Zusammenstellung der Besatzungen am 25.abends
und am 26.6.43 nach Oberursel überführt. Bis jetzt 32 Tote. Kennzeichen der Maschinen und weitere Einzelheiten folgen.

                                        LGK XI-Ic L -

...t Abschüsse 25.6.43.

Typen: Boeing- Fortress. Alle Maschinen 100% Bruch.

1.) 08.54 Uhr Achternholt b. Wardenberg s.w. Oldenburg. Zulassungsnr. 230143, 6 Gefangene, 4 Tote. Flakabschuss.Oldenburg birgt

2.) 08.59 Uhr Munderloh- Dingstede s.o. Oldenburg. Kennzeichen F.O. Kards X. Flakabschuss. 9 Tote, 1 Gefangener. Oldenburg birgt.

3.) 08.50 Uhr Gross- Bollenhagen w. Brake, keine Kennzeichen, 6 Gefan gene, 3 Verwundete in Varel, Sanderbusch und Berne, 1 T ter. Flak.Wesermünde birgt.Ass.1 - 3 wird auch v.Jägern beansprucht

4.) 09.04 Uhr Neu- Arensberg s.w. Zwischenahn. Keine Kennzeichen. Flak n. Jäger. 5 Tote, 2 Gefangene. Zwischenahn birgt.

5.) 09.10 Uhr Rehderfeld n. Aschendorf. Keine Kennzeichen. Flak u. Jäger. 6 Gefangene, 1 Toter, 1 Vermisster.Plantlünne bi

6.) 09.12 Uhr Brual, w. Cloppenburg, keine Kennzeichen. Flak u . Jäge 5 Gefangene, 1 Toter. Plantlünne birgt.

7.) 09.40 Uhr Müll b. Dörpen, s. Aschendorf, keine Kennzeichen. 2 Ge fangene, 8 Tote. Flak u. Jäger. Plantlünne birgt.

8.) 09.15 Uhr Gross- Bersen, s. Sögel, keine Kennzeichen. Flak u. Jäg 7. Gefangene, 3 Tote. Quakenbrück birgt.

9.) 09.10 Uhr Wiste s.o. Sögel, Kennzeichen : R. 1820/87 A T T C 5 A 020292. 5 Gefangene, 1 Verwundeter in Lingen, 1 Tote Flak u. Jäger. Quakenbrück birgt.

10.) 09.09 Uhr Im Dollart. Maschine nicht zu bergen, keine Kennzeichen Flak u. Jäger. 1 Gefangener. Jeverb birgt.

11.) 08.34 Uhr 20 km nördl. Wangerooge in See, Jäger.

12.) 08.45 Uhr 20 km   "   Langeoog   "   "   "

13.) 08.46 Uhr 10 km   "   Norderney   "   "   "

14.) 08.47 Uhr 10 km   "   Spickeroog   "   "   "

15.) 08.49 Uhr 20 km   "   "   "   "   "

16.) 08.50 Uhr 10 km   "   "   "   "   "

17.) 08.52 Uhr 10 km   "   "   "   "   "

18.) 09.00 Uhr 20 km   s.o. Helgoland   "   "   "

19.) 09.01 Uhr 20 km nördlich Wangerooge" "   "

20.) 09.02 Uhr 25 km s.w. Helgoland   "   "   "

21.) 09.04 Uhr 30 km w. Helgoland   "   "   "

22.) 09.03 Uhr 15 km n.w. Wangerooge   "   "   "
23.) 09.04 Uhr 30 km w. Helgoland   "   "   "

24.) 09.05 Uhr 30 km n. Norderney   "   "   "

Der ursprünglich gemeldete Abschuss bei Lahn ist identisch mit Wieste. 1 Abschuss 1 km nördlich Winschooten liegt auf holländischem Gebiet un wird von Leeuwarden geborgen.
Bei 5 Gefangenen konnte Zugehörigkeit zur Besatzung nicht festgestellt werden.

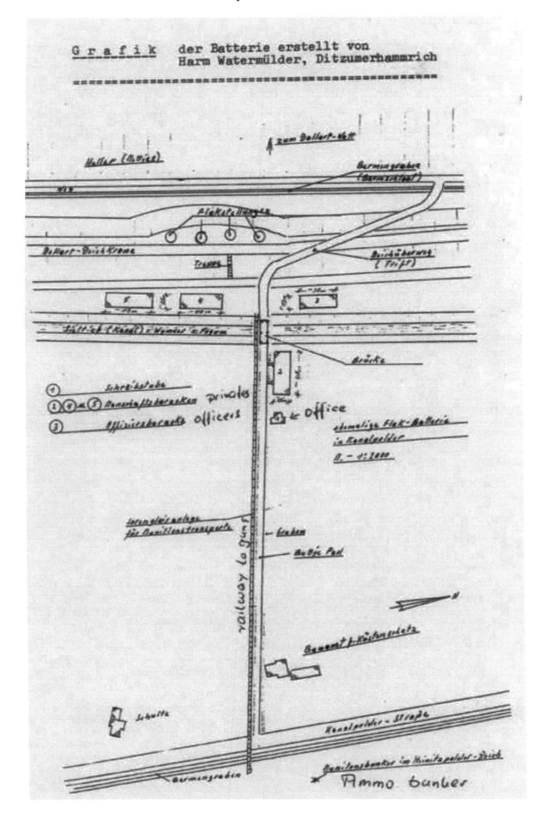

Army Air Base Headquarters
Kearney, Nebraska
May 17, 1943

Inclosure Extract

Headquarters
Crew # A-1—AP –42-30043

Col	Budd J. Peaslee	O-17061	CO
2nd Lt	Duane A. Conkey	O-797238	CO Sq
Capt	James H. Foister	O-443165	Hq Nav
1st Lt	Charles D. Bonnett	O-727080	Hq Bomb
Capt	Warren M. Ringgold	O-465450	Hq S-4
Maj	Ralph E. Switzer	O-356995	Gp Sur
M/Sgt	Ellwood N. Ford	19098504	CO Sq
Sgt	Julius E. Ratliff	38172241	Hq Comm
M/Sgt	Morris Blank	6995404	Gp Insp
M/Sgt	Bernie T. McNally	34163147	Sq Flt Chf

Crew # A-2 –AP –42-30065

Maj	Selden L. McMillin	O-346338	Asst Gp CO
2nd Lt	Herman Wollenweber	O-672010	CO Sq
1st Lt	Clayton M. Olson	O-649686	Hq Stat O
M/Sgt	Herman L. Efland	1AO28311	Sq Line Chief
M/Sgt	John M. Oreto	33121699	Sq Comm Chief
M/Sgt	Vernon T. Salmon	14039703	Sq Line Chief
M/Sgt	Edwin H. Christy	17013843	Sq Insp
M/Sgt	Arthur A. Connor	39259072	Hq S-3 Clk
M/Sgt	John J. Sulik	33104631	Sq Flt Chief

Crew # A-3 –AP –42-30076

1st Lt	Robert E. Langlois	O-662805	Sq Opr O
2nd Lt	Arthur W. Nelson	O-392287	Sq Opr O
1st Lt	John M. Palmer	O-856419	Sq Eng O
1st Lt	Thomas G. Piffiner	O-856524	Sq Eng O
M/Sgt	Marvin D. Hudson	14030328	Sq Line Chief
M/Sgt	Robert V. Gibbons	6148976	Sq Line Chief
M/Sgt	Joseph N. Funk	17018058	Sq Comm
1st Lt	Ray H. Moneymaker	O-1289461	Sq S-2
2nd Lt	Joseph W. Bell	O-672449	CO Sq

ATC Navigator

Crew # A-4 –AP –42-30142

Capt	William E. Gilmore	O-406671	Sq Opr O
1st Lt	Gordon K. Stallings	O-662834	Sq Opr O
1st Lt	Edgar C. Campbell	O-855299	Sq S-4
2nd Lt	Charles L. Moon	O-916920	Hq S-2
1st Lt	Wilfred J. McNeill	O-569254	Sq S-2
M/Sgt	Edward A. Coon	39176118	Sq Arm Chief
M/Sgt	Circy L. Smith	18048462	Sq Flt Chief
T/Sgt	Harold M. Carodiskey	33349410	Hq S-1 Clk
S/Sgt	Delbert P.Radant	19171096	Hq Comm

ATC Navigator

Crew # A-5 –AP-42-30036

1st Lt	Gordon Hankinson	O-729850	Asst Gp Opr O
2nd Lt	Victor G. Kress	O-671969	CO Sq
WO jg	Henry A. Stackhouse	2119072	Sq Bomb Sight O
1st Lt	Elwin R. Kircher	O-563522	Hq S-4
M/Sgt	Homer D. Brown	6304751	Sq Flt Chief
S/Sgt	Lyman Graham	6810203	Hq S-4
M/Sgt	Joseph L. Ramsey	18060313	Sq Eng Insp
M/Sgt	John E. Fisher	19005209	Sq Flt Chief
M/Sgt	Ralph G. Farlow	12013835	Sq Comm
ATC			

Crew #41 –AP –42-30041 (544th Bomb Squad Crews 41-49)

1st Lt	Kelmer J. Hall	O-728648	Pilot
F/O	Bradley B. Summers	T-238	Copilot
1st Lt	James D. Crary	O-728348	Navigator
1st Lt	Herbert Schindler	O-661664	Bombardier
T/Sgt	Kenneth Harland	13033323	Engineer
S/Sgt	Max B. Veber	17067790	Assistant Engineer
T/Sgt	Edward R. Keathley	19053628	Radio Operator Gunner
S/Sgt	Holgate J. Dean	11055383	Assistant Radio Operator Gunner
S/Sgt	Donald L. Harden	37087900	Armorer Gunner
S/Sgt	Clifford W. Spradlin	34266598	Assistant Armorer Gunner

Special Orders #96 AAB Hq., Kearney, Nebraska, May 17, 1943

Crew #42 –AP –42-30039

1st Lt	Edwin S. Halseth	O-665681	Pilot
2nd Lt	Stephen R. Fabian	O-736496	Copilot
2nd Lt	William F. McGeehan	O-790272	Navigator
2nd Lt	Charles J. Deignan	O-734438	Bombardier
T/Sgt	Robert O. Burnes	39604984	Engineer
S/Sgt	Walter M. Pollard	14090963	Assistant Engineer
S/Sgt	Frank L. Delmonte	13097009	Radio Operator Gunner
S/Sgt	David E. Kay	18160198	Assistant Radio Operator Gunner
S/Sgt	John S. Bagdis	31142144	Armorer Gunner
S/Sgt	Donald A. Rutan	32369888	Assistant Armorer Gunner

Crew #43 –AP –42-29956

2nd Lt.	Jesse D. Hausenfluck	O-665305	Pilot
2nd Lt	Donald B. Mackenzie	O-735619	Copilot
2nd Lt	Charles W. Everson	O-795222	Navigator
2nd Lt	Robert J. Kennedy	O-734709	Bombardier
Pvt	John T. Kilcourse	3304193	Engineer
S/Sgt	John C. Blauer	19060153	Assistant Engineer Gunner
S/Sgt	Sebastian Bucheri	31108556	Radio Operator Gunner
S/Sgt	John R. Kelley	19071826	Assistant Radio Operator Gunner
S/Sgt	Raymond P. Gregori	19128120	Armorer Gunner
S/Sgt	James A. Traylor	14150399	Assistant Armorer Gunner

<u>Crew #44 –AP –42-30073</u>

1st Lt	Thomas J. Estes	O-792569	Pilot
F/O	James M. Merritt	T-200	Copilot
2nd Lt	John J. Dubois	O-733416	Navigator
2nd Lt	Davis H. Davis	O-734436	Bombardier
T/Sgt	David L. Cochran	18115008	Engineer
S/Sgt	James M. Self	35477817	Assistant Engineer Gunner
S/Sgt	Fred S. Wagner	16124954	Radio Operator Gunner
S/Sgt	William J. O'Donnell	33324361	Assistant Radio Operator Gunner
S/Sgt	George Ursta	13026695	Armorer Gunner
S/Sgt	John V. Selgo	13041058	Assistant Armorer Gunner

Special Orders #96 AAB Hq., Kearney, Nebraska, May 17, 1943

<u>Crew #45 –AP –42-29960</u>

F/O	Gordon B. Erickson	T-60135	Pilot
2nd Lt.	Clifford C. Lartt	O-797007	Copilot
2nd Lt	Francis M. Hackley	O-796529	Navigator
2nd Lt	Don W. Irvine	O-734698	Bombardier
T/Sgt	Robert H. Penly	32281820	Engineer
S/Sgt	Frank J. Wingerter	15090270	Assistant Engineer Gunner
S/Sgt	Lawrence J. Reandeau	32435712	Radio Operator Gunner
S/Sgt	Paul G. Welch	33350091	Assistant Radio Operator Gunner
Pvt	Charles Mankowitz	32459221	Armorer Gunner
Pvt	James P. Coburn	15043914	Assistant Armorer Gunner

<u>Crew #46 –AP –42-30031</u>

Capt	Alfred C. Nuttal	O-404094	Pilot
F/O	Howard C. Burgoon	T-60131	Copilot
2nd Lt	David B. Wilmot	O-670198	Navigator
2nd Lt	Tom J.E. Hunt	O-732619	Bombardier
T/Sgt	Edward L. Peckham	32286378	Engineer
S/Sgt	Rolsnd H. Jenkins	14080507	Assistant Engineer Gunner
S/Sgt	Harold S. McFarland	33019662	Radio Operator Gunner
S/Sgt	William Aguiar	31036351	Assistant Radio Operator Gunner
S/Sgt	Henry J. Ullmer	36210809	Armorer Gunner
S/Sgt	George Ashworth	31170831	Assistant Armorer Gunner

<u>Crew #47 –AP –42-3118</u>

2nd Lt	Thomas A. Cuddeback	O-515820	Pilot
F/O	Luther E. Adair, Jr.	T-277	Copilot
2nd Lt	George R. Singer	O-736898	Navigator
2nd Lt.	James F. Dillon, Jr.	O-734440	Bombardier
S/Sgt	Albert J. Suchy	33264147	Engineer
S/Sgt	Delmer F. Priest	35328165	Assistant Engineer Gunner
S/Sgt	Edward T. Bessey	33278458	Radio Operator Gunner
S/Sgt	Phillip J. Fink	32380197	Assistant Radio Operator Gunner
Sgt	Albert F. Westlake	6910061	Armorer Gunner
S/Sgt	John H. Riley	11046366	Assistant Armorer Gunner

Crew #48 –AP –42-30048

2nd Lt	Delton G. Wheat	O-515818	Pilot
2nd Lt	Donald G. McMullen	O-672350	Copilot
2nd Lt	Thomas L. Ketcham	O-780133	Navigator
2nd Lt	Robert J. Brown, Jr.	O-734419	Bombardier
S/Sgt	Thomas B. Randolph	35477614	Engineer
S/Sgt	Warren L. Pursch	38157209	Assistant Engineer Gunner
S/Sgt	Theodore W. Finck	35433828	Radio Operator Gunner
S/Sgt	John J. Katuzney	31143855	Assistant Radio Operator Gunner
S/Sgt	Dero Hurst	18126300	Armorer Gunner
S/SGT	Ralph C. Wood	35367816	Assistant Armorer Gunner

Crew #49 –AP - 42-30049

2nd Lt	John R. Way Walter	O-793872	Pilot
2nd Lt	L. Harvey Richard	O-672350	Copilot
2nd Lt	P. Sherrer Thomas	O-736896	Navigator
2nd Lt	J. Corrigan	O-734432	Bombardier
S/Sgt	William R. Feagin	35477792	Engineer
T/Sgt	William C. Hill, Jr.	33364781	Assistant Engineer Gunner
S/Sgt	Benjamin J. Puzio	32471005	Radio Operator Gunner
S/Sgt	Edmund S. Gadomski	32371324	Assistant Radio Operator Gunner
S/Sgt	George D. McCalley	34190111	Armorer Gunner
S/Sgt	Raymond E. Dodge	17109015	Assistant Armorer Gunner

Crew #51 –AP –42-3231 (545th Bomb Squad Crews 51-59)

1st Lt	Richard T. Carrington	O-728581	Pilot
2nd Lt	Harvey C. Esty	O-672340	Copilot
1st Lt	James R. Martin-Vegue	O-728223	Navigator
1st Lt.	M.H. Smithwick	O-729511	Bombardier
T/Sgt	Phillip E. Scmidlapp	35110121	Engineer
S/Sgt	Joseph A. Scholand	37280903	Assistant Engineer Gunner
T/Sgt	Salvatore J. Perrotti	32245272	Radio Operator Gunner
S/Sgt	Floyd M. Wingate	37369181	Assistant Radio Operator Gunner
S/Sgt	Walter C. Parkins	34124122	Armorer Gunner
S/Sgt	Win R. Smalley	37418175	Assistant Armorer Gunner

Special Orders #96 AAB Hq., Kearney, Nebraska, May 17, 1943

Crew #52 –AP –42-3216

1st Lt	Floyd C. Edwards	O-665291	Pilot
2nd Lt	Paul P. Gordy	O-736507	Copilot
2nd Lt	Robert M. Koenig	O-795264	Navigaror
2nd Lt	Victor T. Kelly	O-734469	Bombardier
S/Sgt	Charles F. Tate	35478363	Engineer
T/Sgt	Walter A. Miller	36178539	Assistant Engineer Gunner
S/Sgt	Robert P. Goldman	16101071	Radio Operator Gunner
S/Sgt	Leon Svirsky	31168482	Assistant Radio Operator Gunner
S/Sgt	Edward F. Guzy	36335975	Armorer Gunner
S/Sgt	Alfred Meyer	6979689	Assistant Armorer Gunner

Crew #53 – AP – 42-3218

2nd Lt	Lloyd R. Armstrong	O-665266	Pilot
2nd Lt	Joseph A. Vanderhaegen	O-735475	Copilot
2nd Lt	Eugene T. Wilson	O-795327	Navigator
2nd Lt	William B. Kinney, Jr.	O-734471	Bombardier
T/Sgt	Lloyd S Estes	39092810	Engineer
S/Sgt	Alvin E. Renfro	34136691	Assistant Engineer Gunner
T/Sgt	George H. Carroll	12053073	Radio Operator Gunner
S/Sgt	Jack L. Mason	16069918	Assistant Radio Operator Gunner
Sgt	Robert A. Grimes	6983789	Armorer Gunner
S/Sgt	Fillman C. Thurman	18077086	Assistant Armorer Gunner

Crew #54 – AP – 42-3222

1st Lt	FrankG. Mattes	O-665319	Pilot
2nd Lt	Arthur J. Thompson, Jr.	O-735471	Copilot
2nd Lt	Wayne L. Wentworth	O-795523	Navigator
2nd Lt	Adam Konefal	O-734474	Bombardier
T/Sgt	John C. Dudley	16053949	Engineer
S/Sgt	Edward J. Garcia	19064757	Assistant Engineer
T/Sgt	Homer T. Fletter	36345794	Radio Operator Gunner
S/Sgt	James C. Rhodes	16014609	Assistant Radio Operator Gunner
Pvt	Thomas Hay	11068329	Armorer Gunner
S/Sgt	John P. Thompson	13028470	Assistant Armorer Gunner

Special Orders #96 AAB Hq, Kearney, Nebraska, May 17, 1943

Crew #55 – AP – 42-3235

Capt.	Raymond P. Ketelsen	O-421115	Pilot
2nd Lt	L.W. Myer	O-733702	Copilot
2nd Lt	J.C. Crouch	O-797275	Navigator
2nd Lt	T.H. Brzoznowski	O-735948	Bombardier
S/Sgt	J.L. Larue	39182308	Engineer
Pfc	Kenneth E. Christensen	38130722	Assistant Engineer Gunner
S/Sgt	J. Davidson	35327696	Radio Operator Gunner
Pvt	James T. Carter	6950609	Assistant Radio Operator Gunner
S/Sgt	D.L. Butcher	16011010	Armorer Gunner
S/Sgt	Floyd Hubble	36519335	Assistant Armorer Gunner

Crew #56 – AP – 42-30045

2nd Lt	Raymond W. Manning	O-73805	Pilot
2nd Lt	Norman A. Gauntt	O-672793	Copilot
2nd Lt	R.O. Henley, Jr.	O-670124	Navigator
2nd Lt	Warren B. Dillon	O-735179	Bombardier
T/Sgt	Paul L. Overbaugh	34202988	Engineer
S/Sgt	Howard F. Avery	36395293	Assistant Engineer Gunner
T/Sgt	Arthur E. Brittain	13096046	Radio Operator Gunner
Sgt	Willard E. Freeman	32454255	Assistant Radio Operator Gunner
S/Sgt	Robert J. Quaranta	12141817	Armorer Gunner
S/Sgt	Joseph P. Williams	32453552	Assistant Armorer Gunner

Crew #57 –AP –30139

Rank	Name	Serial	Role
2nd Lt	James R. Roberts	O-735113	Pilot
2nd Lt	Robert L. Lecates	O-515827	Copilot
2nd Lt	David P. Warrilow	O-736919	Navigator
2nd Lt	Francis R. Farwell	O-735185	Bombardier
T/Sgt	Leon F. Ausmus	38097896	Engineer
S/Sgt	Frank H. Bowen	34169468	Assistant Engineer Gunner
T/Sgt	George W. Jumper	35416700	Radio Operator Gunner
S/Sgt	James R. Billingsley	36068397	Assistant Radio Operator Gunner
S/Sgt	Eldore L. Daudelin	11068163	Armorer Gunner
S/Sgt	Henry G. Lemmerman	32457061	Assistant Armorer Gunner

Special Orders #96 AAB Hq., Kearney, Nebraska, May 17, 1943

Crew #58 –AP –42-30143

Rank	Name	Serial	Role
2nd Lt	Ralph J. Hall	O-515825	Pilot
2nd Lt	Rodney W. House	O-521615	Copilot
2nd Lt	Robert M. Janson	O-670745	Navigator
2nd Lt	Anthony Palazzo	O-734731	Bombardier
S/Sgt	Homer J. Cocklin	33014913	Engineer
S/Sgt	Reamond M. Smiley	33268256	Assistant Engineer Gunner
S/Sgt	Smith J. Davis	33285324	Radio Operator Gunner
S/Sgt	Albert R. Valcour	31201024	Assistant Radio Operator Gunner
S/Sgt	James S. Parrish	16074461	Armorer Gunner
S/Sgt	Paul E. McNeal	16074525	Assistant Armorer Gunner

Crew #59 –AP –42-3230

Rank	Name	Serial	Role
2nd Lt	Robert J. Oblinski	O-737710	Pilot
2nd Lt	Harry R. Swift	O-798697	Copilot
2nd Lt	Richard E. Granpre	O-797308	Navigator
2nd Lt	Douglas H. Turner	O-735218	Bombardier
S/Sgt	Ernest M. Trickett	35405056	Engineer
Sgt	William J. Counihan	17053961	Assistant Engineer Gunner
S/Sgt	Oliver E. Reed	35355941	Radio Operator Gunner
S/Sgt	George F. Werbanec	33288705	Assistant Radio Operator Gunner
Pfc	George W. Waterman	12136487	Armorer Gunner
S/Sgt	Harold J. Cooke	34430596	Assistant Armorer Gunner

Crew #61- -AP –42-30026 (546th Bomb Squad Crews 61-69)

Rank	Name	Serial	Role
1st Lt	Phillip A. Algar	O-728536	Pilot
F/O	Richard V. Wolf	T-251	Copilot
1st Lt	Frank A. Celentano	O-728340	Navigator
1st Lt	James C. McClanahan	O-727647	Bombardier
Pvt	Roland B. Laviolette	11015940	Engineer
S/Sgt	Loring C. Miller	39840477	Assistant Engineer Gunner
Cpl	Kenneth M. McKay	19080984	Assistant Radio Operator Gunner
Sgt	Francis Gerow	12024140	Radio Operator Gunner
S/Sgt	Casner R. Majewski	36346741	Armorer Gunner
Sgt	John W. Schimenek	16022229	Assistant Armorer Gunner

Crew #62 –AP –42-30005

1st Lt	Lykes S. Henderson	O-389900	Pilot
F/O	Paul F. Shinsky	T-131	Copilot
2nd Lt	Claudius E. Belk	O-795180	Navigator
2nd Lt	Andrew C. Conway	O-734430	Bombardier
S/Sgt	Ivon J. Schultz	37190789	Engineer
S/Sgt	George H. Smith	39388100	Assistant Engineer Gunner
Sgt	Howard Baker, Jr.	16042061	Radio Operator Gunner
Sgt	Ralph E. Hemmick, Jr.	16093121	Assistant Radio Operator Gunner
Sgt	Joseph A. Lally	38197263	Armorer Gunner
S/Sgt	John M. Price	39452617	Assistant Armorer Gunner

Crew #63 –AP –42-30032

1st Lt	William Dietel, Jr.	O-665286	Pilot
2nd Lt	Kenneth C. Dutton	O-736493	Copilot
2nd Lt	Herbert W. Funk	O-794870	Navigator
2nd Lt	Clyde W. Davis	O-734435	Bombardier
S/Sgt	Howard J. Adams	16051094	Engineer
Cpl	Edward Amory	32226989	Assistant Engineer Gunner
S/Sgt	Ardell H, Bollinger	13097189	Radio Operator Gunner
Pfc	Wyman D. Martin	14067288	Assistant Radio Operator Gunner
Sgt	Jack L. Mason	35393685	Armorer Gunner
S/Sgt	Lawrence E. Lunmyer	33248116	Assistant Armorer Gunner

Crew #64 –AP –42-30033

1st Lt	James H. Kelly	O-665313	Pilot
2nd Lt	Russell R. Faulkiner	O-736497	Copilot
2nd Lt	Wilbourne E. Blount	O-795187	Navigator
2nd Lt	John E. Ryberg	O-734745	Bombardier
S/Sgt	Leonard M. Nealis	38023306	Engineer
S/Sgt	Roland L. Killin	37177382	Assistant Engineer Gunner
Sgt	Jerome B. Beaupre	36505591	Radio Operator Gunner
S/Sgt	Dennis J. Lane	32337502	Assistant Radio Operator Gunner
Sgt	Peter T. Yaskow	32142363	Armorer Gunner
S/Sgt	Aloysius W. Mizgorski	33287505	Assistant Armorer Gunner

Crew #65 –AP –42-30046

2nd Lt	Clayton R. Wilson	O-515816	Pilot
2nd Lt	Dewey C. Brown	O-673704	Copilot
2nd Lt	Fred E. Bloesch	O-797250	Navigator
2nd Lt	Herman D. Stevens	O-735213	Bombardier
S/Sgt	Vern D. Long	39174786	Engineer
S/Sgt	Herbert E. May	39089440	Assistant Engineer Gunner
S/Sgt	John M. Derochers	33248462	Radio Operator Gunner
Sgt	Ellis H. Klein	11041241	Assistant Radio Operator Gunner
S/Sgt	George J. Kendall	6121691	Armorer Gunner
S/Sgt	Jack F. Hook	35336384	Assistant Armorer Gunner

Crew #67 –AP –42-30030

2nd Lt	Edgar E. Ulrey	O-735501	Pilot
F/O	Charles W. Bishop	T-60127	Copilot
2nd Lt	Anthony J. Grimaldi	O-670729	Navigator
2nd Lt	Wilbert Y.K. Yee	O-735224	Bombardier
S/Sgt	Bruno E. Edman	36198223	Engineer
S/Sgt	Leonard J. Kelly	39173397	Assistant Engineer Gunner
S/Sgt	Cecil G. Morton	15080142	Radio Operator Gunner
S/Sgt	Howard D. Parks	39311920	Armorer Gunner
S/Sgt	Joseph M. Kalas	33361307	Assistant Radio Operator Gunner
S/Sgt	James T. Yeater	37185385	Assistant Armorer Gunner

Crew #68 –AP –42-30037

Capt.	George W. Harris, Jr.	O-399610	Pilot
2nd Lt	Ellwood D. Kowalski	O-793416	Copilot
2nd Lt	Samuel A. Eggers, Jr.	O-794787	Navigator
2nd Lt	Leo A. Murphy	O-734727	Bombardier
S/Sgt	George A. Bossinger	33365644	Engineer
S/Sgt	Edward C. Costello	12034337	Assistant Engineer
S/Sgt	Jean L. Blaise	36244473	Radio Operator Gunner
Sgt	Eugene W. Penick	17024507	Assistant Radio Operator Gunner
S/Sgt	David J. Hardin	14124092	Armorer Gunner
S/Sgt	Harry A. Micknight	16051589	Assistant Armorer Gunner

Crew #69 –AP –42-3004

2nd Lt	George W. Evans	O-672784	Copilot
2nd Lt	Joseph Rosio	O-520047	Pilot
2nd Lt.	Leonard J. Fink	O-796510	Navigator
2nd Lt	Sidney Casden	O-734426	Bombardier
Pvt	Otho E. Masterson	16054934	Engineer
S/Sgt	John H. Houghton	34290923	Assistant Engineer
S/Sgt	Lester Brown	20820476	Radio Operator Gunner
S/Sgt	Anthony F. Cucinatta	12034633	Assistant Radio Operator Gunner
S/Sgt	John H. Kuberski	32298859	Armorer Gunner
Sgt	Lee Lewis	16051589	Assistant Armorer Gunner

Crew #71 –AP –5850 (547 Bomb Group Crews 71-79)

1st Lt	James W. Smith	O-661982	Pilot
2nd Lt	Robert B. Kilmer, Jr.	O-671962	Copilot
1st Lt	Robin E. Taber	O-663429	Navigator
1st Lt	Francis J. Meyer	O-731085	Bombardier
T/Sgt	Robert H. Buckley	19074146	Engineer
S/Sgt	Stanley F. MacArthur	32373547	Assistant Engineer
TSgt	John J. Reichwein	35356402	Radio Operator Gunner
S/Sgt	Lynn T. Jones	19072171	Assistant Radio Operator Gunner
Pvt	William F. Igou	34333114	Armorer Gunner
Sgt	David A. Pratt	31151081	Assistant Armorer Gunner

Crew #72 – AP – 42-5843

1st Lt	Ralp R. Pulcipher	O-665337	Pilot
2nd Lt	Merle Johnson	O-741911	Copilot
2nd Lt	William Eudey	O-735983	Navigator
2nd Lt	Paul S. Givens	O-729432	Bombardier
T/Sgt	Judson L. Dacus	14978782	Engineer
Sgt	Joe M. Hawkins, Jr.	15117276	Assistant Engineer
Pvt	Asbury L. Perkins	6284668	Radio Operator Gunner
S/Sgt	Willard D. McLain	17088525	Assistant Radio Operator Gunner
Sgt	Albert F. Gase	35328989	Armorer Gunner
S/Sgt	Thomas E. Furrey	13043315	Assistant Armorer Gunner

Crew #73 – AP - 42-5848

2nd Lt	Donald P. Ogilvie	O-665330	Pilot
2nd Lt	Edmund S. Goulder	O-736509	Copilot
2nd Lt	John W. Barkley, Jr.	O-735966	Navigator
2nd Lt	William H. Wilson	O-2043778	Bombardier
T/Sgt	Emment A. Hood	38104051	Engineer
Sgt	Nathan J. Berg	31092445	Assistant Engineer Gunner
T/Sgt	James R. Murray	32393817	Radio Operator Gunner
Sgt	Bernard M. Kain	353204 79	Assistant Radio Operator Gunner
Sgt	John R. Dudla	31169488	Armorer Gunner
S/Sgt	James W. McKeon	31203048	Assistant Armorer Gunner

Crew #74 – AP – 42-5838

2nd Lt	Frederick G. Disney Don	O-403534	Pilot
2nd Lt	R. Dithomas Alexander	O-736490	Copilot
2nd Lt	J. Bredacs, Jr. Bernarr H.	O-795390	Navigator
2nd Lt	Nelson	O-733306	Bombardier
T/Sgt	Harold F. Hammond	16052869	Engineer
Pvt	Robert E. Lineham, Jr.	35166364	Assistant Engineer
S/Sgt	Maryville R. Galloway	34360049	Radio Operator Gunner
Cpl	Clarence M. Stewart	37184183	Assistant Radio Operator Gunner
Sgt	Joseph J. Kilb	32470338	Armorer Gunner
Pvt	James L. Knutson	16073804	Assistant Armorer Gunner

Crew #75 – AP – 42-5849

2nd Lt	George W. Riches	O-733727	Pilot
2nd Lt	Richard J. McCray	O-742514	Copilot
2nd Lt	Donald J. Irwin	O-736862	Navigator
2nd Lt	William Boomhower	O-735164	Bombardier
T/Sgt	Bernard H. Anderson	31092217	Engineer
S/Sgt	William T. Waller	14074156	Assistant Engineer Gunner
S/Sgt	Guy E. Smith	35483124	Radio Operator Gunner
S/Sgt	Freeman S. Penny	16125337	Assistant Radio Operator Gunner
S/Sgt	Stanley S. Martin	39832711	Armorer Gunner
S/Sgt	Ralph E. Lavoie	11098344	Assistant Armorer Gunner

Crew #76 – AP – 42-30131

2nd Lt	Francis J. Witt	O-665748	Pilot
F/O	T.L. Carter	T-120976	Copilot
2nd Lt	Arthur C. Harris	O-670732	Navigator
2nd Lt	Joseph Derer	O-731364	Bombardier
T/Sgt	Edward A. Thomason	34121576	Engineer
S/Sgt	Michael J. Vodilko	35380958	Assistant Engineer Gunner
S/Sgt	William F. Sears	17041787	Radio Operator Gunner
S/Sgt	Francis M. Seager	37221170	Assistant Radio Operator Gunner
S/Sgt	Claude R. Leslie	35507564	Armorer Gunner
S/Sgt	Rufus F. Douglas	12013980	Assistant Armorer Gunner

Crew #77 – AP – 42-5851

1st Lt	George B. Keck	O-730520	Pilot
2nd Lt	Raymond A. Gaither	O-672790	Copilot
2nd Lt	William W. Juart	O-796543	Navigator
2nd Lt	Arthur H. Bryant	O-735167	Bombardier
T/Sgt	Milton J. Deville	18133971	Engineer
Pvt	Billy J. Jackson	18072064	Assistant Engineer
S/Sgt	Frank E. Hollingsworth	34207347	Radio Operator Gunner
Sgt	Walden A. Hughes	13065674	Assistant Radio Operator Gunner
S/Sgt	Theodore Paduch	32489613	Armorer Gunner
S/Sgt	Alfred Reise	16124429	Assistant Armorer Gunner

Crew #78 – AP – 42-5852

Capt	Maurice G. Dillingham	O-1699192	Pilot
2nd Lt	Johnny A. Butler	O-663844	Copilot
2nd Lt	Edward J. Knowling	O-736868	Navigator
2nd Lt	Joseph W. Baggs	O-735155	Bombardier
T/Sgt	Howard J. Turlington	14073757	Engineer
S/Sgt	Preston A. Davis	18136189	Assistant Engineer Gunner
S/Sgt	Armando N. Ordaz	38112884	Radio Operator Gunner
S/Sgt	Marion C. Rogers	34278719	Assistant Radio Operator Gunner
S/Sgt	William D. Wolven	1219628	Armorer Gunner
S/Sgt	Bunia Martin	38200313	Assistant Armorer Gunner

Crew #79 – AP – 42-5853

2nd Lt	Horace J. Frink	O-736503	Pilot
2nd Lt	Leon Fields	O-672341	Copilot
2nd Lt	Lester O. Hegstead	O-670736	Navigator
2nd Lt	Clyde P. Carlson	O-735170	Bombardier
T/Sgt	William C. Ralston	33263982	Engineer
S/Sgt	Clyde A. Savage	35328426	Assistant Engineer Gunner
S/Sgt	Roy W. Griffith	14107839	Radio Operator Gunner
S/Sgt	William A. Shelton	18066018	Assistant Radio Operator Gunner
S/Sgt	Archie Retherford, Jr.	35370807	Armorer Gunner
S/Sgt	Julius F. McNutt	12138659	Assistant Armorer Gunner

B-17 crew list lost on 12 June 1943 Training mishap
B-17F-85-BO   42-30036   384th Bomb Group, 546 Bomb Squad

Pilot	+ 2/Lt	Ellwood D. Kowalski
Co-pilot	+ 2/Lt	Charles L. Griffin
Navigator	+ 2/Lt	Samuel A. Eggers Jr.
Bombardier	+ 2/Lt	Leo A. Murphy
Radio Operator	+ S/Sgt	Jean L. Blaise

B-17s with crew lists lost on the 29 May 1943 raid on St. Nazaire, France.

The B17F-70-BO KY*G 42-29792 305th Bomb Group, 366th Bomb Squadron

Rank	Name	Role
1/Lt.	+James C. Perry	Pilot
1/Lt.	+Robert S. Roddy	Co-pilot
2/Lt	+Herbert P. Korenko	Navigator
2/Lt	+Russel B. Rose	Bombardier
T/Sgt	+Charles L. Futch	Engineer
T/Sgt	+Harold R. Perry	Radio Operator
T/Sgt	+John R. Gemmel	Ball Turret Gunner
S/Sgt	+Michael Macinsky	Left Waist Gunner
S/Sgt	+Ralph A. Vitello	Right Waist Gunner
S/Sgt	Raymond H. Allaby	Tail Gunner

B17F-35-BO RQ*U 42-29838 "The Concho Clipper" 351st Bomb Group, 509th Bomb Squad

Rank	Name	Role
Lt Colonel	J Russel Jr.	Pilot
2/Lt	Leo Grikstas	Co-pilot
2/Lt	Roy P. Stealey	Navigator
1/Lt	Charles B. Woehrle	Bombardier
S/Sgt	Charles T. Eaton	Engineer
T/Sgt	+James F. Welk	Radio Operator
S/Sgt	+Nahannie Bader	Ball Turret Gunner
T/Sgt	+Wayne I. Baldwin	Waist Gunner
S/Sgt	+Maurice A. McLaughlin	Waist Gunner
S/Sgt	Fredrick D. Williams Jr.	Tail Gunner

B17F-27-BO PU*A 41-24601 "Yardbird" 303rd Bomb Group, 360th Bomb Squad

Rank	Name	Role
1/Lt	Joseph E. Trojan	Pilot
1/Lt	+Thomas S. Vaughan	Co-pilot
1/Lt	Parlew W. Madsen Jr.	Navigator
1/Lt	Jack W. Stewart	Bombardier
S/Sgt	+Paul H. Prescott	Engineer
S/Sgt	Cecil E. Craft	Radio Operator
S/Sgt	Joseph R. Sunderlin	Ball Turret Gunner
S/Sgt	Martin A Semonick	Left Waist Gunner
S/Sgt	Frank W. Bartless	Right Waist Gunner
S/Sgt	Lincoln T. O'Connell	Tail Gunner

B-17F-70-BO LF*F 42-29773 379th Bomb Group, 526th Bomb Squad

Rank	Name	Role
Capt.	John O. Hall	Pilot
1/Lt	Willard S. Thomas	Co-pilot
2/Lt	William J. Koves	Navigator
2/Lt	James M. Griffith	Bombardier
S/Sgt	Michael H. Belock	Engineer
T/Sgt	+Frank A. Adrick	Radio Operator
Sgt	+Robert M. Vanderstraeten	Ball Turret Gunner
S/Sgt	+Clarence E. Gallamore, Jr.	Left Waist Gunner
S/Sgt	+George F. Hague	Right Waist Gunner
Sgt	+Robert G. Kuehl	Tail Gunner

+ Indicates killed in action

B17F-25-DL FR*F 42-3113 379th Bomb Group, 525th Bomb Squad

1/Lt	Arthur P. Hale	Pilot
2/Lt	Stewart M. Sharp	Co-pilot
2/Lt	Bernard Andruskiewicz	Navigator
2/Lt	Jerry B. Ahorn	Bombardier
T/Sgt	Charles M. Ford	Engineer
Sgt	Joseph E. Lasiter	Radio Operator
S/Sgt	Chester A Whitney	Ball Turret Gunner
S/Sgt	Chester T. Moore	Left Waist Gunner
Sgt	Lee S. Hilton	Right Waist Gunner
Sgt	Laurence E Josselyn	Tail Gunner

B17F-55-BO JJ*Z 42-29531 305th Bomb Group, 422nd Bomb Squad

1/Lt	Marshall R. Peterson	Pilot
2/Lt	Harold E. Bentz	Co-pilot
2/Lt	Lawrence F. Madelberg	Navigator
2/Lt	F.R. Perrica	Bombardier
S/Sgt	Hilton Hilliard	Engineer
T/Sgt	John J. Freeborn	Radio Operator
S/Sgt	Peter P. Milasius	Ball Turret Gunner
T/Sgt	George P. Smith	Left Waist Gunner
S/Sgt	+Perry C. Mathews	Right Waist Gunner
S/Sgt	Salvadore S. Tafolya	Tail Gunner

B-17F-75-BO LF*G 42-29878 "Lady Godiva" 379th Bomb Group, 526th Bomb Squad

1/Lt	Theodore M. Peterson	Pilot
2/Lt	Jack W. Bourn	Co-pilot
2/Lt	Woodrow P. Moore	Navigator
2/Lt	J. Warren Rosacker	Bombardier
T/Sgt	Maynard M. Spencer	Engineer
T/Sgt	John M. Scott	Radio Operator
S/Sgt	William E. Blubaugh	Ball Turret Gunner
S/Sgt	Paul E. Cribelar	Left Waist Gunner
Sgt	William T Ayres	Right Waist Gunner
S/Sgt	Gideon A. Brown	Tail Gunner

B17F-70-BO KY*M 42-29742 305th Bomb Group, 366 Bomb Squad

1/Lt	James G. Stevenson	Pilot
2/Lt	Robert J. Curtis	Co-pilot
F/O	Clinton A. Bush	Navigator
2/Lt	C. Veach	Bombardier
T/Sgt	C.L. Bitton	Engineer
T/Sgt	Frederick T. Hunter	Radio Operator
S/Sgt	Chester W. Hack	Ball Turret Gunner
S/Sgt	+Ralph Erwin	Left Waist Gunner
S/Sgt	J. S. Chew	Right Waist Gunner
S/Sgt	Alex R. Algado	Tail Gunner

+ Indicates killed in action

B-17s with crew lists lost on the 11 June 1943 raid on Wilhelmshaven, Germany.

B-17F-25DL 42-3099   FO*R   379th Bomb Group, 527th Bomb Squad

Pilot	1/Lt	William Pinson	Top turr.	S/Sgt	+William Sendzick
Copilot	F/O	+Reed Lamb	Ball turr.	S/Sgt	+Harold Anderson
Navg.	2/Lt	+Davis Murdock	Right Waist	T/Sgt	+Harry Northery
Bomb.	2/Lt	+Roy Self	Left Waist	S/Sgt	+Larus Snydal
Radio.	T/Sgt	+Carol Lohman	Tail Gunner	S/Sgt	+Cleon Biddle

B-17F-25-DL   42-3114   FR*T   379th Bomb Group, 525th Bomb Squad

Pilot	1/Lt	Noel Britten	Top turr.	T/Sgt	Gerald Stratton
Copilot	2/Lt	Patrick Rea	Ball turr.	S/Sgt	Floyd Tichnell
Navg.	2/Lt	Olympio Cassera	Right Waist	T/Sgt	John Rogers
Bomb.	2/Lt	Matthew Driscoll	Left Waist	Sgt	Michael Holinka
Radio.	S/Sgt	Daniel Kenney	Tail Gunner	S/Sgt	Ellis Vance

B-17F-25-DL   42-3138   FO*M   379th Bomb Group, 527th Bomb Squad

Pilot	1/Lt	+Burrel Newman	Top turr.	S/Sgt	+Leo Gunther
Copilot	2/Lt	+John Culler	Ball turr.	S/Sgt	+James Griffin
Navg.	2/Lt	+George Jackson	Right Waist	S/Sgt	+Joseph Butterfield
Bomb.	2/Lt	Thomas Kelley	Left Waist	T/Sgt	+Harold Dudley
Radio.	S/Sgt	+Edward Hyvonen	Tail Gunner	S/Sgt	Raymond Lauters

B-17F-75-BO 42-29915 "Thunder God" WA*U" 379th Bomb Group, 524th Bomb Squad

Pilot	1/Lt	+Raymond Zucker	Top turr.	T/Sgt	+Julius Lee
Copilot	2/Lt	+Abram Birch	Ball turr.	S/Sgt	+John Sneed
Navg.	2/Lt	+Harry Anderson	Right Waist	S/Sgt	+James Keeler
Bomb.	2/Lt	+Anthony Amaya	Left Waist	S/Sgt	+Paul Hammond
Radio.	T/Sgt	+Russel Good	Tail Gunner	S/Sgt	+Michael Froehlich

.B-17F-75-BO   42-29875   FO*L 379th Bomb Group, 527th Bomb Squad

Pilot	Capt	+George Hammrick	Top turr.	S/Sgt	+Lother Nichols
Copilot	2/Lt	Sam Gossen	Ball turr.	T/Sgt	+William Fleck
Navg.	2/Lt	+Hal Herrick	Right Waist	T/Sgt	+James Mitchell
Bomb.	2/Lt	+Walter Kozel	Left Waist	S/Sgt	+Warren Crain
Radio.	T/Sgt	+Anthony Zarro	Tail Gunner	S/Sgt	+Jasper Gallegos

B-17F-25-VE 42-5809 *Mary Jane* 379th Bomb Group, 526th Bomb Squad

Pilot	1/Lt	Walter Carnal	Top turr.	T/Sgt	Dean Wyland
Copilot	2/Lt	William Davidson	Ball turr.	S/Sgt	Donald Shoman
Navg.	2/Lt	Mortis Konier	Right Waist	S/Sgt	Edward Allen
Bomb.	2/Lt	Leslie Gross	Left Waist	S/Sgt	Monico Rodriquezl
Radio.	T/Sgt	Leonard Cruzan	Tail Gunner	S/Sgt	Murel Ellis

B-17F-25-DL 42-3148 379th Bomb Group, 527th Bomb Squad

Pilot	1/Lt	+William Brinkman	Top turr.	T/Sgt	+Clarence Watkins
Copilot	2/Lt	William Cochran	Ball turr.	S/Sgt	+Alfred Mitchell
Navg.	2/Lt	William Homes	Right Waist	S/Sgt	+Robert Todd
Bomb.	2/Lt	+Donald Andrews	Left Waist	S/Sgt	+Ralph Smith
Radio.	Sgt	+William Carver	Tail Gunner	S/Sgt	+Frank Murphy

B-17F-50-BO 42-5430 "Good Enuf" 303rd Bomb Group, 359th Bomb Squad

Pilot	1/Lt	+Rolland Haines	Top turr.	T/Sgt	Robert Garcia
Copilot	2/Lt	Mayer Kramer	Ball turr.	S/Sgt	Allen Foster
Navg.	2/Lt	Dominick DeLorenzo	Right Waist	S/Sgt	Robert Morgan
Bomb.	2/Lt	Anthony Morse	Left Waist	S/Sgt	+Raymond Martin
Radio.	T/Sgt	+Kenneth Kalk	Tail Gunner	S/Sgt	+Charles Davis

+ Indicates killed in action

B-17F-65-BO 42-29693 "Lonesome Polecat" 95th Bomb Group, 412th Bomb Squad

Pilot	1/Lt	+Malcolm Mackinnon	Top turr.	S/Sgt	+George Babich
Copilot	F/O	+Eugene Wood	Ball turr.	S/Sgt	+Richard Cavanaugh
Navg.	2/Lt	+Richard Miller	Right Waist	T/Sgt	+Alexander Mareck
Bomb.	2/Lt	+Windell Neely	Left Waist	S/Sgt	+John Davoren
Radio.	T/Sgt	+John Vail	Tail Gunner	S/Sgt	+Stanley Bennett

Two B-17s with crew lists lost on the 13 June 1943 raid on Kiel, Germany

B-17F-80-BO 42-29940 XM* 94th Bomb Group, 332nd Bomb Squad

Pilot	1/Lt	+Andrew Loog	Copilot	2/Lt	Robert W. Campbell
Navigator	2/Lt	+Francis J. McGee	Bombardier	1/Lt	+George M. Hale Jr
Engineer	T/Sgt	+Howard W. Payne	Radio man	T/Sgt	+Richard M. Himes
Ball turret	S/Sgt	+Eugene Walczynski	Waist Gunnner	S/Sgt	+Richard C. Russell
Waist Gunner	S/Sgt	+Scott J. Wilson	Tail Gunnner	S/Sgt	+Edward C. Layne

B-17F-90-BO 42-30164 BG*E 95Bomb Group 344th Bomb Squad

Pilot	Cpt	+Harry Stirwalt	Radio Man	T/Sgt	+Robert Forest
Copilot	Maj	+Alan Wilder	Ball Turret	S/Sgt	+Charles Benson
Navigator	1/Lt	+Walter Thimm	Left Waist	S/Sgt	+Angelo Triches
Navigator	!/Lt	Willard Brown	Right Waist	S/Sgt	+Odes Boyd
Bombardier	1/Lt	+Robert McNutt	Observer	1/Lt	Vincent Gannon
Engineer	T/Sgt	+Walter Drotleff	Commander	Br/Gen	+Nathan B Forrest III

B-17s with crew lists lost on the 22 June 1943 raid on Antwerp. Belgium

B-17F-80-BO VE*M 42-30016 "Iron Gut Gert" 381st Bomb Group, 532nd Bomb Squad

Pilot	1/Lt	Earl Horr	Radio Operator	S/Sgt	Robert Mandell
Copilot	2/Lt	William Roberts	Ball Turret	S/Sgt	+Charles Henry
Navigator	2/Lt	+George Griffith	Waist Gunner	S/Sgt	Hubert Clark
Bombardier	2/Lt	Chester Hoover	Waist Gunner	S/Sgt	Everett Hodsdon
Engineer	S/Sgt	Glenn Chapin	Tail Gunner	S/Sgt	Arthur Jones

B-17F-80-BO VP*G 42-30021 381st Bomb Group, 533rd Bomb Squad

Pilot	1/Lt	+John Martin	Radio Operator	Sgt	+Hugh Goswick
Copilot	F/O	+Robert Marsh	Ball Turret	S/Sgt	+Leonard Fornaro
Navigator	2/Lt	Harry Long	Waist Gunner	S/Sgt	+Glenn Witts
Bombardier	2/Lt	Wallace Hoag	Waist Gunner	Sgt	+John Hutchinson
Engineer	Sgt	+James Lantto	Tail Gunner	S/Sgt	+Bill Geary

B17F-25-VE SO*U 42-5853 384th Bomb Group, 547th Bomb Squad

Pilot	1/Lt	Fredrick Disney	Radio Operator	T/Sgt	+M R Galloway
Copilot	2/Lt	+Dan Thomas	Ball Turret	Sgt	+Robert Linehan
Navigator	2/Lt	+Alexander Bredacs	Waist Gunner	Sgt	+Clarence Stewart
Bombardier	1/Lt	+Bernard Nelson	Waist Gunner	S/Sgt	Joseph Kilp
Engineer	T/Sgt	+Harold Hammond	Tail Gunner	Sgt	James Knutson

B-17F-85-BO JD*V 42-30076 384th Bomb Group, 545 Bomb Squad

Pilot	2/Lt	Robert Oblinski	Radio Operator	T/Sgt	+Ernest Trickett
Copilot	2/Lt	Harry Swift	Ball Turret	S/Sgt	George Webanec
Navigator	2/Lt	Richard Grandpre	Waist Gunner	S/Sgt	+George Waterman
Bombardier	2/Lt	+Douglas Turner	Waist Gunner	S/Sgt	William Counihan
Engineer	T/Sgt	Oliver Reed	Tail Gunner	S/Sgt	+Harold Cooke

+ Indicates killed in action

Noted MIAs from the 25 June 1943 Hamburg Raid
B-17F-75-BO 42-29892 FO*N 379th Bomb Group 527th Bomb Squad

Pilot	+1/Lt	Douglas Groom	Co-pilot	2/Lt	+Frank Pulaski
Nav	2/Lt	Arthur Bellmyer	Bombardier	2/Lt	Thomas Mortenson
Eng	S/Sgt	Howard Brinkman	Radio	T/Sgt	+Thomas Lyons
Ball turret	S/Sgt	James Bowers	Right Waist	Sgt	+Thaddeus Burzycki
Left waist	S/Sgt	Ralph Weaver	Tail gunner	S/Sgt	+Frank Mills

This was the original Brinkman ship.

The B-17 crew lost on Hamburg raid with unidentified flyer originally assumed to be Crawford
The flyer with the neck wound and his crew were also lost on the 25 June 1943 Hamburg raid
B-17F-80-BO 42-30027 Schrader Crew VP*E 381st Bomb Group, 533 Bomb Squad

Pilot	1/Lt	+Robert K Schrader	Co-pilot	Capt	+John H. Hamilton
Nav	2/Lt	+Edward J Rogers	Bombardier	2/Lt	+Edward J Samara
Eng	T/Sgt	+William K Cutting	Radio	Sgt	+ William W Yarnell
Ball turret	Sgt	+Cecil A Pruiett	Right Waist	Sgt	+Stephen Kurnafil
Left waist	S/Sgt	+Theodore Leidecker	Tail gunner	S/Sgt	+Lewis E Frisbee*

Frisbee was buried in Wittmond Cemetery as an unknown and was recorded as having numerous
fractures after falling from an airplane. This unknown was believed to be Charles Crawford or John
Way until the AGRC provided documentation identifying Frisbee.

B-17 crew from 100th Bomb Group lost on Hamburg raid of 25 June 1943
42-3260 XR* "Angel's Tit" 100th Bomb Group 349th Bomb Squadron

Pilot	1/Lt	+ Alonzo P. Adams	Co-pilot	F/O	+George Z. Krech
Navigator	2/Lt	Nicholos Demchak	Bombardier	2/Lt	+Jesse D Gurley
Engineer	T/Sgt	+John K. Sullivan	Radio Oper.	T/Sgt	+James D Purcell
Ball turret	S/Sgt	+John G Kruzich	Left waist	S/Sgt	+Edmonde J Walker
Right waist	S/Sgt	+Norman Asbornsen	Tail gunner	S/Sgt	+Bryant Hutchinson

Nine KIA; those not killed in the crash would have drowned in the frigid waters of the North Sea
north of the German Frisian Islands. The lone survivor was the navigator, Second Lieutenant
Nicholas Demchaka, who was recovered by a German vessel. The only remains recovered was the
pilot, First Lieutenant Alonzo P. Adams.

B-17F-15-DL 42-3023 FR*F "Boozeness" 379th Bomb Group, 525th Bomb Squad

Pilot	1/Lt	+Thomas J. Simones	Co-pilot	2/Lt	Jack N. Schmitt
Navigator	2/Lt	Harold W. Aebischer	Bombardier	2/Lt	Thornton H. Baker
Engineer	T/Sgt	+Fred Polcover	Radio operator	T/Sgt	Gerald D. Metthe
Ball Turret	S/Sgt	+Joseph P. Noonan	Left waist	S/Sgt	+Norbert H. Meyer
Right waist	S/Sgt	Fredrick B. Hart	Tail gunner	S/Sgt	+Norman Schoolcraft

B-17 crew from 100th Bomb Group lost on Hamburg raid of 25 June 1943
B-17F-85-BO 42-30038 XR* 100th Bomb Group 349th Bomb Squadron

Pilot	1/Lt	+Paul J Schmalenbach	Co-pilot	F/O	+George W Cox
Navigator	1/Lt	John F Brown	Bombardier	2/Lt	+Jack L Clark
Engineer	T/Sgt	+Eugene M Beck	Radio Oper	T/Sgt	Frank J Podbielski
Ball turret	S/Sgt	Norman C Goodwin	Left waist	Sgt	+Anthony J Russo
Right waist	S/Sgt	William C. Lucas	Tail gunner	S/Sgt	+Lewis W Priegel

Six flyers KIA as 42-30038 exploded North of the German island of Wangerooge after an intense
battle between the tail gunner and the wounded fighter pilot. The four POWs were recovered by a
German vessel between Wangerooge and Schilling. The recovery location indicates the weatherman
got one thing right: the winds were out of the west-northwest sending the parachutists back toward
Germany.

+ Indicates killed in action

B-17F-85-BO SU*G 42-30049 "Miss Deal" 384 BombGroup, 544 Bomb Squad

P	2/Lt	+John R. Way	CP	2/Lt	Stephen R Fabian
N	2/Lt	Robert M. Janson	B	2/Lt	Thomas J. Corrigan
E	T/Sgt	William C. Hill Jr	RO	S/Sgt	Edmund S. Gadomski
BTG	Sgt	+Charles E. Crawford	LWG	S/Sgt	+William R. Feagin
RWG	S/Sgt	+ Raymond E. Dodge	TG	Sgt	Albert F. Westlake

MIA 25 June 1943 crashed in the Dollart west of the German Dutch frontier.

B-17F-25-VE SO*M 42-5850 "The McMillin Ship" 384 BombGroup, 544 Bomb Squad

P	Maj	Seldon L. McMillin**	CP	1/Lt.	James W. Smith
N	Cpt	James M. Foister	B	1/Lt	Francis J. Meyers
E	T/Sgt	+Robert H. Buckley	RO	T/Sgt	John J. Reichwein
BTG	S/Sgt	Lynn T. Jones	LWG	Sgt	David A. Prat
RWG	S/Sgt	Stanley W. McArthur	TG	1/Lt	Arthur W. Nelson

MIA 25 June 1943 crashed at Smalbroek, Holland

B-17F-25-VE 42-5839 FR*X 379 BombGroup, 525 Bomb Squad

P	F/O	+Kenneth A. Quade	CP	F/O	+George R. Barnett
N	2/Lt	William G. Hughes	B	2/Lt	+Wallace J. Cosper
TTG	T/Sgt	+Chester L. Burnes	R/O	T/Sgt	+James E. Edinger
BTG	S/Sgt	+Raymond S. Heron	LWG	S/Sgt	+Hugo Pettinatti
RWG	S/Sgt	+Joseph F. Owensby	T/G	Sgt	+ Kingsley D. Nelson

MIA on 25 June 1943 at 0915 hours following viscous attacks by German fighters. Crash site approximately 13 kilometers east of Oldenburg, Germany.

42-30143 B-17F-90-BO JD*Q "Yankee Powerhouse"   384 Bomb Group, 545 Bomb Squad

P	2/Lt	+George W. Riches	CP	2/Lt	+Richard J. McCray
N	2/Lt	Donald J. Irwin	B	2/Lt.	Joseph Deper Jr
E	T/Sgt	Bernard H. Anderson	RO	T/Sgt	Freeman S. Penney
BTG	S/Sgt	Guy E. Smith	LWG	S/Sgt	Ralph E. Lavoi
RWG	S/Sgt	+William T. Waller	TG	S/Sgt	+Stanley S. Martin

MIA 25 June 1943 Crashed near Oldenburg, Germany

B-17F-50-BO 42-5390 PU*L The Avenger 303Bomb Group, 360Bomb Squad

P	1/Lt.	+Joseph F. Palmer	CP	2/Lt.	+Robert M. Sheldon
N	2/Lt.	Claude M. Kieffer	B	Sgt.	Leonard C. Applequist
E	S/Sgt	+Elmer E. Duffey	RO	T/Sgt	+Edmund Gullage
BTG	S/Sgt	+Burl M. Owens	LWG	S/Sgt	+Samuel A. Holder
RWG	S/Sgt	+Norman E. Hornbacher	TG	S/Sgt	Alva E. Hodges
Ph	S/Sgt	James L. Stringer Photographer			

MIA 25 June 1943 Crashed at Borgsweer, Holland at 0915.

Pilot Load List for 25 June 1943
384th Mission #: 2 8th AAF Mission #: 67 Flight Time: 5.40
Target: Hamburg, Germany. AC T/O: 18 AC Attacking: 8 Aborts: 11 Losses: 3
Bomb Load: 20 Tons (500 pound G.P.) Ammunition Used 9,201 rds .50 cal

Maj S McMilln	42-5850	SO*M	Missing In Action
Lt T Estes	42-3188	SU*F Miss Carriage	
Lt J Butler	42-5852	SO*T The Natural	
Lt W Dietel	42-30032	BK*D Sky Queen	
Lt R Pulcipher	42-30043	SO*V Ruthless	
Lt J Way	42-30049	SU*G Miss Deal	Missing In Action
Lt G Riches	42-30143	JD*Q Yankee Powerhouse	Missing In Action
Lt G Keck	42-30065	SO*O	

Luftwaffe record of Boeing-Fortress that crashed in the Dollart on 25 June 43 at 09.09.
Maschine nicht zu Bergen, keine Kennseichen. Flak u. Jager. 7 Gefangener.Jeverb birgt.

+ Indicates killed in action

Pistol Packin Mamma crew list for the Gelsenkircheen raid of 12 August 1943
B-17F-90-BO 42-30142 "Pistol Packin Mamma" SU*L 384th Bomb Group 544th Bomb Squad

Pilot	2/Lt Jesse D. Hausenfluck	Radio Oper	S/Sgt	John R. Kelly
Copilot	2/Lt Donald B. Mckenzie	Ball Turret	S/Sgt	James A. Traylor
Navigator	2/Lt Charle W. Everson	Right Waist	S/Sgt	Sebastian Bucheri
Bombardier	2/Lt Robert J. Kennedy	Left Waist	Sgt	John C. Blauer
Engineer	S/Sgt John T. Kilcourse	Tail Gunner	Sgt	Raymond P. Gregori*

Gregori received the Silver Star for his actions on this raid. He was Charles Crawford's roommate at Grafton Underwood and owner of the 384th's mascot Delbert McNasty.

B-17 crewman KIA by Runaway 50 on the La Borget raid 16 August 1943 was the radio operator Melvin Feigenbaum. Other crewmembers of "The Dallas Rebel" were lost on the Anklam Raid
B-17F-70-BO SU*D 42-29814 "The Dallas Rebel" 384th Bomb Group 544th Bomb Squadron

Pilot	1/Lt	+John Ingles	Radio Man	T/Sgt	+Lawrence Smith
Copilot	2/Lt	+Harry Pratt	Ball Turret	S/Sgt	+John Farley
Navigator	2/Lt	+Charles Ruman	Waist Gunner	S/Sgt	+Carl Janes
Engineer	T/Sgt	+Clarence Morrison	Tail Gunner	S/Sgt	+ Joseph Brescia

Noted Crews from the Schweinfurt Regensburg raids.
The B-17 crew that fought to the end refusing to bail out on the Schweinfurt raid
B-17F-70-BO 42-29830 FR*X "Peter Wabbit" 379th Bomb Group 525 Bomb Squad

Pilot	1/Lt	+Erwalt Wagner	Radio man	T/Sgt	+Benjamin Radensky
Copilot	1/Lt	+William Barnard	Ball turret	S/Sgt	+Francis Donahue
Navigator	1/Lt	+Joseph Hilderbrand	Left waist	S/Sgt	+Marvin Charlson
Bombardier	2/Lt	+Kenneth Gibbs	Right waist	S/Sgt	+Eldred Andrus
Engineer	T/Sgt	+Henry Cushman	Tail gunner	S/Sgt	+Dean Yates

B-17F-65-BO 42-29728 SU*J "El Rauncho" Salvaged after crash landing following Schweinfurt raid

Pilot	1/Lt	Randolph Jacobs*	Radio operator	T/Sgt	Doy Cloud
Copilot	2/Lt	Eugene A Boger	Ball turret	S/Sgt	Donald Gorman
Navigator	2/Lt	John Curtin	Left waist	S/Sgt	Larry Wagner
Bombardier	1/Lt	James E. Seibel	Right waist	T/Sgt	Aldo Gregori
Engineer	S/Sgt	Jack Goetz	Tail gunner	S/Sgt	Robert Compton

B-17F –75-BO 42-29896 FO*Y "Tondelayo" 379 Bomb Group, 527 Bomb Squad P

	2/Lt	Bohn E. Fawkes Jr	CP	2/Lt	Charles A. Mauldin
N	2/Lt	Elmer S. Bendiner	B	2/Lt	Robert L. Henjny
TTG	T/Sgt	Lawrence H. Reedman	RO	S/Sgt	Andrew W. Parker
BTG	S/Sgt	John A. Leary	LWG	S/Sgt	Walter J Gray
RWG	S/Sgt	Harry L. Edwards	TG	S/Sgt	Michael Arooth

Crew List 6 September 1943 when Tondelayo ditched in the English Channel
Same ship and crew for the 17 August 1943 Schweinfurt raid

"Dear Mom" 42-30389 QE*Z 94th Bomb Group, 331st Bomb Squadron MIA 17 Aug 1943

Pilot	Lt	+Bernard Nayovitz	Radio man	T/Sgt	Arthur McDonell
Copilot	2/Lt	+James Smith	Ball turret	S/Sgt	+Jack Loveless
Navigator	2/Lt	+Murlyn Burnett	Left waist	S/Sgt	Jacob Dali
Bombardier	2/Lt	+Robert Allison	Right waist	S/Sgt	Beverly Geye
Engineer	T/Sgt	+Albert Beyke	Tail gunner	S/Sgt	James Tolbert

Lost to fighters enroute to Regensburg

+ Indicates killed in action

42-30315 B-17F-95-BO   CC*S "Peg of My Heart" 390th Bomb Group, 569th Bomb Squad
MIA 17Aug 43 after attack on Regensburg

Pilot	2/Lt Stephen Rapport	Radio man	S/Sgt	William Carter
Copilot	2/Lt Elmer Holloway	Ball turret	S/Sgt	Theodore Obsharsky
Navigator	2/Lt Grover Boyd	Left waist	S/Sgt	Joseph Russell
Bombardier	2/Lt Charles Ryan	Right waist	S/Sgt	Blair Neal
Engineer	T/Sgt John Scott	Tail gunner	S/Sgt	Ricardo Robledo

Crash landed north of Berne, Switzerland. Salvaged by the Swiss

B-17 and crew successfully returned from Raid on Munster Rail Yards then hit a hangar
B-17F-60-BO 42-29557 SO*S "Yankee Girl" 384th Bomb Group 547th Bomb Squad

2/L	+William E. Kopf	Pilot	S/Sgt Herbert E. Yeryar	Radio Operator
2/Lt	+Alfred W. Scott	Copilot	S/Sgt +Clyde C. Smith	Ball Turret
Lt	+Toscha E. Massey	Navigator	S/Sgt +Anthony R. Perroni	Waist Gunner
Lt	Eugene W. Connor	Bombardier	S/Sgt +Leroy Bernard	Waist Gunner
T/Sgt	Kenneth G. Swift	Engineer	S/Sgt +Elton W. Buddmeyer	Tail Gunner

The fortress was salvaged and all crewmembers returned to duty.
Crew then participated in the 2nd Schweinfurt raid on 14 Oct 1943 with a loss of 7 crewmembers

B-17 lost on return from the Munster rail yard raid on 10 October 1943
B-17F-35-B0 42-5086 BK*B "Wahoo II" 384th Bomb Group 346th Bomb Squad

2/Lt	William M. Wilson	Pilot	S/Sgt James H. Compton	Radio Operator
2/Lt	Carlos J. Rabby	Copilot	S/Sgt David Heintzelman	Ball Turret Gunner
Lt	Robert K. Belk	Navigator	S/Sgt Murray R. Stamm	Waist Gunner
Lt	Richard K. Crown	Bombardier	S/Sgt F.O. Miller	Waist Gunner
Sgt	Lester Birnbaum	Engineer	S/Sgt Frank P. Greene	Tail Gunner

The fortress was salvaged and all crewmembers returned to duty after crash landing at Eye, Suffolk.
The only casualty was a cow. Crew completed 25 missions on 20 March 1944.

B-17 lost on raid of the Munster rail yard on 10 October 1943
B-17F-95-BO 42-30273 BG*F "Patsy Ann III" 95th Bomb Group, 334 Bomb Squad

2/Lt	+William E. Buckley	Pilot	T/Sgt +Ralph E. Piner	Radio Operator
2/Lt	Fredrick J. Kennie	Copilot	S/Sgt +Harry F. Balmer	Ball Turret
2/Lt	Robert Barto	Navigator	S/Sgt +Leo Baron	Waist Gunner
2/Lt	Edison P. Janney	Bombardier	S/Sgt Donald Reinhart	Waist Gunner
T/Sgt	+Richard W. Sluder	Engineer	S/Sgt Edward Burlingham	Tail Gunner

The Jacobs crew lost on their 28th raid:
B-17G-5-BO 42-31211 "Reno's Raider" BK*H 384th Bomb Group 546th Bomb Squad

Commander	Cpt	+Randolph Jacobs	Engineer	T/Sgt	+William Clements
Pilot	1/Lt	+Earl Allison	Ball Turret	Sgt	+Vernon Kaufman
Navigator	1/Lt	John Curtin	Waist Gunner	S/Sgt	Kenneth Hougard
Bombardier	1/Lt	+Jack Nagel	Waist Gunner	Sgt	James Grimmett
Radio Man	T/Sgt	William Laubenstein	Tail Gunner	2/Lt	Lester Hall

MIA crew lost while attacking Villacoublay airfield on 26 June 1943
*B-17F-85-BO   SU*K 42-30048 "Flak Dancer" 384th Bomb Group, 544th Bomb Squadron

Pilot	2/Lt	Delton Wheat	Radio man	S/Sgt	Theodore Finck
Copilot	2/Lt	+David McMullen	Ball Turret	S/Sgt	John Katuzney
Navigator	2/Lt	Thomas Ketcham	Left Waist	S/Sgt	+Ralph Wood
Bombardier	2/Lt	Robert Brown	Right Waist	S/Sgt	Warren Pursch
Engineer	S/Sgt	George Bossinger	Tail Gunner	S/Sgt	Dero Hurst

+ Indicates killed in action

MIA crew lost on a Wyoming mountain while enroute from Pendleton,O to the European Theatre
B-17F-55-DL 42-3399 "Scharazad 318th Squadron

Crew Position		Crew Position	
Pilot	Lt +William R. Ronaghan	Radio Operator	Sgt +Charles E. Newburn
Unknown	Lt +Leonard H. Phillips	Unknown	Sgt +Lewis M. Shepard
Unknown	Lt +Charles H. Suppes	Unknown	Pvt +Lee V. Miller
Unknown	Lt +Anthony J. Tilotta	Unknown	Sgt +Ferguson T. Bell, Jr.
Unknown	Sgt+James A. Hinds	Unknown	Sgt +Jake E. Penick

B-17 crew list lost on 27 September 1943 raid on Emden
B-17F-120-BO "Fisher Fortress" 42-30793 QJ*E 96th Bomb Group, 399 Bomb Squad

Pilot	2/Lt Cecil B. Fisher	Co-pilot	F/O +Alfred Drabnis
Navigator	2/Lt +Lester A. Leonard	Bombardier	2/Lt Stewart E. Cooper
Engineer	T/Sgt Gordon S. Nutt Jr	Radio Operator	S/Sgt Daniel Cook
Ball Turret	S/Sgt Wilbur L. Bornschein	Left Waist	S/Sgt Paul W. Sweeney
Right Waist	S/Sgt Joseph J. McKenna	Tail Gunner	S/Sgt Morrison T. Miller

Pilots load list 22 June 1943
Date: 22 June   384th Mission # 1   8AF Mission #: 65   Flight Time: 4.23
Target: Antwerp, Belgium
A/C T/O 20   Spare: 2A/C Attacking: 20   Aborts: 0   Losses: 2
Bomb Load: 50 tons (M-44-Dem. G.P.)   Ammunition Used: 38,305 rds .50 cal

Col B J Peaslee	42-30043 SO*V Ruthless B-17F-85-BO*	
Lt D P Oglive	42-5848 SO*R Patches	
Lt L S Henderson	42-30005 BK*A Salvage Queen	
Lt C R Wilson	42-30046 BK*H Merrie Hell	
Lt J Rosio	42-30040 BK*B Piccadilly Commando	
Lt. P M Algar	42-30006 BK*J Battle Wagon	
Lt W Dietel	42-30032 BK*D Sky Queen	
Lt J H Kelly	42-30033 BK*G Little America	
Lt F Edwards	42-3216 JD*S The Joker	
Lt L Armstrong	42-3218 JD*R Doris Mae	
Lt F Mattes	42-3222 JD*P Deuces Wild	
Lt R Carrington	42-3231 JD*M The Inferno	
Lt G Riches	42-5849 SO*N Hell's Belles II	
Lt M Dillingham	42-5850 SO*M	
Lt J Butler	42-5852 SO*T The Natural	
Lt F Disney	42-5853 SO*U	Missing In Action
Lt G Keck	42-30065 SO*O	
Lt R Oblinski	42-30076 JD*V	Missing In Action
Lt J Roberts	42-30139 JD*O Snuffy	
Lt R Hall	42-30143 JD*Q Yankee Powerhouse	

*B-17F-85-BO is the production block number for 100 B-17s including *Miss Deal's* 42-30049. This block of B-17s represented changes or continuing general improvements from the previous blocks of B-17Fs noted changes from previous blocks that were included were additions of bomb release control, bombardier windshield wiper, auxiliary power plant, radio compartment upper hatch gun, provision for auxiliary power plant to operate electrical system, improved brake and wheel assembly and the addition of fuel tanks (Tokyo) in the outer wing assembly. The engines for this production block of B-17s were rated at 1,200 horsepower at 25,000 feet and 1,380 at war emergency. Her normal design bomb load was 6,000 pounds while her normal designed ferry weight was 56,500 pounds and her empty design weight was 38,000 pounds. She was designed for a crew of 10 and her armament design was for 11, 50 caliber machine guns, 4,430 rounds of ammo, and a maximum of 6 each 1,600-pound bombs.

+ indicates killed in action   xxiv

Noted MIA B-17s and crews lost on the 25 July 1943 raid on Hamburg
B-17F-25-DL   42-3088 SU*G "Sugar Puss" 384th Bomb Group, 544th Bomb Squad

Pilot	1/Lt	+Clarence Christman	Co-pilot	2/Lt	Rodney W. House
Navigator	2/Lt	+Vern B. Dennett	Bombardier	2/Lt	William H. Sears
Engineer	T/Sgt	Albert W. Detrick	Radio Oper	T/Sgt	+John J. Gillis
Ball Turret	S/Sgt	+Robert A. Leonard	Left Waist	S/Sgt	Carl V. Hill
Right Waist	S/Sgt	S.G. Stephenson	Tail Gunner	S/Sgt	+Jerome Goubeauz

Five of the crew became POWs, while five were KIA

B-17F-25-DL   42-3122 JD*N "April's Fool" 384th Bomb Group 545th Bomb Squad

Pilot	2/Lt	Ralph J. Hall	Co-pilot	2/Lt	Rodney W. House
Navigator	2/Lt	R.O. Henley	Bombardier	2/Lt	Warren B. Dillon
Engineer	T/Sgt	Homer J, Cocklin	Radio Oper.	T/Sgt	Paul F. Henry
Ball Turret	S/Sgt	Albert R. Valcour	Left Waist	S/Sgt	Raymond C. Smiley
Right Waist	S/Sgt	James S. Parrish	Tail Gunner	S/Sgt	Paul E. McNeal

Estes crew on the 4 January 1944 Kiel mission
The crew of "Sissy" when Fred Wagner fell out of the bomb bay
B-17G-15-DL   42-37848 BK*E   "Sissy" 384th Bomb Group 544th Bomb Squad

Commander		Capt	Alfred C.Nuttal		
Pilot	1/Lt	Thomas J. Estes	Co-pilot	F/O	James M. Merritt*
Navigator	1/Lt	John J. Dubois	Bombardier	1/Lt	David H. Davis
Engineer	T/Sgt	David L. Cochran	Radio Oper.	S/Sgt	Fred S. Wagner
Ball Turret	S/Sgt	George Ursta	Right Waist	S/Sgt	William J. O'Donnell
Left Waist	S/Sgt	James M. Self	Tail Gunner	S/Sgt	Burton C. McDuffie

While the crew was from the 544th Bomb Squad 42-37848 was assigned to the 546th Bomb Squad

The two crews of "Patches" after being heavily damaged by fighters
B-17F-25-VE 42-5848 "Patches"   384th Bomb Group, 547th Bomb Squadron

Pilot	2/Lt	Donald Ogilvie	Co-pilot	2/Lt	Edmund S. Goulder
Navigator	2/Lt	John Barkley	Bombardier	2/Lt	+Wliam H.Wilson
Engineer	T/Sgt	Emmett Hood	Radio Oper.	T/Sgt	+James Murray
Ball Turret	T/Sgt	James McKeon	Left Waist	S/Sgt	Joe M. Hawkins
Right Waist	S/Sgt	Bernard M. Kain	Tail Gunner	S/Sgt	John R. Dudla

Wilson and Murray were lost on the Schweinfurt raid of October 14, 1943

B-17F-25-VE 42-5848 "Patches"384th Bomb Group, 547th Bomb Squadron Pilot   2/Lt

		William R Harry	Co-pilot	2/Lt	Ivan L Rice
Navigator	2/Lt	David H Black	Bombardier	2/Lt	Charles P Mannka
Engineer	T/Sgt	Curry A Reed	Radio Oper.	T/Sgt	Edward P Simpson
Ball Turret	S/Sgt	John C Mckenner	Left Waist	S/Sgt	Willard Cronin
Right Waist	S/Sgt	Thomas S Wheeler	Tail Gunner	S/Sgt	Leroy Parent

Lt. Harry was awarded a Silver Star for his actions in piloting "Patches" back to England.

B-17 lost on the 30 December 1943 Ludwigshaven raid
B-17G-10-BO "Sea Hag" 42-31274 SU*O 384th Bomb Group 544th Bomb Squad

Pilot	1/Lt	Randolph Jacobs*	Radio oper.	T/Sgt	Doy Cloud
Copilot	2/Lt	Winthrop Jackson	Ball turret	S/Sgt	Donald Gorman
Navigator	2/Lt	John Curtin	Left waist	S/Sgt	Larry Wagner
Bombardier	1/Lt	David Davies	Right waist	T/Sgt	+Aldo Gregori
Engineer	S/Sgt	Jack Goetz	Tail gunner	S/Sgt	Robert Compton

This B-17 ditched with loss of one crewman. Nine of her crew were rescued and returned to duty.

+ indicates killed in action

Acknowledgments and Bibliography

List of Individuals Interviewed Partial
From the 379th Bomb Group members, family and friends
Mrs. Betty Banks
Kyle Brinkman
Walter Bzlbziak
William H. Cochran
Arvid Dahl
Howard Fibel
J. Gore
John Gray

Lou Kline
Ed Milner
J.A. Morrow
Jim Roberts
Sam Satariano
David Willey
Woody Woodruff

From the 384th Bomb Group members, family and friends
Robert Austen
Quentin Bland 384th Historian
Joe Carnes
Ellen Corrigan
Levi Lestetr Davis
Darvin Dodge
Floyd Dodge
Stephen Fabian
Berry Feagin
Walter Feagin
Mary Way Gier
Mrs. Charlotte Gadomski and Family
Jack Goetz
Gene Goodrick
Paul Gordy
Raymond Gregori
Bill and Betty Harvey

Shirley Smith Haskell
Paul Mantle
Nathan Mazer
Selden McMillin Jr
Mark Meehl
Tony Palazzo.
Marc Poole
Fred Preller
Pat Rollins
Ted Rothschild
William Smisek
Henry J. Stadelman
Melissa Trawick
James Traylor
A. J. and Denise Watkins
Albert and Marie Westlake
Lloyd Whitlow

Other Bomb Group Members, family and friends
William Dixon (100th)
Bill L Owen (303rd)
Janice Watterson Snyder (100th)

Dutch and German researchers
Jan A. Hey
Ab A. Jansen
Roel Kisteman
Franz Lenselink
Harm Pastoor
Dr. Harmut Rudolph

Lenny Schrik
Jan Stegmeijer
Father Gerad Thuring
Olaf Timmermann
Patrick Righart van Gelder
Sicco de Vries

Miscellaneous information sources and Individuals that assisted in my search

B-17 Combat Crewmen and Wingmen	Doug Gross
Bulletin Air War 1939-1945	P.J. Grimm, J. Woortman, I.M. de Jong
Independent Computer Software Consultant	J. Morgan Braly

DPMO, JPAC, AHRC-PER, and other DOD Personnel

Tracy Brown	Corrine Hagan
Heather Harris	Major Paul Madrid
Randolph Van Meter	Thomas P. Lauria
Dr. Mark Russel	Johnie Webb

Archives II, National Archives, College Park, MD
Robin Cookson

American Graves Registration Command (AGRC) and American Graves Registration Services (AGRS)

Neuville-en Condroz   cemetery plot chart images
Narrative and Report of Investigation of Search for John R. Way and Charles E. Crawford by the American Graves Registration Command (AGRC)
Captain Herbert L. Swanson AGRC
Narrative and Report of Investigation of Search for John Way and Charles Crawford by Hendrick Veigh AGRC

Total Army Personnel Command

Individual Deceased Personnel File (IDPF)
Thomas M. Jones, Department of The Army, U.S. Human Resources Command Alexandria, VA

National Personnel Records Center

Military Personnel Records
St. Louis, MO

Web Sites

The Luftwaffe Archives & Records Reference Group (www.lwag.org)	
Tony Woods Documents	Bomb Group web sites of the 8th Army Air Force
aces/ww2hbk.htm	Lufrtwaffe Archives and Records Reference Group
armyairforcesforum.com	
missingaircrew.com	
aviationarchaeology.com	

Ministers, Political Figures and Offices

The Mayor of Wittmund, Germany
The Mayors office of Finsterwolde, Holland
The Bunker Museum, Emden, Germany
Klinikum Hans Susemihl Krankenhaus (Hospital), Emden, Germany
The Minister of the Northern Water District of Holland, Delfzijl, Holland

Congressman Jeb Hensarling and and his assistant Margaret Smith
Senator John Cornyn and his assistants
Robert J. Newberry, Acting Deputy Assistant Secretary of Defense

Writers of Letters to Gay Crawford
Bertha Andrews
Thomas   Corrigan
Charles Crawford
Gaynell Crawford
Dr. James M. Crawford
Anna Dodge
Elvin Doll
Mr. and Mrs. Ed. Feagin
Margaret Feagin
Edmund Gadomski
Mrs. G. Gadomski
Hazel Hill
Mrs. Margaret Janson
Robert Janson
Col. "Budd" Peaslee
Chaplain Dayle R. Schnelle
Mary T. Way

Writers of Letters to Gaynell Crawford
Stephen Fabian
Mrs. D. Westlake
American Red Cross

Letters to or from Dr. James M. Crawford
Bertha Andrews
Family of Thomas Corrigan
Gaynell Crawford
General Robert H. Dunlap
Edmund Gadomski
American Red Cross
Maj. General J.A.Uli

The John R. Way collection of Letters to his family
Charles E. Crawford memorabilia and collection of Letters to and from his Family

Books

Verliesregister 1939-1945	Frans Auwerda, Peter Grimm, Ivo de Jong, Jos Stok, Erwin van Loo, et. al
The Wild Blue	Stephen E. Ambrose
The Fall of Fortresses	Elmer Bendiner
Claims to Fame The B-17 Flying Fortress	Steve Birdsall, Roger Freeman
Losses of the US 8th and 9th Air Forces	Stan D Bishop and John A Hey
Combat Legend B-17 Flying Fortress Combat Crew	Martin Bowman, John Comer
B-17 Flying Fortress Units of The Eighth Air Force (Part 1 and Part 2	Martin Bowman
Hitler's U-Boat Fortresses	Randolph Bradham
Flying Forts	Martin Caiden
A Dying Breed	Neal B. Dillion
Keep the Show on the Road The History of The 384th Bombardment Group	Linda and Vic Fayers-Hallin and Quentin Bland
Bomber Offensive the Devastation of Europe	Noble Frankland
The B-17 Flying Fortress Story	Roger A. Freeman
Overpaid, Oversexed, & Overhere	Juliet Gardiner
Once Upon a Town	Bob Greene
Guide to Axis Fighters of World War II	Bill Gunston
Air War Europa: America's Air War Against Germany in Europe and North Africa 1942-1945: Chronology	Eric Hammel
B-17s Over Berlin	Ian L. Hawkins

Air Heroes of World War II	Robert Jackson
The B-17 Flying Fortress	Robert Jackson
Flying Fortress	Edward Jablonski
Terror From The Sky	Edward Jablonski
Tragic Victories	Edward Jablonski
Wings of Fire	Edward Jablonski
Sporen Aan De Hemel	A.A. Jansen
Wespennest Leeuwarden	A.A. Jansen
Messerschmitt 109	D.A. Lande
Masters of the Air: America's Bomber Boys Who Fought the Air War Against Nazi Germany	Donald L. Miller
The Men Who Bombed The Reich	Bernard Nalty, Carl Berger
Half a Wing Three Engines and a Prayer	Brian D. O'Neill
As Briefed	Walter Owen
Heritage of Valor; the Eighth Air Force in World War II	Budd J. Peaslee
The Greatest Raid of All	C.E. Lucas Phillips
Shades of Kimbolton, A Narrative of the 379th Bombardment Group	Derwyn D. Robb
The Greatest Aces	Edward H. Sims
The Blond Knight of Germany	Raymond F.Toliver
Target Germany: The Army Air Forces' Offical Story of the VIII Bomber Command's First Year Over Europe	U.S. Army Air Force

Made in the USA
San Bernardino, CA
15 January 2015